IDENTITY'S STRATEGY

Studies in Rhetoric/Communication
Thomas W. Benson, Series Editor

IDENTITY'S STRATEGY

RHETORICAL SELVES IN CONVERSION

Dana Anderson

The University of South Carolina Press

Published by the University of South Carolina Press
Columbia, South Carolina 29208

www.sc.edu/uscpress

Manufactured in the United States of America

16 15 14 13 12 11 10 09 08 07 10 9 8 7 6 5 4 3 2 1

Library of Congress Cataloging-in-Publication Data

Anderson, Dana, 1971–
Identity's strategy : rhetorical selves in conversion / Dana Anderson.
p. cm.— (Studies in rhetoric/communication)
Includes bibliographical references and index.
ISBN-13: 978-1-57003-706-1 (cloth : alk. paper)
ISBN-10: 1-57003-706-X (cloth : alk. paper)
1. Conversion. 2. Autobiography—Authorship. 3. Identity (Psychology) 4. Self. I. Title.
BL639.A53 2007
204'.2—dc22
2007015640

This book was printed on Glatfelter Natures, a recycled paper with 50 percent postconsumer waste content.

CONTENTS

SERIES EDITOR'S PREFACE

Dana Anderson's *Identity's Strategy: Rhetorical Selves in Conversion* is a theoretical and critical investigation of *identity* as an inescapably rhetorical strategy. It also examines autobiographical narratives about the experience of conversion as rhetorical strategies of identity under extreme conditions. Professor Anderson argues that—taken as a rhetorical strategy rather than as a transcendent philosophical category—*identity* is understood as a matter of common sense and that the concept of identity is fundamental to the ongoing processes of self-definition, self-interpretation, and self-presentation.

Because identity is taken for granted as a category, it forms the substance for other, more visible rhetorical strategies. Anderson turns to Kenneth Burke for a framework for understanding the rhetoric of identity, tracing Burke's analysis of identity/identification and showing how Burke's description of the rhetoric of constitutions may be understood as explaining how the substance of identity is constituted in and as rhetoric.

Anderson then traces out the implications of his preliminary findings in probing theoretical and critical investigations of four twentieth-century American autobiographical accounts that describe various radical challenges to their authors' identities. In chapters on Dorothy Day's *The Long Loneliness*, David Brock's *Blinded by the Right*, Deirdre McCloskey's *Crossing*, and John G. Neihardt's *Black Elk Speaks*, Professor Anderson explores how the radical refashionings of self described by these conversion narratives are also reconstitutive appeals to their readers. *Identity's Strategy* is an illuminating rereading of Kenneth Burke in the light of contemporary theory and a provocative revision of the notion of identity in rhetorical studies.

THOMAS W. BENSON

ACKNOWLEDGMENTS

Writing about identity has certainly heightened my awareness of all the people who are in some way essential to who I think I am. So too has it made me aware of those people who have been essential to this book, and I want them to know how much I appreciate them.

In his kind tutelage on everything from prose style to putting, Jack Selzer has been an ideal mentor and friend. I look forward to many more years of owing him and his caring family a debt that I hope this book begins to repay.

John Schilb has shared more insight and enthusiasm with me than I can convey or had any right to expect. What I have tried to articulate here is much improved for his incomparably broad and deep understanding of rhetoric in the world, a virtue surpassed only by his unflagging good humor. Christine Farris, Kathy Smith, and Steve Watt helped me find the institutional and intellectual support I needed at crucial times, doing so with friendship that has proved so much more valuable. I am particularly indebted to Paul Gutjar and Ray Hedin for their ears for tone and their examples of charitable scholarship.

Greg Clark offered much valuable advice about rhetoric, identity, and life along the way, and I thank him and Steven Mailloux for joining me on a panel that greatly shaped and strengthened my inquiry. Cheryl Glenn, Jeff Walker, Marie Secor, Fred Antczak, Rosa Eberly, and Steve Browne all graciously pointed me toward texts and ideas that I doubtfully would have encountered on my own. Jon Olson continues to make the idea of praxis both concrete and human in a way that I have tried to enact here and will always try to emulate.

I am especially grateful to those who have commented on specific portions of this book. John Eakin and the participants in the Lifewriting Colloquia of the Indiana University Institute for Advanced Study thoughtfully challenged me to see lifewriting for the complex—and utterly essential—human discourse that it is. Debra Hawhee and Jan Fernheimer both read crucial sections on

Burke with care and tremendous insight. Sandy Stelts's mastery of the Kenneth Burke papers at the Pattee Library of Penn State University was instrumental in this project, as was Phil Runkel's command of the Dorothy Day–Catholic Worker Collection at the Raynor Memorial Library of Marquette University. I thank them both for their assistance. I am also grateful to Scott Sanders, Nick Williams, Andrew Miller, Mary Favret, Joan Linton, Ivan Kreilkamp, Mark Decker, Ross Wolin, John Muckelbauer, Mark Longaker, Blake Scott, Keith Gibson, Krista Ratcliffe, Matthew Johnson, and Bill Fitzgerald for influential conversations at key moments. Gary Hatch, Penny Bird, Lance Larsen, and Brandie Siegfried may not recognize their influence herein, but they should know that I see it everywhere. Jesse Crisler already knows I wouldn't be writing this at all if it weren't for his instruction and kindness.

I am fortunate to have worked with so many exceptional students, especially those who let me besiege them with questions about identity. Alex Borowicz, Camilla Stefl, Camille Constantin, Hannah Smith, Katie Crank, Aaron Lambert, Sara Salman, Conor Duggan, and Kyle Kartz have all taken the time to help me when they had better things to do. My graduate students in my seminars on narrative, agency, and Kenneth Burke, and especially Rick Johnston, Maura Smyth, and Laura Johnson challenged me to be both relevant and readable.

My good friends Mark and Gayle Decker, Matt and Amy Decker, Jason Lindquist, Jeff and Susan Daniels, and Julie Flott have given me rewarding companionship that has been as vital to this book as any text or archive. To David Nash, Brenda Andrus, Bryce Knudsen, Jon Ebbert, Matt Hoyt, Ken Spafford, Mark Gardner, and Nobleza Gaucha, my longtime compatriots, I say thank you for your warmth and constant generosity of spirit.

I am grateful to everyone at the University of South Carolina Press and their anonymous reviewers for a truly enriching experience in bringing this book to completion.

I thank Kenneth Burke for exuberant heterodoxy in a world of decorous specialization.

My parents, Don and Mary Jane, have been both the means and the ends of my writing. I hope that some portion of this book might salve my mother's lament that I didn't become a writer of commercial jingles and answer my father's demand that I demonstrate once and for all what a "rhetoritician" does for a living. For *Eddy Duchin* at the Warner, for Pirates games, and for always being there, I love and thank you. I cannot sufficiently thank my sisters, Jordan, Emily, and Michelle, and their families, for their goodwill and for bringing joy to vacations, holidays, and every day. Carmen Fernandez, for giving me my wife, supporting my family, and believing in me always, deserves so much more than a line in a book, but at least I can give her that. Te quiero, Uchi, and for a very long time to come. Jared Gorton has been the brother I never had, but the one I would have picked, even if he refuses to enjoy Disney World. Thank you for your cheer during timely breaks that got my family through tough days.

My son, Ethan, continues to motivate me to ensure that the fruits of my labor are not only good but good for something.

Last and most of all, I thank my wife and resident muse, Thalia. Since our earliest days sitting together in "Principles of Literary Criticism," your love has inspired me to be better, and you are patient when I am not. Your sacrifice, support, and trust over our many years together have immeasurably deepened the substance of both my scholarship and my life, and even though you are too modest to care for dedications, this book, like my love, is for you.

ABBREVIATIONS

Autobiographies

BE	John G. Neihardt, *Black Elk Speaks*
BR	David Brock, *Blinded by the Right: The Conscience of an Ex-Conservative*
CM	Deirdre McCloskey, *Crossing: A Memoir*
LL	Dorothy Day, *The Long Loneliness*

Works by Kenneth Burke

ATH	*Attitudes toward History*
DOC	"The Dialectic of Constitutions"
GM	*A Grammar of Motives*
PC	*Permanence and Change*
PLF	*The Philosophy of Literary Form*
RM	*A Rhetoric of Motives*

1

Introduction

Conversion, Identity, and Rhetorical Common Sense

Each person has a repertoire of autobiographies appropriate for different cultural settings, and most people are skilled at constructing new autobiographies for novel occasions.

J.-P. De Waele and Rom Harré,
"Autobiography as a Psychological Method"

As I went to Damascus with authority and commission from the chief priests, at midday, O king, I saw in the way a light from heaven, above the brightness of the sun, shining round about me and them which journeyed with me. And when we were all fallen to the earth, I heard a voice speaking unto me, and saying in the Hebrew tongue, Saul, Saul, why persecutest thou me? . . . And I said, Who art thou, Lord? And he said, I am Jesus whom thou persecutest.

Acts 26: 12–14

Try to map the road to conversion, and you're going to need Damascus as a cardinal point. If it thus seems somewhat unremarkable for me to begin with this commonplace of conversion narratives, I hope you'll allow one more brief return to the familiar Syrian road where both a convert and a paradigm were born.

In the New Testament book of Acts, Luke writes of Saul, a Pharisaic legend in his own time for his zeal in persecuting Christians, and the journey to Damascus on which he literally saw the light. Within that light, knocking him to the ground, blinding him, was a being who declared himself to be the very Jesus whose teachings—and followers—Saul so eagerly sought to purge from Jewry. Confronted with the divinity of what he had been excoriating as a heresy, Saul could do little else but to inquire of this being where he should go from here: "Lord, what wilt thou have me to do?" (Acts 9:6). Where he goes, he goes now as Paul, a renaming to seal his reconstitution as a man who will become Christian discipleship incarnate.

Along with this new missionary life, Paul also established, albeit indirectly, the idea of "conversion" that is expressed in the term's Latin root, *conversio:* it is a *turning,* a "reorientation of the soul . . . a consciousness that a great change is involved, that the old was wrong and the new is right" (Nock 7). Forsaking a dark, misguided past for a brighter, righter future he now turned to face, Paul became a touchstone by which conversion is still measured, "enshrined in Western thought" as the epitome of profound personal change (Coleman 17). When that other autobiographer who has so influentially defined conversion undergoes his own transformation beneath a certain fig tree, who else's words would we expect that he should be divinely directed to *tolle lege*—take up, and read?

The miraculous character alone of Paul's conversion experience makes it interesting. But from a rhetorical perspective, just as interesting are three comparatively banal moments that follow his vision—namely the three recorded instances in which he shares the story of his transformation (also in the New Testament). That Paul retold this story at least three times isn't surprising. Without presuming to know the mind of his god, it seems a justifiable surmise that his experience on the road to Damascus was a spectacular one in part so that it would merit retelling, an anecdote sure to attract the many ears he would subsequently bend on the missionary journeys that occupied the remainder of his life. Seeing the once-entombed, now-resurrected Jesus in a light from heaven, hearing his voice, and then being healed of your resultant blindness by one of this Christ's chosen apostles does make for an excellent *prooemium,* as the Greek rhetoricians would term it: it is a much more alluring call to hear Paul's oration than if he had undergone a comparatively cerebral conversion—say, as a consequence of years of careful study of the Torah. (One can hardly imagine the market-embroiled Jews or Gentiles who would be lured away from their to-do lists by a stranger's declaration of "Let me tell you how I have changed my mind.")

But retelling any story opens it to inconsistencies, and Paul's retellings are no different. And while some of the divergences in his narratives seem minor enough, others beg explanation. For example, how does this conversion by way of an overpowering, blinding, and certainly terrifying vision square with his description of these events in his letter to the Galatians as a "call[ing] by grace" (Gal. 1:15)? The fact that Paul's words have weathered nearly two millennia of textual transmission might explain some of the inconsistencies in his narratives: for instance, his traveling companions hear the voice that speaks to him in one version, but not in another; they remain standing in one, but fall to the ground in another. Perhaps he simply misremembers some of these jots and tittles as he tells his story, caught up instead in the prevailing message of his vision—that working against this Jesus is to work one's own undoing, to "kick against the pricks" (Acts 9:5). Or maybe there is malevolence behind the inconsistencies. Maybe Paul is, as Nietzsche argues, a liar, and a bad one at that, failing to keep straight the details of his own invented, hallucinogenic miracle.[1] History boasts no small lineup of those who have sought—and found—personal gain through greater fictions than this.

Another possibility, however, can explain some of the more significant differences in Paul's portrayals of his conversion, such as that in the Galatian letter I have just mentioned. If one grants that even relatively minor changes of life can be complicated matters, then his sense of having become a "new creature" through his transforming epiphany was surely far from simple (Gal. 6:15). Perhaps this new sense of self that his transformation yielded—a self-understanding we today would term his sense of *identity*—was complex enough to accommodate a range of possible expressions, rich with as many meanings as means for conveying them. Is the telling of stories about ourselves not fundamentally an exercise in emphasis? In composing these self-stories, do we not, as De Waele and Harré assert, necessarily shape them in response to the "cultural setting" and other specifics of the occasion in and for which we compose them, whatever personal realities we mean them to express? Is it not tenable to suggest, then, that Paul, a rabbi formally schooled and skilled in the art of rhetoric, would have recognized the malleability of his own self-story and, along with it, the persuasive potential of sharing this story in a certain way for a certain audience?[2]

Returning to Galatians for a moment, Paul's letter there is a sermon on grace for an audience of fellow Christians—recent converts like himself who were trying to reconcile their former lives beneath the Law of Moses with this new gospel's much less concrete prescriptions. As Paul sought to convey, their happiness waited on a road he had already walked: only in releasing their hold upon the outward, conspicuous observances of tradition could they become, like him, new creatures in a gospel that bade them to live not by sight but by faith. Adding even this rudimentary awareness of audience and purpose to a reading of Paul's letter helps to illuminate why his opening narrative about his conversion here mimetically downplays the outward and obvious (heavenly voices and blinding lights) and emphasizes the intangible—the inscrutable mercies of God, the *grace*—behind his miraculous reversal. Paul's other narratives about his self-transformation are at least as varied as the immediate audiences to whom he addresses them. Whatever he felt to be the realities of his conversion, sharing this experience was not a matter of delivering some stock, trans-situational message; rather, it was an act of triangulating the meaning of this experience in relation to *whom* he addressed in sharing it and *what* he aimed to accomplish in the sharing. One interlocutor of Paul's conversion narrative, the Roman honorific King Agrippa, even responds to him in words that make it difficult to miss the rhetorical in his self-storying: "Almost thou persuadest [*peitheis*] me to be a Christian" (Acts 26:28). However one determines what is ultimately "correct" in the different accounts of Paul's conversion, John Gager argues for one vital consideration in arriving at such a judgment, a "new law" about reading Paul: "*if you miss his rhetorical strategies, you will get him wrong*" (13, emphasis in original).[3]

This is not a book about Paul. But it is a book about life-altering experiences like his—*conversions,* or transformations that, whether sacred or profane, bathed in blinding lights or shrouded in psychological interiority, are as self-defining, or redefining, for the people who have written about them as Saul's conversion was for the Paul it brought into being. Autobiographical narratives of such conversions, as I look to them here, tell us something about one important rhetorical strategy Paul demonstrates in speaking and writing about his own conversion—the rhetorical strategy of *identity,* the influencing of others through the articulation of our sense of *who we are.* In light of the many fields where identity is both a key critical term and a central object of study—psychology, sociology, philosophy, anthropology, to name but a few of the concept's major shareholders—the nature of a specifically rhetorical interest in identity bears some explaining. One way of viewing identity rhetorically, as I am suggesting, is to view it as a kind of persuasive strategy, as a means of moving audiences toward certain beliefs or actions. From this more-or-less traditional rhetorical perspective (one I do not directly challenge herein), identity matters less as something that one "is" and more as something that one *does* in language; or, more exactly, identity matters as something that one does to an audience through the expression of who or what one is. Considering the rhetorical dimensions of such expression means focusing on the interrelated questions of how identities are "made" in the texts that articulate them, what they are made of, and how they are made persuasive.

Conversion narratives lend themselves uniquely to such questions. In telling the story of an "encompassing transformation that touches every facet of an individual's life—physical, spiritual, emotional, psychological, and political" (Schauffler 6)—these narratives invite an especially focused look at how identity is both a subject for these authors *within* their autobiographies and a rhetorical means by which they pursue aims in the world *outside* their texts. Seeking to transform readers as definitively as the authorial transformations they portray, conversion narratives offer a singular window on the workings of identity's strategy.

Does Rhetoric Need Identity? A Doxology

The central claim upon which all this rests—that the expression of identity, one's sense of self-understanding, is a powerful means of persuasion—should strike few as novel. The "identity politics" of the past quarter century has done nothing if not cast in high relief the rhetorical dimension of identity, its usefulness as a tool for social and political change, stereotypically so in the leverage of specific identity categories (the equally stereotypical triumvirate of race, class, and gender). Perhaps we are so accustomed to this dynamic of identity that we all the more heartily concur with the judgment Edward Said pronounced almost a decade ago—that "identity as such is about as boring a subject as one can imagine" (7).

What I offer here, however, is in part a counterpoint or corrective to this very general sense of identity's utilitarian potential, and perhaps even the attendant ennui at its ubiquity. For with them has settled an equally general sense of *how* identity accomplishes the cultural, rhetorical work it does. Looking at how conversion narratives wield identity toward changing the beliefs and actions of the audiences they address, I outline a means for bringing identity's rhetorical functions more clearly into the critical foreground. The joint poetics and rhetoric of identity I develop, a framework for discussing both how identity is made or constituted in these narratives and how it is then exercised toward persuasive ends, will, I hope, contribute to making the strategic dynamics of identity a more deliberate, more precisely explored area of rhetorical theory. At the same time, I have tried to elaborate this framework in a way that invites application in areas of study beyond rhetoric, especially those areas that I have drawn on to articulate identity's persuasive functions, including autobiography, cultural and philosophical anthropology, and narrative theory.

Yet in arguing for increased rhetorical attention to identity, I am well aware of the contestation I invite. The term can be something of a firebrand in even the most polite theoretical circles. Whatever the various labels that have been fashioned for our dominant current perspective on human being and human knowing—poststructuralism, social constructivism, the postmodern condition—a pronounced effect of this perspective has been the virtual abandonment of "identity" as a valid theoretical concept. The word smacks of a certain naive modernism, of enlightened, unified, atomistic individuals freely doing and becoming as is their fancy. The "essentialist" conception of the human person that identity seems to connote—of an agential self that exists prior to and ultimately outside the forces of language, culture, and history—has become a favored target of critical theory since poststructuralism. Not without reason, one of its particularly fervent crusades has been to topple this one-word legacy of the Cartesian *cogito*, "to dismantle the concept of identity" (Moya 2).

The prolonged sorties against identity have been effective. In the "crisis of concepts" that characterizes our post-postmodern effort to talk about the human person (Schrag 3), identity has become part of the problem, not the solution.[4] At worst, identity is a malevolent ideological minion, the mystifying calling card of a transcendental subject that never existed. At best, it is "a nonissue—a muddle that should be skipped in favor of clearer terrains" (Lie 3). And perhaps it is even an outright bore. Why, then, should rhetoric risk the critical disfavor, the indictments of backwardness and (gasp) *humanism*, the yawns, in owning any interest in such a *verbum non grata?* More than just an interest, does rhetoric dare to profess a need for—perhaps even a responsibility to—the concept of identity that should prevent rhetoric's march in the well-attended parade of disavowal? Certainly the assorted "post-" critiques of identity that I allude to have been valuable, especially in revealing how the term has served to naturalize different ideologies of selfhood; consequently, I do not invoke *identity* here in the essentialist terms of the not-so-distant past, as a word for some ineffable, unified, and stable substance—that irreducible something that makes us a discrete, induplicable *I*.

But if identity is considered not in these *ontological* terms but in *experiential* ones instead, as a word not for what a person or self "really" is but rather for a person's ability to articulate a sense of self or self-understanding, then the concept should indeed hold a place within rhetoric's critical vocabulary of the person.[5] Allow me to couch my defense of this claim in a brief anecdote that, while fictitious, should yet ring true. As I converse with a neighbor I know to be somewhat bookish, my remarks might turn toward one of my recent favorites, Yann Martel's *Life of Pi.* I tell him that I not only enjoyed the book heartily, but that it has fundamentally changed the way I view my relation to the animal kingdom as well: I now have a much more robust understanding of the interdependence of human and nonhuman life forms, an understanding that humbles me as I come to grips with a revised conception of my responsibilities to other living creatures.

Even if my neighbor has not read Martel's excellent book, and regardless of his own reception of the story's message about the hierarchy of being in the world, my neighbor can make sense of my claims about its effects on me, provided that I can be sufficiently articulate about them. When I tell him that I no longer think of myself in the same terms, he does not balk at the idea. He does not besiege me with questions about this object I refer to as "my self," its knowability, or how it is, exactly, that I am able to revise my understanding of it on the simple act of reading a work of fiction. "I feel as though my identity is significantly different," I might continue, putting a fine point on things, and he will know what I mean. He will know that, if I were asked to clarify, I would explain that I now have a different answer to the question of "who am I?" than

I did before reading Martel's moving novel. He may dispute the veracity of my claims to a changed, less anthrocentric self—he has just seen me yelling at my cat moments before our chat—but he understands the possibility of what I'm saying nonetheless. He understands, I safely assume, that my identity is an evolving sense of who I am. It may be more or less central in my thinking, more or less fixed or fluid, and more or less open to being further calcified or radically shaken by experiences with things such as books, pets, and conversations with one's neighbor.

My neighbor and I could have such a conversation in part because of the shared understanding of self and identity we both bring to our discussion, an understanding we have both elicited without explicitly having to acknowledge. That we might speak together about the "identity" I feel I have is, in this way, "common sense": the idea is intelligible to us both, accepted, and something we believe a majority of others like ourselves would also deem intelligible and acceptable. Were my neighbor to find my experience of personal change interesting enough, he might share it with a friend of his, expecting, as I did, that the ideas of self and identity it deals with already have referents in the mind of his audience. However hypothetical my anecdote, this commonsense, implicit understanding of identity is far from a fiction. It is the same commonsense understanding that undergirds a recent composition reader's assertion of what it believes are comprehensible claims about the relationship between writing and the self. "We all have multiple identities," the text (titled *Identity Matters*) confidently pronounces; "You have the freedom to interrogate your own beliefs and attitudes and to examine multiple factors that determine your identity" (1), and writing is an effective vehicle for such excursions into the ineluctable heterodoxy of our self-knowledge. I am not faulting the text for its panoramic claims about identity and language, for not engaging in some Foucaultian excursus on the trammeling quandaries of selfhood they mask. On the contrary, from the experiential orientation to identity I wish to elaborate here, it is much more telling that the authors of the reader engage in no such efforts to clarify a grand abstraction such as identity for their intended audience of first-year college students. They assume these students will know from experience what identity is, that they have identities and can talk about them, and that they will know and recognize the identities of others when they see them in the prose collected therein. They further assume that the graduate instructors and faculty who teach with this text will also know these things about identity, and know them thoroughly enough to improve the knowledge of others about them as well.

This commonsense understanding of identity in contemporary culture grounds both rhetoric's need for the term and rhetoric's responsibility to the activities that happen in its name. As long as it seems a basic, even inherent feature of human selfhood (and perhaps especially Western selfhood) that people can formulate and share answers to the question of "who I am," this conviction will continue to inform and authorize a range of discursive acts—acts as different and pervasive as conversations, textbooks, and autobiographies. The persuasive ends of such acts of identity expression are uniquely rhetoric's task to parse and critique.

Identity itself may be a concept of modern coinage, but the charge that rhetoric attend to the commonsense and conventional about such an aspect of contemporary human experience is an ancient one. This concern for the culturally common, particularly as it functions in discourse, is as old as rhetoric's long tradition as a doxastic art—as a faculty of persuasion "concerned with such things as are, to an extent, within the knowledge of all people" (Aristotle, *On Rhetoric* 1354a).[6] As Aristotle explains, *endoxa,* or "generally accepted opinions," are the starting point of rhetoric; unlike first principles (*arkhai*), which are knowledge claims universally regarded as true, endoxa are beliefs that are widely held, yet still open to disputation—beliefs "which commend themselves [or, in George Kennedy's translation, "which seem right"] to all or to the majority or to the wise" (*Topics* 100b, Forster's translation). In their character as questionable, yet typically unquestioned, *doxa* are "the positive inverse of *adoxa* and *paradoxa,* shameful and problematic opinions" (Amossy, "Introduction" 371).[7]

Understanding identity rhetorically begins with understanding how such doxa about identity govern its meaning and possible uses in a given culture. As "the ensemble of norms (beliefs, values, motifs) invested in discourse" (Sarfati 493) about identity, these doxa inform how identity might be utilized in an attempt to shape the conduct and convictions of a given audience, for they determine what kinds of claims about identity are intelligible in the first place. My neighbor's unproblematic reception of my claims to a changed identity, to a revised sense of the "who" that is me, for example, bespeaks a mutual invocation of our doxa about identity—mine in making what I take to be meaningful identity claims, my neighbor's in interpreting them as such. A necessary concomitant to civic life, this shared foundation of commonly held beliefs explains how, as Steve Pile and Nigel Thrift observe, "in everyday life, certain words are bandied around with thoughtless abandon, such as body, self, person, identity and subject"; despite the complexities they encompass, such terms yet "seem to need no further explanation" and "appear obvious" in the discourse between people of similar enculturation (2).[8] Doxa often assume this peculiar status of being, as the expression goes, those ideas we think *with* rather than think *about;* they are, as Aristotle summarizes, "the 'given'" in discourse (*Rhetoric* 1355b). This "givenness" seems especially true of our cultural understanding of self, identity, and other such terms regarding the nature of the person. Indeed, it is precisely the taken-for-granted-ness—and hence the power—of how such doxastic elements define personhood that Clifford Geertz targets in his now-axiomatic assertion: "there is no such thing as human nature independent of culture" (51).

Within the general doxa that define the person, *identity* names the commonly held belief that human selves are capable of—and arguably incapable of functioning without—some sense of self-definition, some answer to the question of "who I am" in the culture, society, and world they inhabit. Created through a capacity for self-interpretation seen largely as the essence of human selfhood, identity is one's understanding of oneself as a self.[9] Of course this *self* that is a person's interpretive object in creating identity is as culturally, doxastically governed in meaning as is *identity*; accordingly, those features that a culture holds as foundational or intrinsic to selves—gender, race, ethnicity, or family relationships, for example—often most powerfully influence the ongoing process of self-interpretation that informs one's identity. Such features become something that every identity must reflect: they are the norms of "undamaged human personhood" (Taylor, *Sources* 27), the "attributes [that] the person finds it difficult or disturbing to imagine himself or herself without" (Perry 190). Counterposed to these imperatives of self-interpretation, other aspects of identity seem to be largely matters of choice: for example, how profession or religion factor into one's sense of self, if such features factor in at all. Presenting a theory of agency to justify this picture of identity as a nexus of determination and choice is not my intention here. Rather, in the doxastic perspective I am trying to outline, what matters is how powerfully commonsense (or powerful *because* commonsense) this dynamic of identity is—that identity is sometimes a matter of choice, sometimes a matter of acceptance. Accounting for the interplay between the two is a main component of the poetic of identity constitution I develop in chapter 3.

Whatever their particular configurations of inherencies and allegiances, identities serve certain truth functions in culture that drive their importance. The most basic such function is the use of identity as that which identifies another: identity is what we invoke in order to correctly, consistently single out a person as a specific individual. The "truth" of identity in this sense surely means more to the identifier than the identified, little more than a sign that one is a verifiable human someone, by name, appearance, fingerprint, or other sufficiently reliable attribute. Simple as it may be, this sense of identity as that which makes us demonstrably unique (what Erving Goffman has called "personal identity") is a load-bearing girder in the foundation of culture. Think of the consequence in the realm of fiction alone if dissembling double agents who trade on our national security can no longer be ferreted out, their secret, true identities finally revealed. Think of the much more pressing consequences if the Internet criminals who recently acquired an estimated forty million credit card numbers aren't prosecuted for identity theft. Identity allows us to say *you are known*, and on this hinges any ability to hold people accountable as the authors of specific actions. For this reason alone, even if having an identity were of no personal concern to us at all, civil society would yet ensure that we had one anyway.

But identity performs a much more complex truth function as well, and one that is central to how identity persuades. A term not just for what others regard as verifiable proofs of who we are, identity also names that which we regard as true about ourselves—those "deepest and most enduring features of our unique selves that constitute who we believe ourselves to be" (Williams 7). When I know another's identity in this richer sense (a close friend of mine's, for example), I know more than how to find her in a crowd: I know something of the truths of personal experience that anchor and define her sense of self. I know something of what endures about her beneath the changes she makes in accordance with her changing situations. However different she might appear to me in the array of contexts and roles she occupies—more authoritative as an instructor than as a mother, less detail-oriented as a canasta partner than as a housekeeper—I know some of the claims she would make to articulate who she really, truly is. *I am Argentine. I am an agnostic. I am a married woman and a mother of two. I am a five-years-sober alcoholic. I am a breast cancer survivor.* To change any of these or other defining features of her self-understanding would require some kind of experience greater than the changes of character or persona her average day elicits, an experience as real and personally true as whatever aspect of her identity it alters. In short, it would require something like a conversion—"a self-transformation, a change in what one *is*" (Stromberg 18).

In reflecting what is thus "accepted by individuals to be true of themselves independent of time and location" (Williams 7), identities express what can be called the personal truths or personal realities of an individual's experience. And because personal experience is *personal*, directly accessible only to the person who has experienced it, the identities we build out of our personal experiences are unique points of rhetorical authority. "We cannot judge the truth of a writer's sense of his or her own lived experience," Candace Spigelman comments (81); the immediacy or singularity of experience that insulates it from the direct apprehension of others effectively renders us de facto authorities on what our individual personal experiences mean—and what they mean, if anything, to our identities, regardless of counterinterpretations. If I were in Paul's traveling company on the Damascan road, for example, I might contend with him about the truthfulness or accuracy of one of his renditions of our miraculous experience—the voice he claims to have heard, the light he says he saw. (Depending on the narrative, one of these phenomena would have escaped my notice.) But how do I prove or disprove the reality of his sense of being called to the service of Jesus? How do I contend with him about the meaning of what for him is a transformative personal truth? Just as our "personal experience cannot be nullified or negotiated" by others (Spigelman 77), identity suggests that, at some point, we must accept a person's word for what is real and true about who they are, for their words are all we have. As exegetes of ourselves, we are not easily trumped.[10]

This sense of truth in identity also has ethical and material implications at least as powerful as these rhetorical implications. For when people have something they thus regard as true *about* themselves, they also have something they can be—and are often expected to be—more or less true *to*. If grading is something I do as part of my profession but not something that defines who I am, I can give a friend an overly generous evaluation of a short story he's written without losing much sleep. However, if my sense of self is anchored in my devotion to the sensitive, yet unflinchingly accurate appraisal of writing, then my action—my self-betrayal—could occasion serious personal turmoil. Forcing me to admit that I'm not the critic I thought I was, it may leave me wondering who I really, truly am: it might initiate an identity crisis. Left unresolved, this crisis may even become a diagnosable identity disorder. Offering such a diagnosis, of course, would not be the bailiwick of the theorist, who is still free to question "Who needs identity?," and perhaps to grow weary at the banality of the question before positing an answer. But when a mental health professional plies a sophisticated personality index to verify identity's absence, when medications are prescribed to assuage its lack (as insurance workers determine who will foot the bill), and when therapies are enacted to facilitate its return, the broader cultural discourse registers an unequivocal validation of what it already knew about identity, and what it knew about who needs it. You need it. We need you to have it. And if you don't, it can cost us all.[11]

This is a far from complete catalog of the commonsense "givens" about identity in contemporary culture, meant less as a definition of *identity* than as an illustration of the experiential or doxastic orientation to the term that the following chapters assume. From this doxastic perspective, what people "have" when they have identity is a personally defining, culturally informed, and to some extent expressible self-interpretation. An umbrella term for all the "ways in which a person can tell others 'who I am'" (Deaux 224), *identity* is a deeply held sense of the realities of oneself, shaped by particular doxastic commonplaces about the nature of human selfhood. For rhetoric to work from such a doxastic perspective on identity—an emphasis on how identity is experienced and articulated in culture—is to focus on how commonsense beliefs about identity and selfhood function in discourse, informing the actions of rhetors and audiences alike in specific discursive exchanges. And while there is merit in the "critical rhetoric" that would adjudicate the veracity of these commonly held beliefs, rhetoric should first ponder both how and why such doxastic elements are employed, their appropriateness to the implicit or explicit aims of a given text. Is gender *really* every bit as much a part of one's "soul" as it is a matter of external "performance," as Deirdre McCloskey asserts in her memoir about her conversion from male to female? This is one kind of question to ask about identity in her text. But whether McCloskey's intended audience buys the soulful, "felt" nature of gender identity beneath the surface of performativity, and whether this advances her argument for the more humane treatment of transgendered people, as I discuss in chapter 6: these are questions of another sort—rhetorical questions, the kind with rhetorical answers, aiming to enlarge our understanding of how language shapes human conduct. Our justifiable, productive skepticism about the falsehoods that common sense might fob off as self-evident truth does not justify the neglect of the persuasive effects that these falsehoods accomplish. The rhetorical responsibility to identity is a responsibility to scrutinize the persuasive work that identity performs in its manifold particular instantiations, work that gets done even if the identity driving it "is" every bit the ontological lie for which it is often suspect. To summarize this orientation in the words of Kenneth Burke, whose work has most influenced my approach here, rhetoric's concern should be "primarily with the analysis of *language* rather than with the analysis of '*reality*'" (GM 317).

This pragmatic approach to identity as a rhetorical engagement guides a variety of recent texts across the far-ranging study of rhetoric. Yun Lee Too's *The Rhetoric of Identity in Isocrates: Text, Power, Pedagogy*, for example, reveals how Isocrates exercised a "complex rhetoric of self" in attempting to craft his authority as both speaker and teacher in fourth-century Athens (4). A much different book, Wendy Hesford's *Framing Identities: Autobiography and the Politics of Pedagogy* explores how historically marginalized groups have utilized autobiography ("an especially weighty discourse of identity") as a counterforce to the power structures of the academy, "expos[ing] the partiality and presumptions of institutional histories and truths" (xx–xxiv). And in a book whose perspective shares much with my own, Stephen Browne's *Angelina Grimké: Rhetoric, Identity, and the Radical Imagination* examines how Grimké "symbolically fashioned" a "public self" in the service of nineteenth-century moral reform efforts. Grimké's influential advocacy of causes such as abolition and the emergent women's rights movement evidences how she found her most potent "available means of persuasion" in the depiction of her own identity; she found, as Browne summarizes, "that in creating herself she might transform the world" (1–4). If identity matters to rhetoric, then it matters in just the capacity these texts suggest—as a way to account for the expression of self-understanding as rhetorical action. Rhetoric needs identity not for what it might say or occlude about what we "really" are but rather for what it might reveal about how language moves us. Rhetoric needs identity because it can help to explain how in the claims we make about who we are we might also come to *transform the world.*

Measuring the Means and Ends of Identity Constitution

That the term *identity* appears frequently in books throughout rhetorical studies (as well as articles, conference presentations, and conference titles) does not mean, however, that any established or consistent framework guides inquiry into identity's rhetorical potentials. Definitions or clarifications about how the concept is being used rarely accompany such references to identity, and neither the recent *Encyclopedia of Rhetoric* nor the *Encyclopedia of Rhetoric and Composition* includes an entry for the term. On the whole, *identity* in rhetorical theory reflects the same commonsense, taken-for-granted status it exhibits in culture generally, a status that is at least twofold risky. Contentment with an uncritical notion of identity threatens to lead rhetoric, like other branches of theory, to see the ensuing theoretical ungainliness of such generality as endemic to "identity" itself, as further indictment of the concept's speciousness, and as yet more evidence for abandoning it. Worse yet, just as nature abhors a vacuum, leaving identity vacuously unspecified invites all manner of dubious supposition to slip in, even those pernicious essentialisms now three decades in the dismantling. In the absence of clear rhetorical formulations, identity drifts in vagueness, unproductive beyond evoking in us the commonsense nod of thinking that we know what someone means when they say it.

One area of rhetorical theory to suggest productive alternatives to this vagueness is the study of "constitutive rhetorics" or "constitutive discourse." As John Hammerback explains, constitutive rhetorics aim to "change . . . the character or self-identity of audiences"; they aim to "redefine" or "reconstitute" audiences "in ways that impel . . . them to enact the rhetor's substantive agenda" (18). Work in this area draws on a range of preeminent rhetorical thinkers, including Wayne Booth, Edwin Black, and especially Kenneth Burke.[12] Maurice Charland's "Constitutive Rhetoric: The Case of the *Peuple Québécois*" (the namesake of constitutive rhetoric), for example, draws on Burke's concept of identification to illustrate how the 1979 white paper of the Quebec sovereignty movement constituted an independent Francophone state by "call[ing] its audience into being" (134). That is, the document constituted its audience as a "peuple Québécois" in the rhetorical act of depicting this Québécois identity, and those who identify with this depiction become constituted in its terms. If a constitutive rhetoric succeeds, then it succeeds in just this way: it accomplishes a "rhetorical transformation" of an audience's sense of self, a transformation that often "requires auditors to adopt an altered identity and often to act out a new way of life" (Hammerback and Jensen 46).

I am indebted to the consideration identity has received within this rubric of constitutive rhetoric. My divergence from this work, however, is perhaps best illustrated by comparing how constitutive rhetoric has treated the kind of identity-formative experience that is my focus—conversion. As Hammerback and Jensen elaborate, *conversion* is an apt synonym for the kind of "rhetorical transformation" that audiences undergo as a result of a successful constitutive rhetoric. Typical cases of such transformation might include "the born-again Christian, the cult member, the newly converted political zealot, and many others [who] see themselves as different in fundamental ways from their former selves. They have experienced something more profound than a mere change in belief or attitude" (47). Both Charland and Black also describe this moment of an audience's rhetorical reconstitution, their acceptance of an altered identity (what Black has described as a "second persona"), as a moment of conversion (Charland 142; Black, "Idioms" 46–50).[13] But whereas constitutive rhetoric has focused on how rhetors constitute *the identities of audiences*, moving them to adopt the "altered identities" that such conversions entail, I instead want to consider how rhetors constitute *their own identities* through experiences of conversion in ways that would persuade. That is, rather than examine how a constitutive rhetoric has moved an audience member to adopt the new identity of "converted political zealot," I instead want to explore how this converted political zealot might narrate the story of this identity transformation, and narrate it in ways that would transform the audience or situation the text addresses, perhaps seeking to win further converts to the political zeal that has come to redefine this new convert's identity. (This is, in fact, just the errand I undertake in my reading of David Brock's *Blinded by the Right* in chapter 5.)

Thus while I draw on what have been insightful examinations of rhetoric's potential to transform identity, no constitutive approach exists for the analysis of what I call *first-person identity constitution.* Certainly rhetoric is interested in how rhetors portray themselves in the first person as a means of persuasion. Burke's simplest instance of identification is, after all, the identity assertion of "the politician who, addressing an audience of farmers, says, 'I was a farm boy myself'" (RM xiv). And long before Burke and identification, there were *ethos* and *persona,* key rhetorical and literary terms that differently assess how the person of the rhetor is a factor in persuasion. Rather than supplant these mainstays, I instead want to expand the basic rhetorical vocabulary of the person they represent. A fuller set of concepts for analyzing how rhetors assert self-understanding and self-definition toward persuasive ends helps to sharpen the focus on identity's rhetorical workings; at the same time, it clarifies the specific contributions that terms such as *ethos* and *persona* can be expected to make toward understanding identity's strategic function.

To develop this perspective on first-person identity constitution, I turn to the theorist who has most influenced both constitutive rhetoric and rhetoric's more general thinking about identity: Kenneth Burke. Decades before *identification* became rhetoric's reigning term of inquiry into matters of identity, Burke pored over what he termed "the problem of identity" manifested in human symbol use. Not some monolithic crisis he intended to solve, this problem is rather more of a perpetual concern for the complex, often enigmatic interactions between individuals and collectives by which both come to be defined. More specifically, Burke's "problem of identity" involves not simply the formation of such individual and collective identities in language but their *transformation* as well, the "ritualistic naming and changing of identity" that Burke saw as the driving force of all symbolic action (ATH 268).

Chapter 2 briefly lays out this problem of identity, its emphasis on how "changes of identity occur in everyone" (ATH 269), as a foundation for the more specific theory of identity constitution I develop in chapter 3. Breaking Burke's overarching, expansive "problem of identity" into three component grammatical, rhetorical, and symbolic problems of identity clarifies how Burke saw these distinct senses of transformation at work in the linguistic transaction of identity. Each of these problems is unique in emphasis; yet they share a common focus in their concern for revealing the manifold "uses, abuses, and techniques of identity transformation" that language enables (Eddy 20). Delineating these three perspectives, their individual emphases and their shared overall purpose, greatly illuminates how Burke's prevailing interest in "the possibilities of linguistic transformation" bears specifically on matters of identity (GM 338). And given that transformation is itself the "primary connotation" of conversion (Smith, "Concept" 55), this chapter's refined sense of the complex transformations that drive identity well sets the stage for an analysis of such identity transformation at work in specific narratives. Readers unfamiliar with Burke might use this chapter as something of a Fodor's guide to the agendas of the two actualized texts and one unfinished text of the motives trilogy at the center of his work; Burkophiles for whom these are familiar texts should yet find value in how they are read specifically with an eye toward articulating the place of identity in each, including the unfinished "A Symbolic of Motives" and the "study of individual identity" that Burke promised to offer therein ("Addendum" 222).

Building on this understanding of identity and its transformations as a crucial Burkean problematic, chapter 3 then presents a framework for analyzing the textual means and rhetorical ends of first-person identity constitution.

My primary text for developing this framework is Burke's "The Dialectic of Constitutions." Underrepresented in Burke studies generally and somewhat ironically absent from studies of constitutive rhetoric, Burke's theory of the workings of constitutions in the latter third of *A Grammar of Motives* can inform an enlightening model of identity as a rhetorical strategy—as a "substance designed to serve as motives for the shaping or transforming of behavior" (GM 342). Burke himself signals the connection between this neglected portion of *A Grammar of Motives* and questions of identity when he notes in *A Rhetoric of Motives* (five years following *A Grammar of Motives*) that the identities of individuals are "unique 'constitutions'" (21). In likening the substance of individual identity to the substance of constitutions, Burke provocatively intimates that identities exhibit the same shifting, context-dependent (or "scenic"), and inherently strategic nature as do their documentary analogues. As I illustrate in this chapter, the same tools that Burke provides for gauging the substantiating, strategic functions of these documents—circumference, the "agon" of constitutional principles, and the audience-addressed nature of constitutions—apply equally in measuring the poetic construction and the rhetorical aims of identities constituted in autobiographical narrative. Moreover, in suggesting that identity and constitutions are both animated by the same dialectic of merger and division, the same "central moltenness" that is substance itself (GM xix), Burke offers a way of thinking about identity that ultimately subtends the well-parsed workings of identification. For to speak of identification is to invoke the consubstantiality at which identification aims, the sharing of substance between rhetor and audience. Such consubstantiality, however, presupposes an answer to a question that is too infrequently asked: Before substance can be shared, where, exactly, does it come from? The answer lies in constitutions.

The narratives I then turn to in fleshing out this model of first-person identity constitution all share as their centerpieces the experience of conversion. In the gamut of personal changes that people might experience, what makes conversions unique? As John E. Smith distinguishes, conversions result in a kind of change that, in comparison to other types of personal alteration, is "difficult to locate or determine." The "convert" is a person who "is in some sense changed, but the change seems not to be a difference *in* this or that feature of the person's life, but a change of person as if a new being now dwelt where another had lived before. . . . The change is so radical and so completely alters the being of the person that we are inclined to speak of a 'new' person being involved" (55). Clearly, all conversions involve change, but not all changes are conversions, transformations of an individual's very sense of who or what he or she is; in Paul's phrasing, the convert is one who is so changed to have been rendered a "new creature." The narratives of such profound personal redefinitions that I discuss here are all twentieth-century texts, primarily because of the great variety of conversion experiences that autobiographies of the last century, and perhaps especially of the last few decades, have brought to light. However much some of the conversions they treat may fall outside the religious contexts in which conversion is typically examined, these experiences of personal transformation yet manifest some of the most traditionally defined effects of conversion: whether a change of religion, or political conscience, or gender, these conversions all play a "significant role in the construction of identity, pointing a life in a particular direction, giving it aim. . . . provid[ing] a coherent center from which to conduct one's life" (Rambo 31–36). The different kinds of conversions in the narratives I discuss thus share this defining commonality as identity-transformative experiences, yet they diverge enough to illustrate that such transformations are far from an exclusively religious concern. To further define my approach here, my interest in the narratives that conversions inspire stands apart from studies of "conversion discourse" or "conversion rhetoric"—studies less about assessing rhetorical effects than establishing the tropologies and conventional structures that define the conversion narrative genre. While I believe certain patterns emerge across the narratives I examine, these patterns are incidental to my aim of demonstrating how identity functions within these narratives as a means of transforming the broader situations they address. I should also note that I intend to offer solely rhetorical judgments about the different conversions that these narratives present. My interest begins and ends with their nature as private experiences made public in text for a world of potential readers—and for a range of specific purposes, as I contend.

I begin my consideration of these narratives in chapter 4, applying the previous chapter's model of first-person constitution in a reading of Dorothy Day's *The Long Loneliness* (1952). The third of five autobiographical texts by this legendary Catholic social activist, *The Long Loneliness* narrates the story of Day's unlikely synthesis of religion and radicalism, a synthesis that undergirds the still-functioning Catholic Worker Movement she established following her conversion. Constituting her transformed identity as a representation of this synthesis, Day employs her conversion as an argument for the validity of her movement—a validity that needed dramatic reassertion for a 1950s public that had become more than suspicious of her antiestablishment religiosity. Responding to this skepticism, her conversion narrative, rather than just the story of her transformed self, becomes as well an attempt to transform public understanding of how religious faith can inform radical social intervention. To conclude this initial illustration of how an identity's narrative constitution can be analyzed as a strategic constitution—as an "instrument . . . for the shaping of human relations" (GM 341)—the chapter defines conversion in terms of this Burkean constitutional perspective.

Chapter 5 builds on this beginning by taking up a question I raised earlier about identity in rhetorical theory, a question sure to be on the mind of any rhetorician interested in self-presentation: What is the relationship between identity and ethos in measuring how the person of the rhetor is a factor in persuasion? My text for exploring this relationship is one of the most controversial political autobiographies of the past quarter century, David Brock's *Blinded by the Right: The Conscience of an Ex-Conservative* (2002). In this narrative of his conversion from fact-bending "right-wing attack dog" (11) to ethical, nonpartisan political watchdog, Brock faces a challenge unique within the narratives I consider here: the challenge of credibility. How can an admitted career liar tell a believable tale of personal transformation? How can Brock detail the transgressions of his past within a "vast right-wing conspiracy" while yet preserving the possibility of being forgiven by readers in the present? As Brock's attempt to meet this dual ambition for credibility and redemption demonstrates, persuading readers that he is truly changed and trustworthy is the work of ethos. It is also, however, the work of identity, the expression of Brock's self-understanding and its dramatic revision through the conversion he describes. Illuminating a strategy whereby character and identity cooperate toward realizing Brock's rhetorical aims, the chapter argues that there is more than simply room to consider identity in persuasive self-representation. If rhetoric is to fully assess the ways in which the person is persuasive, there is a clear need for this consideration as well.

Chapter 6 significantly expands both the scope of conversion and the sense of what it can change about identity through a reading of Deirdre McCloskey's *Crossing: A Memoir* (1999). In this detailed account of how Donald McCloskey came to accept the reality of her own female gender identity, McCloskey presents the conversion experience through which she realized this identity as an argument for the "reality" of gender identity beneath one's powers of self-fashioning or choice. Articulating a concept of identity as "both made and not made" (177), McCloskey thus contends that there are limits to our agency in determining who and what we are. In light of these limits, both the medical establishment that "treats" the "disorder" of transsexuality and society generally in its perception of transsexuality as a conscious choice need to dramatically revise their understanding of gender and identity. In short, they need to abandon the model of "prudence" upon which this understanding is predicated, one that, in its insistence that choice defines the alteration of one's gender, must inevitably hold transsexuals accountable for choosing imprudently.

Declaring one's identity in narrative, however, is but one way that such an expression of who one is can perform rhetorical work. What happens to a narrated identity's rhetorical possibilities when its narrator is no longer around to manage it—when its meaning and significance become entirely public domain? Chapter 7 examines this question by looking at one of the most widely read and widely contested narratives of Native American experience, John G. Neihardt's *Black Elk Speaks: Being the Life Story of a Holy Man of the Oglala Sioux* (1932). A narrative of Black Elk's visionary transformation into a vessel of redemption for the troubled Lakota Sioux nation, its account of Black Elk's failure in his divine calling constitutes him as the tragic embodiment of Plains Indian decline. Or does it? Drawing on Burke's consideration of how the scenes a constitution occupies can come to transform that constitution, I examine how changes in the contemporary "scenes" that *Black Elk Speaks* addresses have inspired his reconstitution in at least three distinct ways. This dialectic between a constitution and the "constitution *beneath* the constitution" (PLF 111), one where transformation is always potentially mutual, qualifies that identities may be potent rhetorical strategies, but they can never be the final arbiters of their meanings or rhetorical effects.

As a brief conclusion, chapter 8 reiterates both the challenge and the potential I have tried to demonstrate in considering identity rhetorically. "What a Constitution would do primarily is to *substantiate an ought* . . . to base a statement as to *what should be* upon a statement as to *what is*," Burke concisely summarizes the purpose of constitutions (GM 358). To borrow his idiom and summarize this final chapter, I hope to have substantiated the case for identity convincingly enough to transform skepticism about its theoretical gaucheness into a renewed consideration of its merits—and its necessity—in the study of persuasive discourse. For whatever else identity is, it is rhetorical. To an understanding of how we move and are moved in language, that ought to matter.

2

Tracing the Circles of Kenneth Burke's "Problem[s] of Identity"

Charts, Prayers, and Dreams of Transformation

All symbolism can be treated as the ritualistic naming and changing of identity.

Kenneth Burke, *Attitudes toward History*

Kenneth Burke's abode in mainstream rhetorical studies is the home that *identification* built. In his pragmatic–linguistic adaptation of this principle of Freudian psychology, Burke has shaped rhetoric's thinking about identity more than any other figure. But his concern with identity well predates his discussion of identification in *A Rhetoric of Motives* as the central mechanism by which identities are formed and transformed. In his third volume of theory and criticism, *Attitudes toward History,* Burke pondered at length the "ritualistic naming and changing of identity" we interminably enact in our symbol use, a proclivity he approached generally as "the problem of identity." The acts of "transcendence" through which we endeavor to become "symbolically endowed with a new identity"; the radical transformations of the "twice-born" whose identities are "at once a continuum and a duality"; the revisions of our "so-called 'I'" that result when "a given structure of society calls forth conflicts among our 'corporate we's'": these and other such "changes of identity [that] occur in everyone" caught Burke's attention in the 1930s—and held it for the rest of his career (263–337). So defining of our lives as language-learned animals is this penchant for self-naming and renaming that its "problem"—its ubiquity, its inevitability—can be seen as the driving force of all human symbolism. The claim that Burke articulates in 1937's *Attitudes toward History* he will prove over and again in the five decades of theorizing that follow it: his career-defining interests in humankind's "life in political communities," in the "characteristic responses of people in their forming and reforming of congregations," are interests that do, in fact, "come to a head in the problem of identity" (1, 263). Burke may not be rhetoric's only answer to questions of identity. But in continually excavating identity as a motive—even the primary motive—of human symbol use, he is one of rhetoric's most promising.

Burke's own powerful claims notwithstanding, however, his complex appraisal of identity and symbolic action is largely uncharted territory. This thread that both ornaments and binds his work has just begun to attract the kind of sustained critical interest that other Burkean concepts have long enjoyed, even ones that seem much less central.[1] This is a curious absence, both from a historical standpoint, if Jonathan Arac is correct in crediting Burke as "the first English-language critic to make extended, crucial use of the terms *identity* and *identification*" (203); and from an internal perspective on Burke's work as well, if Beth Eddy is right in naming identity—and especially identity transformation—as his work's "moral core" (20). One potential reason for this lack of attention to identity in Burke might be the general theoretical antagonism toward the term that characterizes the past three decades of French-inspired poststructuralism. (Burke himself was a target of this antagonism when Fredric Jameson rather famously indicted him in *Critical Inquiry* for his seemingly naive use of identity and hence for perpetuating bourgeois "American myths of the self" [82]). Another possible, and I think probable, explanation for our indefinite sense of identity's nature and significance in Burke is the status of his oft-described, yet never finished volume, "A Symbolic of Motives." More specifically, Burke's frequent nods to "A Symbolic of Motives" as the book that would "round out" his motives trilogy with a "study of individual identity" ("Addendum" 222) might have focused attention on what the work *would have said* about identity, diverting it from what Burke *has,* in fact, already said about the concept in all of his major works from *Attitudes toward History* on.[2]

Without trying to cobble together all that Burke has said about identity, in volumes finished or unfinished, I yet want to create a sense of the concept's richness in his work that encourages a broader application of Burke's engaging, if scattered, remarks on identity. To provide some context for the theory of identity constitution I develop in chapter 3, I want to articulate here a Burkean way of looking at identity—three interrelated ways, really—as something more compelling than identification's tagalong entailment, as something more definite than an abstract, overarching "problem" of human relations. For whatever else identity may be for Burke, our namings, changings, and expressions of identity, like all language, are a form of action upon the world; that is, they are *symbolic actions*. As such, they beg the questions that Burke asks in analyzing symbolic action—questions he hopes to motivate us to ask as well if we are to better apprehend the many "uses, abuses, and techniques of identity transformation" that are indeed among Burke's most enduring concerns (Eddy 20). These questions, as I formulate them here, comprise three distinct, yet complementary perspectives for analyzing identity in language, their emphases corresponding to the texts of Burke's planned trilogy on motives. Taking Burke's cue that "to think through a matter is to trace an ever-widening circle of relationships" (PC 230), I situate *A Grammar of Motives*, *A Rhetoric of Motives*, and "A Symbolic of Motives" as a series of narrowing hermeneutic contexts (or, in one of Burke's adaptations of William James, as narrowing *circumferences*) of Burkean inquiry into identity, each focused on "thinking through" a distinct dimension of identity—and especially identity transformation—as symbolic action. Tracing these three different, "interwoven" (PLF 5), and, as I place them, *concentric* problems within Burke's all-encompassing "problem of identity" opens at least three doors to a more nuanced understanding of identity in his work. Behind each lies great potential for a more practicable sense of identity's rhetorical significance.

Grammatical, Rhetorical, and Symbolic Problems of Identity

In "The Philosophy of Literary Form," the lead essay within the same-titled collection, Burke argues that there are three overlapping or "interwoven . . . subdivisions for the analysis of an act in poetry":

Chart: "the realistic sizing-up of situations that is sometimes explicit, sometimes implicit, in poetic strategies";
Prayer: "the communicative function of the poem"; and
Dream: "the unconscious or subconscious factors in a poem" (5–6).

Burke modifies this tripartite scheme with the publication of the first of his three planned examinations of "motive" four years later, *A Grammar of Motives*, opting instead for the nomenclature of *Grammar*, *Rhetoric*, and *Symbolic*, respectively. The linguistic dimensions of symbolic action that the earlier *chart*, *prayer*, and *dream* were intended to illuminate, however, still correspond directly with the emphases of the later *A Grammar of Motives*, *A Rhetoric of Motives*, and the promised "A Symbolic of Motives." Burke's lucid demonstration in "The Philosophy of Literary Form" of how these chart, prayer, and dream aspects of language come together in effecting symbolic action thus provides a useful précis of what the later motives volumes spell out in much greater detail. Moreover, Burke's concise demonstration of his critical method in this essay explains with a clarity to rival any other part of his work how these overlapping grammatical, rhetorical, and symbolic perspectives, while distinct, share a common interest in the different types of transformations that language enacts. Such transformations are at the heart of a Burkean conception of identity. In part to bring *The Philosophy of Literary Form* into discussions of Burke and identity, and in part to help clarify my own distinctions in what follows, I draw on his schema of chart, prayer, and dream in situating the grammatical, rhetorical, and symbolic circumferences of his hermeneutic inquiry into identity and transformation.

Charting Identity's "Great Central Moltenness" in *A Grammar of Motives*

A Grammar of Motives, the broadest circumference of Burke's motives trilogy, provides a general examination of "the forms necessarily exemplified in the imputing of human motives," "the resources . . . [that] figure in the utterances about motives, throughout all human history" (GM 402, 56). Given Burke's popular dictum that "situation is but another word for motives" (PLF 20; PC 29), *A Grammar of Motives* might be summarized as an inquiry into the most elemental mechanisms of language through which human beings interpret the infinite situations of action they come to perceive and inhabit. To elucidate this process of interpretation, he introduces the pentad (scene, act, agent, agency, purpose), outlines the ratios by which its five terms function in the imputation of motives, and presents "Dramatism" as the title for this methodological perspective, a perspective that, "being developed from the analysis of drama, treats language and thought primarily as modes of action" (GM xxii). In accordance with *chart*'s "realistic" emphasis on "the sizing up of situations" (or, again, the sizing up of *motives*), *A Grammar of Motives* is "concern[ed] with the *terms alone*" that factor into this process of sizing up, an exclusive focus on their function as "resources" or "*principles*" of interpretation (xvi). Burke's deliberate breadth here in elaborating what it means to view "language and thought primarily as modes of action" (xxii) makes *A Grammar of Motives* the least explicit of Burke's motives texts in its consideration of identity. But in its thorough treatment of language as a dialectical terrain of limitless potential transformations, *A Grammar of Motives* establishes the philosophical grounds upon which the more specific rhetorical and symbolic inquiries or problems of identity rest.[3]

This grounding materializes as Burke explores the true architectonic principle of his inquiry into motive: the concept of *substance.* "Men's conception of motive . . . is integrally related to their conception of substance," he notes. "Hence, to deal with problems of motive is to deal with problems of substance" (338). This equation is crucial to understanding his protracted inquiry into substance in *A Grammar of Motives,* particularly its appearance within a volume of a planned trilogy whose titular concept is *motive:* for behind every statement about motive there lies, implicitly or explicitly, some judgment about what a person or situation *substantially is* as well. Burke's concept of "substance" is hardly traditional, as is apparent in the fact that he moves to define the concept within a section titled "Antinomies of Definition." Moreover, that he begins by investigating not "substance" itself but a "paradox of substance" further intimates the deliberate indeterminacy at work in the "definition" he formulates. To briefly summarize, A *Grammar of Motives* approaches all language about motives or substances (and definitions in particular) as inherently ambiguous. "Since no two things or acts or situations are exactly alike," Burke explains in the introduction, "you cannot apply the same term to both of them without thereby introducing a certain margin of ambiguity, an ambiguity as great as the difference between the two subjects that are given the identical title" (xix). This "underlying enigma" of language use, as Burke terms it—that words "used to designate what a thing *is*" can also introduce "something that a thing *is not*"—"will manifest itself in inevitable ambiguities and inconsistencies among the terms for motives" (23, xviii).

Through these inevitable ambiguities and inconsistencies, such statements thus open themselves to the possibility of *transformation*. In Burke's simple example of transformation, two statements so seemingly irreconcilable as "A" and "non-A" can still from some interpretive angle be seen as sharing a common ground where A and non-A meet, a ground where their *opposition* might become *unification*. The transformations by which such oppositional divisions between statements become unifying mergers, and vice versa, are predicated upon these joint ambiguities of language and of substance, for "it is in the areas of ambiguity that transformations take place. In fact, without such areas, transformation would be impossible" (xix). The crux of Burke's grammatical inquiry into acts of linguistic imputation "throughout all human history" is therefore that ambiguity be perceived not as an obstacle to analysis but as a "*resource*"—a resource tapped not through "*terms that avoid ambiguity*" but through "*terms that clearly reveal the strategic spots at which ambiguities necessarily arise*" (xvii–xix).[4]

In total, the "realistic sizing-up of situations," the *charting* of symbolic action that Burke explains as the focus of A *Grammar of Motives*, comprises a dual emphasis. First, it focuses our attention on discerning the terms or "principles" at work in any statement about "what people are doing and why they are doing it" (GM xv). This, of course, would include statements where what people do or why they do it appear to us to involve identity. What general terms or principles inform our discourses about identity, and how do these discourses impute identity as a motive in human experience? Sizing up such terms or principles in this way entails the second crucial emphasis of Burke's grammatical focus on identity: an awareness of the inevitable ambiguities of such terms and principles, ambiguities whereby statements about identity, or any situation or motive of human conduct, might find themselves altered beyond anyone's intentions. One need only briefly survey the evolving academic terminologies of human personhood to grasp the ambiguities endemic to any such discussion. It is precisely this ambiguity inherent in all language use, along with the potential transformations it invites—"strategic" and otherwise—that both anchors and animates Burke's "problem of identity."

Identity's Partisan Prayerfulness in *A Rhetoric of Motives*

A Rhetoric of Motives builds upon and specifies the emphasis on ambiguity and substance in *A Grammar of Motives*. Burke's concern with these issues in *A Grammar of Motives* is, again, deliberately as panoramic as possible, a concern with "universal paradoxes of substance," with "resources of placement and definition common to all thought" (RM 21). In *A Rhetoric of Motives*, however, he narrows his investigation to consider how these issues of ambiguity and substance manifest themselves in the specific—in "*actual statements about motives*," in all the "stratagems which people employ, in endless variations, and consciously or unconsciously, for the outwitting or cajoling of one another" (GM xvi–xvii). "The ambiguity of substance affords, as one might expect, a major resource of rhetoric," Burke notes in *A Grammar of Motives*, anticipating his exploration of this coy understatement in *A Rhetoric of Motives* (51). Indeed, the persuasive potential of ambiguity is so vast a resource that he introduces a new rhetorical instrument with which to fathom it: *identification*. Rhetoric, "the use of words by human agents to form attitudes or to induce actions in other human agents" (RM 41), is typically seen as functioning through its "traditional principle," persuasion. But persuasion, he qualifies, presupposes a conscious awareness in both speaker and audience that would occlude the many unconscious ways in which people are moved toward belief and action. "Even without being subjected to deliberate persuasion, we spontaneously identify ourselves with some groups or other, some trends or other—and we need a term for this kind of persuasion in which (you might say) we spontaneously, intuitively, and often unconsciously, act upon ourselves" (*Dramatism* 27–28). *Identification* thus becomes the "key term" of *Rhetoric*'s effort to probe this "intermediate area of expression that is not wholly deliberate, yet not wholly unconscious. . . . midway between aimless utterance and speech directly purposive."[5] It is Burke's tool for illustrating "how a rhetorical motive is often present where it is not usually recognized, or thought to belong" (RM xii–xiv).

The identifications that language effects can assume myriad forms, all of which bear on treating identity as a kind of symbolic action. As Burke illustrates, identifications range from the "deliberate device[s]" of "the politician

[who] seeks to identify himself with his audience"—a conscious persuasive strategy—to the much less obvious means by which people "become identified with groups more or less at odds with one another" (RM 22). And while *identification* may be the "key term" of *A Rhetoric of Motives,* Burke first explores the concept's possibilities in the much earlier *Attitudes toward History.* Indeed, it is in that text's "Dictionary of Pivotal Terms" that he presents identification as a fundamental mechanism of identity, a tenet that undergirds the entire *Rhetoric of Motives.* In the dictionary's entry on "Identity, Identification" (a conjunction that already asserts the interdependence of the two concepts), Burke presents his oft-quoted maxim that "the so-called 'I' is merely a unique combination of partially conflicting 'corporate we's'" (264). Identification in this conception of the individual names the process by which the "unique combination" of the *I*, of one's sense of identity, is assembled: it is the process of perceiving the self in relation to the various social scenes it occupies, such that acquiring a "new identification" proffers "a new way of defining the individual's identity with relation to a corporate identity" (337). As *Attitudes toward History* argues, and as the later *Rhetoric of Motives* concurs, "'identification' is hardly other than a name for the *function of sociality,*" for "one's participation in a collective, social role cannot be obtained in any other way" (ATH 266–67).

Burke continues this emphasis on identity as a nexus of various social identifications in *A Rhetoric of Motives.* Yet he moves beyond *Attitudes toward History* there as well by more explicitly considering identification in light of the emphasis on substance in *A Grammar of Motives.* More specifically, *A Rhetoric of Motives* conjoins *Attitudes toward History*'s conception of identity as a social, *rhetorical* process with the *Grammar*'s terminological, *dialectical* focus on substance: just as *A Grammar of Motives* provides a dialectical map (or *chart*) through the potential mergers and divisions in the ambiguous heart of any statement about substance, so *A Rhetoric of Motives* would scrutinize these statements not merely as words about substance, but as purposive, *strategic* transformations of substance, as ways of characterizing substance that would serve deliberate suasive ends.[6] The mechanism of this characterization is identification. "To identify A with B is to make A 'consubstantial' with B," goes Burke's well-known phrase (RM 21). For a person to forge an identification with some other individual, a cause, or a corporate unit in which one participates amounts to the assertion that the person and the object of its identification are in some sense at one, identical. As per Burke's paradigm case of identification, to declare that "we" are at war is to declare a common ground of *at war-ness* on which all auditors stand, a shared substance of purpose or intention with which all in earshot would *identify,* however diverse the hearers. (The question of where such a substance comes from before it can be shared in this way is the subject of chapter 3.) Recalling "The Philosophy of Literary Form," such an identification would be an example of the *prayerful* function of an act of language, of how "the poet's inducements can lead us to participate in his poem"—here, the poem's implicit plea that we join in preparations for armed conflict (PLF 5–6). Together, these earlier sociological and later rhetorical uses of identification assert the basic perspective on identity that permeates the whole of Burke's musings on human relations: that identity is not an "essence" that one *has* but "a *process*, a social, symbolic, linguistic process" (Crusius 37, emphasis added). It is a process in which the individual who would occupy even the smallest of roles in the drama of human relations must participate.

Identification is a complicated concept in Burke, one that he develops from multiple angles, at different points in his writings, and one whose resultant multiple senses all have bearing on how Burke theorizes identity. Following *Attitudes toward History*, we can regard identification as "a name for the function of sociality" (268), as a term for the general interdependence of the self and the social through which seemingly endless permutations of identity are cast. These senses of identity and identification both inform the later *A Rhetoric of Motives*, where Burke expands on identification as an instrument of language in its "*partisan* aspects" (RM 22, emphasis in original). Here, Burke demonstrates how identifications can transpire at varying levels of consciousness and can therefore operate with corresponding complexity in language that would bring us into the fold of its ambitions. For example, identification can be the *means* of persuasion, as in such deliberate and "stylistic identifications" as the assertion of shared identity by "the politician who, addressing an audience of farmers, says 'I was a farm boy myself'" (RM xiv); identification can also be the persuasive *end*, or rhetorical *effect* of language, as with the "we" that would drive a diverse audience to identify with a shared national state of pending war.[7]

And finally, by conceptualizing *A Rhetoric of Motives* in terms of the emphasis on substance in *A Grammar of Motives* before it, Burke demonstrates that these senses of identification are all ways of understanding "the possibilities of linguistic transformation" at the level of the rhetorical—at the level of *actual statements* that would move us one way or another. "One need not scrutinize the concept of 'identification' very sharply to see, implied in it at every turn, its ironic counterpart: division," Burke counsels (RM 23). In other words, the resources of ambiguity that *A Grammar of Motives* should diligently chart are every bit as present in the rhetorical; in the same dialectical spirit of transformation through merger and division, statements that rhetorically would bring us to identify in one respect also divide us in another.[8] This nebulous line between union and division, this "central moltenness" (GM xix) from which all such distinctions are forged, melded, and recast, is itself the very nativity of the rhetorical: "In pure identification there would be no strife. . . . But put identification and division ambiguously together, so that you cannot know for certain just where one ends and the other begins, and you have the characteristic invitation to rhetoric" (RM 25). The *Rhetoric*'s perhaps most salient contribution as a component of Burke's "problem of identity," then, is its argument that the identities produced through our many converging and diverging identifications are no more fixed or final than the words that would call them into being, whoever the supplicant and whatever their partisan purpose.

Identity Dreams of Singularity: "A Symbolic of Motives"

Burke's last planned volume of the motives trilogy, "A Symbolic of Motives," would have represented the most specific context for his treatment of identity, as compared to the treatments it receives in *A Grammar of Motives* and *A Rhetoric of Motives.* The scope of motivational inquiry that begins with terms and transformation in general and then narrows to the uses of these terms and transformations in rhetorical discourse, respectively, would here at the symbolic confine itself to the study of "the individual in his uniqueness" (RM 37). As I mentioned earlier, the fact that "A Symbolic of Motives" was never finished does not compromise a discussion of what Burke planned to do at this level. In addition to the fact that many of the selections that had been slated for inclusion in "A Symbolic of Motives" were either published earlier or have been published since (many appearing in 1966's *Language as Symbolic Action*), we also have Burke's numerous descriptions of what "A Symbolic of Motives" would have covered in his works since 1945. Additional help in understanding "A Symbolic of Motives" comes from the fact that both *A Grammar of Motives* and *A Rhetoric of Motives* take considerable pains to situate their respective projects in relation to the culminating "A Symbolic of Motives." For example, the discussion of "scene" in the pentadic reading of philosophical schools in *A Grammar of Motives* devotes nearly ten pages to a section on "Rhetorical and Symbolic Levels," where Burke presents a series of "hypotheses, problems, or undemonstrated propositions" to illustrate the "unconsidered . . . important matters" that *A Grammar of Motives* must defer for consideration in its companion motive volumes (161–70). And part 1 of *A Rhetoric of Motives,* where Burke delimits "The Range of Rhetoric," offers even more numerous statements as to the aim of "A Symbolic of Motives," noting in particular how its focus both differs from and complements that of *A Rhetoric of Motives.*

Taken together, Burke's various descriptions of "A Symbolic of Motives" establish a clear trajectory for its intended "study of individual identity" ("Addendum" 222). A longer passage from *A Rhetoric of Motives* illustrates.

> Our third volume, *Symbolic of Motives,* should be built about *identity* as titular or ancestral term, the "first" to which all other terms could be

> reduced and from which they could be derived or generated, as from a common spirit. The thing's *identity* would here be its uniqueness as an entity in itself and by itself, a demarcated unit having its own particular structure. . . . The *Symbolic* should deal with unique individuals, each its own peculiarly constructed act, or form. These unique "constitutions" being capable of treatment in isolation, the *Symbolic* should consider them primarily in their capacity as singulars, each a separate universe of discourse. . . . a set of inter-related terms all conspiring to round out their identity as participants in a common substance of meaning. (RM 21–22)

The passage amply clarifies the object of study of "A Symbolic of Motives": the nature of an individual or a thing "in itself, "by itself," as "singular." Unlike the *Rhetoric*'s embroilment with the "scrabble" of the "Human Barnyard," "A Symbolic of Motives" might be seen as an interest in each component creature of our linguistic farm-scape in its particularity—not as a representative of a certain species or class, and not as a member of various competing collectives, but as its own never-before, never-again assemblage of the stuff that gives it breath. The squabble of the scrabble is rhetoric's home turf, driven as it is by the "competitive use of the cooperative," by the polemic and mystery of class and classification (RM 46). But in stark contrast to *Rhetoric*'s focus on this competition and partisanship, "within the rules of the Symbolic, the individual is treated merely as a self-subsistent unit proclaiming its peculiar nature" (23). This symbolic concern with the "uniqueness" of any such "individual" or "self-subsistent unit" is a concern with the "identity" of that thing.

But what, exactly, are the "things" or "entities" that "A Symbolic of Motives" would examine in its "study of individual identity"? In explaining the scope of "A Symbolic of Motives," Burke clarifies that these things can be people—or *poets*, more correctly, in that "identity" in his approach is both fashioned and expressed primarily through a person's use of language. Burke indicates in *A Grammar of Motives*, however, that "A Symbolic of Motives" has other interests as well: "the forms and methods of art best illustrate the concerns of the Symbolic"; it is "concerned with modes of expression and appeal in the fine arts, and with purely psychological or psychoanalytic matter" (GM xviii, xvii). And furthering this focus on the "forms and methods of art," Burke claims in his 1953 "Curriculum Criticum" (where he describes his "Symbolic of Motives" as "now in progress") that "the *Symbolic* will seek to treat of further problems that have to do with the intrinsic analysis of texts"; it will "deal with linguistic structures in their . . . *poetic* dimension" (218).

At first, these two emphases—on individuals and on the forms, methods, and analysis of texts—might appear disparate. But Burke sees an easy merger of the two under the head of the poetic more generally, for *poetic*, in its literal sense, would underscore a crucial Burkean similarity between them: that both art and individual identity are *made*. Not only are they both made, Burke points out, but they are both *made of the same materials* as well: "both the character of the individual poem and the character of the individual person embody 'equations' (explicit or implicit assumptions as to what fits with what)" ("Addendum" 222). As far as "A Symbolic of Motives" is concerned, the properties or characters of the individual and of the work of art are therefore interchangeable, allowing for the "identities" of each to be discussed in terms of the other: just as one might speak about the "identity" of a text as it "proclaim[s] . . . its peculiar nature," so one might elaborate on the "methods," "equations," and "modes of expression and appeal" that comprise an individual person's identity.[9]

This convertibility between the characters of the "individual poem" and the "individual person" helps to clarify and integrate the many different descriptions of identity and of the individual that Burke provides in explaining "A Symbolic of Motives." For example, individuals are "demarcated unit[s]," "particular structures"; they are "singulars" and "separate universe[s] of discourse." And in the clauses that will prove most relevant in the next chapter, they are "set[s] of inter-related terms all conspiring to round out their identity as participants in a common substance of meaning"; they are "*unique 'constitutions*'" (RM 21–23, emphasis added). Whether the "individual" in question is a person or an individual text that such a person has produced, Burke's statement on the nature of identity applies equally: "identity is like a unified, mutually adjusted set of terms" (23). To be sure, Burke is not claiming that people are no more than the language they use (or, in the spirit of Burke's logology, no more than the language that uses them). The prelinguistic status of the human body, if nothing else, argues for this recalcitrance and for the "*metabiology*" that Burke develops early on as his theoretical foundation (PC 261).[10] "The Philosophy of Literary Form" also attests to this fact, for the *dream* aspect of symbolic action would turn the attention of "A Symbolic of Motives" toward the "unconscious or subconscious factors in a poem," toward "purely psychological or psychoanalytic matter[s]" that presuppose the physical, biological reality of the human organism beneath identity (PLF 5). And such psychological or psychoanalytic matters, as Burke sees them, are prime Symbolic territory.

In his reading of Coleridge's "The Rime of the Ancient Mariner," for example, Burke notes how "Coleridge's enslavement to his drug" (laudanum) is present in the poem as "a burden[,] the manifestation of which can be trailed through his work," a "burden [that] becomes interwoven with his many other concerns." "To grasp the full nature of the symbolic enactment going on in the poem," he argues in culmination, "we must study the interrelationships disclosable by a study of Coleridge's mind itself" (PLF 22–23). Similarly the section in *A Grammar of Motives* on "Rhetorical and Symbolic Levels" offers an analysis of Lucretius's *De Rerum Natura* anchored in the observation that "there is much evidence in the poem that the author is in some way goaded." The issues that this hypothesis foregrounds are patent examples of the "unconscious or subconscious factors" that Burke's "A Symbolic of Motives" would fathom: "Why so monumental an attempt to assure men that the wrath of the gods will pursue them neither in this life nor in the life hereafter? What unresolved guilt may perhaps reside in this attack upon religions that believe in the punishments of heaven? What was it that would make an Epicurean find in the thought of the soul's mortality the very solace that Christians seek in the thought of immortality?" (162–63). Following his "main ideal of criticism"—"use all that is there to use"—Burke was certain to make a place for the appreciation of such inscrutable, yet nonetheless real psychological dimensions of symbolic action, dimensions that for reason of scope and focus are left implicit in his broader grammatical and rhetorical inquiries (PLF 23).

Burke continually references psychology as a scenic ground of the "Symbolic of Motives" project (with Freud being the most obvious presence in this scene). But his interest in identity here is not primarily *psychological* but rather *linguistic*. As is true not merely of the motives trilogy but of Burke's entire corpus as well, *language* is the overarching perspective from which to theorize human relations.[11] The predominance of this linguistic perspective is communicated by the many descriptions of both identity and the individual I have just presented, all of which are language-oriented—*form, structure, constitution, separate universe of discourse*. Consequently Burke articulates a concept of identity within the symbolic that highlights this linguistic perspective: identity is *like a unified, mutually adjusted set of terms*. To inquire into identity, then, is to inquire into these terms and the processes of adjustment they enact in the singularity of their unique discursive universe—their "conspir[ing] . . . to round out their identity as participants in a common substance of meaning" (RM 23).

In summary, "A Symbolic of Motives," while not completed in Burke's lifetime, is defined by its concern with the particularity of a thing—a "text," a "work of art," or an "individual," all in the "isolation" of this thing's "uniqueness." "We are in pure Symbolic," Burke tells us, "when we concentrate upon one particular integrated structure of motives" (RM 27). Within the Symbolic problem of identity's "stress . . . upon the work [or "thing"] in its internality," one would approach "identity" as a function of the language that the thing embodies—as a function of the terms that "conspire" and "mutually adjust" to "round out" a characterization of its "substance," an effect of the "equations it inevitably embodies in its action as an evolving unity" ("Curriculum Criticum" 217). I have more to say in chapter 3 about such equations and their relationship to identity and rhetorics of self-constitution. But at present, I want to note only that Burke regards such equations as the essence of how a symbolic act accomplishes the "proclaiming and formation of identity"—the joint processes that, as he argues, are at the epicenter of all human relations. Attending to these equations therefore offers a way of broaching Burke's "problem of identity" as it concerns the equally poetic substance of both the individual and the individual text. Whether depicting the changing identity of fictional protagonists, such as in his analysis of Clifford Odets's *Golden Boy*, or proclaiming the lived transformations of identity in individuals that declare themselves "converted," these terminological equations provide a means of discussing how identity is managed in language—or, in the term I explore in the next chapter, how identity is "constituted."

Perpetuating the Problem

In his summary of "identity" as one of three key "PostPhilosophical" themes in the work of Kenneth Burke, Timothy Crusius underscores how differently Burke and poststructuralist theory have responded to "the problem of identity." "Poststructuralism proposes to 'solve' the problem of identity," Crusius asserts, "by doing away with identity" (43). Whether or not this seems like overstatement, its gist is true enough to make abundantly clear how differently Burke regards—embraces—"the problem of identity" he targeted early in his work. Identity for him is a terrain of dialectical transformations, a place where our identifications with and divisions from aspects of the world commingle as we daily define who we are (our substance) and, consequently, how we should act (our motives). As such, the persistence of our refashionings and renamings is a sign to Burke not of identity's theoretical wrongheadedness but of its social indispensability, its generative role in language and human relations. To think of identity as a "problem" for Burke in the same way it has become a problem for much contemporary theory, then, is a gross mischaracterization. Whatever conceptual quandaries may mire "identity" in our day, the only true "problem" of identity for Burke would be the hubris of thinking ourselves capable of somehow *solving* it, of concocting some means to establish—or abolish—identity once and for all, freezing the central moltenness and ambiguity of substance that opens all identity formation to transformation.[12] In total his retort in *Attitudes toward History* to those who would remedy the "psychosis" of identification could just as well be said today of the ongoing naming and changing that, for Burke, *is* identity: "it can't be 'cured,' for the simple reason that it is *normal*" (263).

We might thus do more justice to Burke's "problem of identity" by recasting it as a *problematic* of identity—as a dynamic, an economy, a perpetual interplay between the individual and the world by which both shape, and reshape, their senses of who they are. Understood in this way, his problem of identity thus asks for something more ambitious than solutions. It asks for our continued interest in probing human symbol use to find the spots where this "problem" arises, where grammatical, rhetorical, and symbolic transformations of identity can and do transpire. These spots, Burke reminds, include "strategic spots," places where identity is formed and transformed because of the rhetorical work these transformations might accomplish. Such "symbolic proclamation and formation of identity" may be as calculated and beguiling as the "rebirth ritual" by which a malicious corporate interest hides behind the family-friendly face of the well-known food and drug brands it has just acquired. Or such transformations may be as unanticipated and unwelcome as a world leader's black-and-white identity assertion that would make us either war-supporting patriots or terrorists. Whatever their particularities, our scrutiny of these and the many other potential forms that such "naming and changing of identity" may take will likely lead us to the conclusion upon which Burke settles: "the confused shufflings of identity must go on" (ATH 265). And so must our attention to them.

This chapter has aimed to encourage such attention by providing a guide to Burke's heterogeneous theorizing about identity. Distinguishing within his broad "problem of identity" three interrelated grammatical, rhetorical, and symbolic problems of identity, I hope also to have clarified what their application might look like, along with the potential contribution that each might make to our understanding of identity formation and transformation in human symbol use. And while each of these perspectives has its own distinct emphasis in relation to identity, I have placed these perspectives hermeneutically as a way to emphasize that a common center anchors them all. For more than simply interweaving or overlapping, these grammatical, rhetorical, and symbolic circumferences all radiate from a shared grounding in dialectic: they each emanate from a common focus on "the possibilities of linguistic transformation," on the "unity and division that serves pretty much as the over-all category for everything, and certainly for human relations" (GM 338). Placing them in this way underscores how the rhetorical and the symbolic in Burke are every bit as infused with the ambiguities and transformations that *A Grammar of Motives* would size up.[13] In the rhetorical, these transformations hover in the tension between identification and division, in the very nature of language itself, which can only bind us in one way by rending us in another. At the symbolic or poetic level, transformation names the "what equals what" and the "from what to what" that a work's equations enact, what Burke describes in "Dialectic in General" as "the *dis*position and *trans*position of terms" (PLF 38; GM 402). It is therefore no exaggeration to describe Burke's work on identity, like all his theorizing, as saturated with the transformative.

Equally saturated with identity and transformation are the conversion narratives I examine in this book. Understanding Burke's multilayered interest in identity as a kind of symbolic action, then, should prove helpful now in considering how identity and its transformations are articulated in these narratives (a poetics of their structuring) and how they seek strategic ends in the audiences they address (a rhetoric of their persuasive designs). I begin these tasks in the next chapter by turning to a text that, as promising an aid it might seem to theorizing the constitution of identity, has not had much impact in rhetorical theory. That is, I begin by considering what Burke has to say about the workings of constitutions themselves.

3

Toward a Poetics and Rhetoric of Identity through "The Dialectic of Constitutions"

A constitution is a *substance* **. . . designed to serve as motives for the shaping or transforming of behavior.**

Kenneth Burke, *A Grammar of Motives*

Unique individuals, each its own peculiarly constructed act, or form . . . [are] unique "constitutions."

Kenneth Burke, *A Rhetoric of Motives*

If *A Grammar of Motives*—Burke's "big book"—is often regarded as the most difficult of his tomes to digest, then its "Part Three: On Dialectic" is perhaps largely to blame for such conceptual dyspepsia. Heavy as it may be, however, Burke communicates quite clearly that the part's two companion sections, "The Dialectic of Constitutions" (DOC) and "Dialectic in General," are important ones. "Questions of motivation come to a head in questions of substantiation and transubstantiation," Burke states in the concluding paragraph of "Part Two: The Philosophic Schools," a windup to a final swing in "Part Three" at demonstrating how "human relations are at every turn affected by the nature of verbal dialectic": "And so, in Part III of this book, we shall deal with the dialectic of these two processes. We shall take as our text for substantiation, the theory of Constitutions. And we shall consider transubstantiation as the representative moment of dialectic in general" (GM 320, 338). As Burke explains, these two concluding sections bookend his explanation of dialectic: "The Dialectic of Constitutions" first offers a specific demonstration of the concept of *substance* that the 300-plus previous pages of *A Grammar of Motives* have been discussing; and "Dialectic in General" then demonstrates the types of transformation that the ambiguities of substance invite—processes of *transubstantiation*, the moments wherein "A" becomes "non-A."

Burke's reading of constitutions generally and the U.S. Constitution specifically in "The Dialectic of Constitutions," then, is much more than one of his many insightful readings of popular historical or literary documents. Its stakes are higher than, say, those of descanting "The Vegetal Radicalism of Theodore Roethke," or of uncovering the workings of "order" in Henry James's *The Spoils of Poynton*. In Burke's own characterization, his analysis of the substantiating function of constitutions in "The Dialectic of Constitutions" is a vital half of the *Grammar*'s entire investigation into the workings of substance, an investigation that grounds the whole of his remarks on motive. "In arguing in his *Grammar* for human nature as substantial," Michael Feehan asserts, "Burke looked to constitutions as the pivotal concept, the nearest human analog to the creation" (43). And given that "a concern with substance is a concern with the problem of constitutionality," as Burke states, the relevance of the focus of "The Dialectic of Constitutions" on constitutions in its explication of substance is clear: "Could we do better than select the subject of a Constitution and its typical resources as the anecdote about which to shape our terms?" (GM 338). More than a pointed anecdote for this inquiry into substantiation, "The Dialectic of Constitutions" is ultimately a "representative anecdote" for the entire motives project itself as well. It is an elaborate theoretical exemplum "in which we might see both a summary and convergence of the central issues in the study of human relations" (324).[1]

Understanding the importance of "The Dialectic of Constitutions" within *A Grammar of Motives* makes it easier to understand Burke's disgruntlement at the section's neglect as well. His notes and correspondences indicate that this "countrywide oblivion" continued to miff him well into his later years (Letter to Chesebro). One of his frequent responses to reviewers who seemed to miss the point of *A Grammar of Motives* was that they should have read "The Dialectic of Constitutions."[2] Burke notes in a 1972 letter to William Rueckert that he is preparing a presentation for Clark University, "pleading anew for my pages (in GM) on 'the Dialectic of Constitutions.'" Another letter to Rueckert five years later expresses his "great delight" at how a French political theorist's monograph "did wonders" with "The Dialectic of Constitutions" ("which often didn't even so much as get mentioned by domestic thinkeroos"; Rueckert, *Letters* 183, 210). And as late as 1989, Burke's remarks on "Language and Power" at the Conference on College Composition and Communication in Seattle, one of his last appearances at an academic conference, included a call for others to join him on a "committee" to help him pursue his work on constitutions.[3]

Despite Burke's call for help, much of the excellent study of his work over the past two decades avails itself but little of the resources that he saw in the grand "summary and convergence" of the major issues of human relations in "The Dialectic of Constitutions." Within the handful of scholars who have in some way engaged this crucial text, Robert Wess and Gregory Clark both demonstrate the merits of giving this section the closer look Burke would have liked. Wess's *Kenneth Burke: Rhetoric, Subjectivity, Postmodernism,* for example, elucidates the overall purpose of "The Dialectic of Constitutions" by showing how the section is, as Burke claims, a "generative model for the study of language as symbolic action" ("Questions" 334). Reading "The Dialectic of Constitutions" as Burke's most powerful argument for the grammatical primacy of *act,* "the claim of claims in the dramatistic view of language as action," Wess movingly articulates how the truly radical power of the "constitutional act" is its power "to go beyond its antecedent situation in transforming it" (181, 146). So great is this power that even the rigged game of ideological prescription itself—its "totalizing set of structuralist combinations in which all possibilities are determined in advance"—might be transformed into something much more humane, a refashioned social game with "rules by which everyone can function materially, and with no rule that benefits anyone at the expense of anyone else" (38). In a more concrete application, and one of obvious relevance to my focus on identity, Clark's *Rhetorical Landscapes: Variations on a Theme from Kenneth Burke* turns to "The Dialectic of Constitutions" to help examine how our experience of landscape can constitute a sense of collective identity. In an eloquent analysis of American tourist artifacts from postcards to World's Fair programs to Burke's own cross-country travel lyrics, Clark plies a Burkean constitutional perspective to illuminate "the ways residents of a vast and diverse nation have been prompted by the symbolic experiences they share as tourists to adopt for themselves a common sense of national identity" (4). Stressing the collective rhetorical transformation—the *reconstitution*—that individuals undergo in thus adopting a shared identity, Clark goes so far as to assert that Burke's "complex of ideas" on the material and rhetorical power of constitutions in "The Dialectic of Constitutions" represents "what we can call, though he never quite used the term, a *constitutive rhetoric*" (124–26, emphasis in original).

I share the common interest of Wess and Clark in using "The Dialectic of Constitutions" to better understand the range of constitutive acts by which we can, and often do, transform ourselves and our world. My focus on conversion differs significantly from the kinds of transformation that they consider, but in a way a that ultimately complements the utility they both find in "The Dialectic of Constitutions." Where Wess uses "The Dialectic of Constitutions" to clarify how Burke's *act* is *constitutive,* I instead consider specific *constitutive acts*—autobiographical narratives and their presentation of the transformed identities of their authors. And where Clark applies "The Dialectic of

Constitutions" toward understanding the rhetorical transformations by which "diverse and divergent individuals" acquire "a shared sense of national identity" (147), I instead focus primarily on the *individual* sense of identity transformation that conversion experiences materialize. What I offer in my reading of "The Dialectic of Constitutions" thus rests somewhere in between their contributions, with Wess's excursus on the transformative power of constitutive acts as a scenic backdrop and Clark's analysis as an extension of the constitutional principles and functions I will discuss.

As I mentioned in chapter 1, my emphasis here on how individuals constitute their identities in texts, what I have been calling *first-person constitution,* is a less explored topic in studies of rhetoric and identity. As I also noted in that chapter, one impediment to more wide-scale analysis of the self-constitutive acts by which individuals articulate their identities in discourse might be some trepidation concerning the view of the individual that such analysis seems to endorse, perhaps even to require. Indeed, my use of *individual* in referring to the person is problematic, as is my reference to "self-constitutive acts": both of these might be seen as archaic humanisms, as proclamations of some self inalienably free to fashion itself as is its whim, "the stable product of its own manufacture" (Battaglia 1). And beyond this concern for the concept of the person underpinning the analysis of self-constitution, there is perhaps little sense of the rhetorical tools for attempting such analysis. In short, what conceptual equipment can rhetoric employ toward analyzing identity as strategic self-constitution, and how can it do so without implying a self that is free to constitute and strategize as it pleases?

Both questions find the beginnings of their answers in Burke's "Dialectic of Constitutions." In demonstrating how constitutions are strategic "instrument[s] . . . for the shaping of human relations" (GM 341), Burke presents specific tools for discussing what I have referred to as the poetic and rhetorical dimensions of constitutions: his discussion is as much a treatise on the materials and means of their composition (a poetics) as it is an analysis of how these constitutions seek to transform the audiences to which they are addressed (a rhetoric). As I follow Burke's suggestion in arguing here, this joint poetics and rhetoric of constitutions applies equally to documents such as the U.S. Constitution and to the "unique 'constitutions'" of individual identity (RM 21). Read in this way, "The Dialectic of Constitutions" provocatively underscores that the same substance-defining, motivating, and audience-transforming functions—*rhetorical* functions—equally animate the national constitution of a "we the people" and the self-constitution of an "I the person."

As context for this joint poetics and rhetoric of identity constitution, I first present an overview of what Burke tells us that constitutions do in "The Dialectic of Constitutions."

How—and What—Do Constitutions Constitute?

> What a Constitution would do primarily is to *substantiate an ought* . . . to base a statement as to *what should be* upon a statement as to *what is.* (*A Grammar of Motives*, 538)

In their introduction to *Identity, Rights, and Constitutional Transformation*, a collection of essays on comparative constitutionalism, Patrick J. Hanafin and Melissa S. Williams review recent political crises that have foregrounded the many powers of constitutions—for example, Indonesian president Suharto's 1998 resignation after having been publicly brought to task for violating "the most basic principles" of the national constitution. In assessing "the place of identity in constitutional formation and transformation," Hanafin and Williams argue that governmental upheavals such as Indonesia's are among the most obvious proofs that "constitutions are not passive vehicles for the expression of already-existing identities and relations of power"; "they can also function as engines" of new identities, articulating new "express[ions of] both community and exclusion, solidarity and domination" (1–2). Following Gayatri Spivak's claim that a "text has no stable identity, no stable origin, no stable end" (xii), Hanafin and Williams assert that "the notion of identity contained within a constitution is always open to disruption"; "writing a constitution is merely the beginning of an unending dialectic between text and people" (2), between the formulation of a collective identity and the individuals whom this constituted collective would subsume. The more recent struggles to draft the constitution for a democratic post-Saddam Iraq only strengthen this assertion.

This "unending dialectic" between constitutions and the things they would constitute is just what attracts Burke to constitutions as representative texts for "deal[ing] with matters of substance and enactment." As he asserts, constitutions seem perfectly suited to a discussion of how substance is decreed in discourse, "for what could be more basic, more 'laid down,' than the law?" (GM 323). In order to elaborate the relationship between constitutions, substance, and motive that he sees as "a solid point of departure" for the study of human relations, Burke begins with a straightforward definition of a constitution: it is "an enactment of human wills" (323). But before explaining exactly what such an "enacting" function entails, he first reviews various "ordinary dictionary usages" of the term *constitution:* a constitution might refer to "the aggregate of all one's inherited physical qualities," or "the fundamental, organic law or principles of government . . . embodied in written documents," for example. The definition of the functions of a constitution that Burke then offers in response, however, is not meant to somehow transcend this range of "ordinary usages." Rather, he means to indicate that, in all of these possible senses of the term *constitution*, "obviously . . . we are dealing with a word that has to do with matters of substance and motive" (341).

Burke's instrument for parsing issues of substance and motive is that which the previous sections of *A Grammar of Motives* have taken such pains to elaborate: the pentad. Not surprisingly, then, his definition of the function of a constitution "covers all five terms": "A legal constitution is an *act* or body of acts (or enactments), done by *agents* (such as rulers, magistrates, or other representative persons), and designed (*purpose*) to serve as a motivational ground (*scene*) of subsequent actions, it being an instrument (*agency*) for the shaping of human relations" (341). While Burke's reference here is to legal constitutions, the following page indicates that legislation is by no means the only sphere of constitutionality that fits the above pentadic bill. "There are constitutions of a purely natural sort, such as geographical and physiological properties, that act motivationally upon us," he explains. In addition, "a given complex of customs and values, from which similar customs and values are deduced, is a constitution" (342). Clearly Burke's aim here is not to narrow his consideration in "The Dialectic of Constitutions" to one particular type or definition of constitution, but rather (in keeping with his general aim for "maximum scope and relevancy") to expand the sense of constitution as far as it may be stretched—to see exactly how deeply such constitutional functions are rooted in the "central issues" of human relations.

This depth of function is profound, to say the least, for the roots of constitutionality run all the way down to the architectonics of substance itself. "A constitution is a *substance*—and as such, it is a set of motives," Burke claims, moving from his pentadic definition of constitutional function to a defense of the claim that prefaces part 3 of *A Grammar of Motives*—that constitutions are the representative text of the dialectical process of substantiation (342). Several pages earlier in "The Dialectic of Constitutions," he offers a partial explanation to the first of the two claims in the above sentence—that of the interdependence of constitutions and substance: "A thing's substance," he elucidates, is "that whereof it is constituted" (337). To *constitute* something, then, is to define its *substance* in a certain way, to proclaim it of one particular nature or another. Thus, as Burke claims following his review of various "ordinary usages" of *constitution*, questions of substantiation do indeed factor into whatever sense of *constitution* we might invoke, for definitions of substance cannot help but result from any such constitutive act. Whether this act be the constitution of a collective, as with the "We the people" of the U.S. Constitution, or the constitution of an individual, as with the deceptively banal proclamation of substance in the assertion "You are a bastard" (GM 57; RM 13–15), the same substance-defining function of a constitution is in operation. "Hence," Burke concludes, "a concern with substance is a concern with the problems of constitutionality" (338). Little wonder, then, why a somewhat crestfallen Burke later puzzled at how scholarship on his work could be absorbed in questions of the former yet disengaged from the latter.

This interrelationship of constitutions and substances is one important claim of "The Dialectic of Constitutions." But what of the second half of Burke's equation—that in defining or "enacting" a substance, a constitution is also "a set of motives"? A clearer sense of this progression between constitution, substance, and motive can be achieved by reviewing Burke's remarks in this section on the different types of "anecdotes" that frame his discussion: the representative, the constitutive, and the admonitory, respectively. The "representative anecdote," as he explains in *A Grammar of Motives* and elsewhere, seeks to "yield representative terms" for the contemplation of something; it articulates a summarizing "vocabulary" that "contain[s] implicitly what the system that is developed from it contains explicitly" (340; 59–60). The function of a representative anecdote could thus be described as normative, inasmuch as it seeks not merely to reduce or summarize a more complex phenomenon, but to do so faithfully—to re-present in the strictest sense that which it encapsulates.[4] The "constitutive anecdote," while similar in its representative aim, is less interested in the faithful description of something *as it is* than in the description of *how it is declared to be that way*. In other words, constitutive anecdotes are abstracted from humankind's varied efforts to decree that something "*substantially is*"—the paradigmatic case being, of course, a constitution. The constitutive anecdote's focus is thus to represent how such acts of substantiation take place. And finally, as Burke continually asserts in "The Dialectic of Constitutions," declarations of how something "substantially is" inevitably lead to declarations of how something *should be*. Such exhortations are the focus of the "admonitory anecdote"; as representations of the ways in which "it *is* so" leads to "*would that it were* so," they reveal the logic by which a decree of what one *substantially is* ushers in the motivational arguments concerning "*what one may become*" and what one "is *in danger of becoming*" (GM 330–34). Given that constitutions are designed to "shape" and "transform" the behaviors of those they would constitute, this admonitory function is quite the point of such design, for "what a Constitution would do primarily is to *substantiate an ought* . . . to base a statement as to *what should be* upon a statement as to *what is*" (358).[5]

Through these three related anecdotes, the complex substantiating and motivating functions of a constitution might be given a more streamlined explanation. First, a situation exists where certain things are understood to be so, as encapsulated within some representative anecdote of this situation. Based on this understanding of how things are, one may then formally, authoritatively declare that such things *substantially are* in a constitution; depending on one's constitutional purpose, one might also declare that things are substantially different than they are commonly held to be—for example, a constitutional declaration that certain rights once absent are now inalienable to all. And finally, this act of substantiation is not an end in and of itself, for it seeks to change the motivations of those within its constitutive reach: in short, the constitutive act is meaningless unless it effectively motivates people to behave differently—to behave in accordance with the substance that the constitution declares they embody. The tactics by which this desired "shaping or transforming of behavior" is accomplished would then be represented in an admonitory anecdote. This anecdotal pattern of representation, constitution, and admonition, then, provides a way of understanding how constitutions serve both substantiating and motivating functions, a way of understanding how constitutions are "substances designed to serve as motives for the shaping or transforming of behavior" (342). To render this claim in the language of Burke's previous pentadic explanation, the purpose of a constitutive act, whether performed by one agent or a group of agents, is to describe a particular scene for the purpose of encouraging certain motives (and therefore discouraging others).[6] In this way, the "enactment of human wills" that is a constitution, whatever its type or scope, might ultimately function as an "instrument (agency)" for the "shaping" and "transforming of human behavior" (GM 341–42).

The power of a constitution thus lies in its power to define substance, and to define it in such a way that those who share this substance then also share in the motives that bear it up. How could one work against "promot[ing] the general welfare" of others within the domain of the U.S. Constitution, for example, yet still be considered "consubstantial" with the "We the people" that this constitution addresses? In this power to decree substance and thereby direct future conduct or motives, constitutional injunctions might appear to be of a power beyond impeachment, of the "'let there be—and there was' sort" (340). But inasmuch as a constitution's power is itself the power of substantiation, any constitutive effort is therefore fair game for the ambiguities and transformations that, as *A Grammar of Motives* asserts, come part and parcel with any statement about substance. As "a decreeing of substance, [and] hence a decreeing of motives," a constitution cannot help but "open the avenues to the ambiguities of substance," even as it would attempt to shunt them off (373). After all, "men cannot themselves create the universe" (xviii), no matter how vast their constitutive power. The behavioral "oughts" that their constitutions would substantiate are threatened at every turn by inevitable mergers and divisions—the dialectics of transformation by which "let there be" becomes "let it be no longer." This dialectical inevitability is where "The Dialectic of Constitutions" concludes, with Burke noting that all constitutions ultimately lead us to "the old problem of unity and diversity" (399). This problem, however, is more properly the domain of "transubstantiation" that Burke next investigates in "Dialectic in General," the counterpoint to his look in "The Dialectic of Constitutions" at how issues of substantiation are inherently issues of constitutionality. The importance of such issues of constitutionality in *A Grammar of Motives* cannot be overstated, given the text's overall concern with the ways that individuals "size up," "chart," or judge the world of situations (motives) that surrounds them: for where there is a judgment—any human judgment—there is a constitution to substantiate it (GM 356).[7]

Outlining the substantiating and motivating functions of constitutions brings me midway in my discussion of "The Dialectic of Constitutions." Having thus considered these interrelated functions of constitutions, I can now examine how these functions relate to the constitution of identity—a linkage that Burke himself suggests in describing individuals as "unique 'constitutions'" (RM 21). How is the identity of the individual like the collective identities more commonly examined as the goal of constitutions? And in what sense does the constitution of an individual's identity enact the same substantiating and motivating functions that Burke identifies in constitutions generally? "The Dialectic of Constitutions" again proves helpful here. In addition to illuminating these substantiating and motivating functions, the section also suggests three possible analytical tools with which to explore these functions in relation to first-person constitution: the concept of circumference in constitutional function, the agon of "voluntaristic" and "necessitarian" principles within a constitution, and the nature of a constitution as a strategic addressed. These tools begin to explain what it means to view individuals as Burke does, as "set[s] of inter-related terms all conspiring to round out their identity as participants in a common substance of meaning." Moreover, these tools begin to explain how to account for this "rounding out" of identity, both poetically and rhetorically, in actual texts that seek to persuade through the changing identities of their authors.

Circumference: The Boundaries of Identity

In "Scope and Reduction," the concluding section of part 1 of *A Grammar of Motives*, Burke explores at length how every interpretation of an action (an imputation of motive) is formed in relation to some conception of the scene in which this action is performed. This key assertion represents what the pentad describes as a "scene–act ratio." The range of possible scenes in which one might situate an action is expansive, he notes, and so, correspondingly, are the different interpretations of the act that such a choice of scene would yield. The scene of a man cutting down a tree, for instance, might give us little to go on in interpreting this act beyond the simple restatement of the tree's apparently deliberate felling. Broaden this scene a bit to reveal that the tree is part of a public park and the act becomes something different—an act of vandalism, perhaps, or an act of malicious self-centeredness, its perpetrator a man deserving of public censure. Step out even further, however, to reveal that the more inclusive scene surrounding the park is a country at war, threatened now with utter impoverishment, and that the tree-cutting man is one of many residents who have reluctantly turned to their town's public foliage as their last resort for firewood, and we have an entirely different act again—an act of desperation, its author a man to be pitied and aided rather than scorned.

Bearing out the section title of "Scope and Reduction," Burke explains that these choices of scene represent different choices of *scope*; in a term borrowed from William James, they are different *circumferences* that one must draw around an act in order to interpret it, encircling it in contexts as broad or as narrow as one chooses, containing it within a range of possibilities that this circumference inscribes. As Burke elaborates, "One has *a great variety of circumferences* to select as characterizations of a given agent's scene. For a man is not only in the situation peculiar to his era or his particular place in that era (even if we could agree on the traits that characterize his era). He is also in a situation extending through centuries; he is in a 'generically human' situation; and he is in a 'universal' situation. Who is to say, once and for all, which of these circumferences is to be selected as the motivation of his act, insofar as the act is to be defined in scenic terms?" The answer to Burke's query, of course, is no one: inasmuch as any interpretation is as open to transformation as any other, no single imputation can represent the absolute, "once and for all" circumference or motivation of a given action. All such selections of circumference are therefore equally "act[s] of faith, with the definition or interpretation of the act taking shape accordingly" (84). And "every circumference, no matter how far-reaching its scope," he claims, "is a reduction" as well in that it serves to simplify or limit that which it contains in order to make it meaningful (96). More than a function of human perception, this reductive necessity of "marking the outer boundaries of the ground that is to be covered" in interpretation is itself inherent in "the very nature of linguistic placement": "To select a set of terms is, by the same token, to select a circumference," Burke postulates. Simply put, to interpret an action is to reduce it, to delimit some specific scope or situation in which this interpretation is meaningful. And given that an action may be thus situated in any number of ways, there are ultimately as many interpretations of an action as there are words to represent it (84).

This inevitable "circumferential logic" of interpretation that Burke outlines—"the contracting and expanding of scene . . . [in the] selection of circumference" (GM 84)—is important to his concept of constitutionality in at least two ways. First, as Wess thoroughly argues, Burke underscores that all constitutive acts involve the assertion of a circumference—that because any constitution is partial, it also necessarily asserts the "outer boundary" of its constitutive power.[8] "Since circumference frames interpretation," Wess explains, "each choice [of circumference], in bringing a situation into being for the first time, constitutes a reality" ("Dialectic" 23). In so doing, this selection of circumference is "substantive, 'constitutive,' quite as was God's creative act" (GM 86). As Burke suggests, a simple summary of this constitutive function of the principle of circumference is that "a new scene would make possible a new act" (85). In other words, "men are continually performing 'new acts,'" for "they are continually making judgments as to the scope or context which they implicitly or explicitly impute in their interpretation" (90).[9] The "act of faith" by which a circumference is selected in interpretation, then, is a "constitutive" act: like a constitution, it substantiates a particular scene in which certain motives are possible.

A second key aspect of circumference in constitutionality concerns the way in which an interpretation makes its choice of circumference apparent. As Burke asserts, the way to discern a constitution's designs for "the shaping or transforming of behavior" is to scrutinize its terminology, for "the motives and motifs featured by [a person or author's] terminology will fix the nature of the constitution which he has enacted" (342, 86). In Burke's example, the language of "the jungle" in the U.S. Constitution would create a nation "conceived in the idiom of pure competition." It is a powerful metaphor, one that could even be expanded to contain the whole of human existence—an extreme widening of circumference demonstrated by certain "ecologists . . . trying to ground a few simple theories of small business not merely in the Constitution of the U.S. but in the very Constitution of the Universe" (331). This idea of "pure competition," then, in the circumference of either the U.S. Constitution specifically or of the Universe generally, would function as what Burke calls the "god-term" of that constitution. Within the various terminological motives and motifs of a constitution, this all-encompassing term "designates the ultimate motivation, or substance, of a constitutional frame" (355).

In thus establishing a circumference of some sort for the scene that it substantiates, a constitution also communicates some term or ideal that signposts this circumferential boundary of its act of substantiation. This circumference simultaneously marks both the "ultimate motivation" to which a constitution aspires and the motivational limit of that which it is capable of constituting. In *The Rhetoric of Religion* (where god-terms are the fourth of Burke's six framing "analogies" between language in its "natural" and "supernatural" realms), Burke elaborates that a god-term is a title "for the situation it refers to," a condensed shorthand for its array of details. More accurately, it is something of an *uber*-title, the "Title of Titles," in that all other aspects of this situation, all other "orders of generalization," can be derived from it. Like the "ideal title" of a book, the god-term "would 'sum up' all the particulars" it contains and "would in a way 'imply' these particulars" (*Religion*, 25–27). Burke's ideas of *god-term* (a situation's overall "title") and *circumference* (a situation's overall boundary or limit), then, are very nearly synonymous, for each is a means of expressing the other. In Charlotte L. Stuart's reading of the U.S. Constitution, for example, all the hopeful decrees of the Preamble amount to a single god-term, articulating the single greatest aspiration of the nation-scene it would create within its borders—*Power* (113). And Burke as well comments on how god-terms and circumference work in tandem, noting that a change in one indicates a change in the other—the "stepping-down of the God-term" representing "a confinement to a narrower circumference," for instance (GM 351).

These aspects of circumference and god-term are essential to Burke's theory of constitutions, for they are the starting point in explaining how a constitution works to delimit and substantiate a particular scene in which particular motives are possible.[10] If we take Burke at his word that his remarks on constitutionality lend themselves to an examination of the individual—that the individual and identity are unique constitutions themselves—then this "circumferential logic" he takes such great pains to elaborate should be equally prominent in the constitution of individual identity. A starting point for the rhetorical analysis of identity constitution, then, is to consider how authors define themselves "in terms of" the various scenes in which they place themselves. Moreover, within these scenes they occupy, how do authors represent their self-definition as a substance that is similarly circumscribed, something with its own "outer boundaries" of both self-understanding and "ultimate motivation"? Inasmuch as such circumferences represent both the limits and the guiding ambitions of a constitution, changes in these circumferential boundaries can signal important changes in the perspective of one's self-interpretation—changes in identity.

A dramatic illustration of the function of circumference in identity constitution is Peter Jenkins's popular 1979 travelogue/conversion narrative, *A Walk across America*. Jenkins, a twenty-something art student at New York's Alfred University, is beginning to come to terms with how little he knows about life, his country, and, ultimately, himself. Disillusioned at everything from Nixon to Vietnam to his recently failed marriage, he feels certain of just one thing: "the hollowness deep down inside of me that hurt bad and never really went away. It had not gone away after wild parties and it always came back after the beer or booze or drugs wore off. It had not gone away after skiing at a chalet in Stowe, Vermont. My generation's giant revival called Woodstock, in the summer of my senior year in high school, gave no lasting relief either. Somehow college and being on my own made the hollowness intensify. It was up to me to search and sift out the answers that I was not so determined to find" (16).

Feeling that the discovery of these answers hinges on the discovery of the world around him, Jenkins and his half-malamute, Cooper, set out with Spartan provisions to walk from New York to New Orleans. The eight-month cook's tour that Jenkins had planned, however, ends up taking almost a year and a half, and Jenkins, equipped with a camera and a commission from *National Geographic* to document his peregrination, narrates this quixotic introduction to America in photographic detail.

Each of Jenkins's sojourns, in places as different as the hovel of an Appalachian mountain man and the dormitory of the New Orleans Theological Seminary, represents a literal change of scene within the text. But beyond these literal scene changes, Jenkins's travels also occasion a more personal change of scene as well—a gradual expansion of the circumference in which he seems to understand himself. In New York, he had seen himself largely through the perspective of his Greenwich, Connecticut, upbringing—a circumference and ultimate motivation that, as he accounts, might be represented by god-terms such as "material prosperity" and "intellectual achievement." Defining himself in terms of such prosperity and achievement had motivated him to seek an education, yet ultimately these motives had left him hollow. But living on the generosity of an African American family in North Carolina, sharing their trailer and their meals of turnip greens and Kool-Aid, he realizes that his focus on himself and on his social advancement might be the exact source of the acute emptiness that embraces him. Subsequent experiences, such as his dog's death at a Tennessee agrarian commune and his befriending of a group of Alabama men (the "Shelby County Drunk Four") who were determined to kill the bearded hippie drug pusher they heard was walking across the country, all teach him of the need to understand others. In other words, the circumference of self-advancement that once characterized the limits of Jenkins's motivation gradually broadens on his walk to become markedly more other-centered. As he thus redraws this widened boundary of his own self-understanding, he becomes capable of selfless, charitable actions that the more narrowly bounded Jenkins simply couldn't conceive of, let alone perform. This relationship between changes in circumference and changes in action demonstrates what Burke describes as the "scenic" function of a constitution, where a constitution "lay[s] down the 'environment' for future acts" (GM 362).

In the course of his narrative, Jenkins eventually comes to fill the hollowness that so long defined him, but only through a paradoxical filling of himself that is the emptying of himself into the service of others. When the time has come for him to stop walking (at least temporarily—subsequent books document his walk from New Orleans to the West Coast), he has walked into and out of nearly as many interpretations of who he is as he has pairs of shoes. Put another way, he has traversed many new scenes in which to situate himself, and many of these scenes have inspired him toward equally new interpretations of the substance that is his identity. Just as Burke summarizes this function of circumference in interpretation generally (and in constitutions specifically) by claiming that "a new scene would make possible a new act," treating the individual and identity as "unique 'constitutions'" allows a paraphrase of this function of circumference as it pertains to acts of first-person constitution: a new scene would make possible a new self and a new identity. In the metaphor for the scene-agent ratio that opens A *Grammar of Motives*—that of the "Container and Thing Contained"—the concept of circumference can be thought of as the constitutional container for the identity it contains, for the "enactment of human wills" that this identity represents. As the outer limit of this "universe of discourse" it circumscribes, a circumference not only delimits a constitution's potential enactments but shapes them as well, unifying them in their motivation toward the god-term—the ideal that simultaneously represents both the length of a constitution's reach and the object of its grasp.

Constitutional Principles and the Agonism of Identity

At the outset of "The Dialectic of Constitutions," Burke announces that his examination of constitutions as "matters of substance and enactment . . . will revolve about the subject of Constitutional principles (or ideals, or wishes)" (323). These principles that comprise a constitution's "enactment of human wills," Burke explains, are of two varieties: the "voluntaristic" and the "necessitarian" (374). Understanding how both types of principles interact within the circumference of a given constitution is essential to understanding how constitutions wield considerable power in their efforts to define substance (and thus to act as "set[s] of motives"), yet are limited in this power as well, their necessarily reductive and partial attempts to "transform human behavior" inevitably falling short of the "ideal" they would enact.[11] In addition, understanding how these principles lend themselves to the dialectical mergers and divisions of transformation that animate all constitutions of substance is essential to explaining how the individual, as a "unique 'constitution,'" might be viewed as "a set of inter-related terms all conspiring to round out their identity as participants in a common substance of meaning" (RM 21–23).

Voluntaristic constitutional principles are those that we most readily identify with the aims and the language of constitutions. A voluntaristic principle for Burke would be any "term having a volitional element" within a constitution—terms articulating "'deals,' 'commands,' [and] 'wishes,'" for example, all of which underscore the "willed" aspect of a constitution's "enactment of human wills." Consider, for example, the wills embodied in a constitution whose act of substantiation has had considerable impact on human relations: the 1955 constitution that merged and declared the shared agenda of the American

Federation of Labor and Congress of Industrial Organizations (and thereby constituting the new substance of the AFL–CIO). That this constitution contains principles of a voluntaristic nature is clear: as the opening sentence of its preamble declares, this constitution "is an expression of the hopes and aspirations of the working people of America" (xxxviii). One key voluntaristic principle within this expression of worker's ambitions is Article II.4, a pledge that members will "encourage all workers without regard to race, creed, color, national origin or ancestry to share in the full benefits of union organization" (xxxix). The human will for equality in labor behind this constitutional principle is evident; also evident is why Burke uses *wish* as a synonym for such voluntaristic principles. As Burke explains, "to insert the 'principle of equality' into a Constitution is to utter a hope that men may become equal or may continue to be equal" (GM 373). Recalling the relationship between constitutive and admonitory anecdotes that Burke elaborates in "The Dialectic of Constitutions," to declare or constitute a state of equality between all workers through this principle is to declare that all workers *should be equal,* to admonish that no worker *should be deprived* of the benefits of organized labor on the basis of race, creed, or nationality. Such voluntaristic principles are the heart of a constitution's hopes to enact a specified body of "human wills"—to substantiate a certain type of scene in which certain types of motives might inhere. In addition, Burke's constant reference to such wills not as "laws" or "declarations" but as *wishes* reminds us of what every constitution's true aim is in its act of substantiation: "to *substantiate an ought,*" "to base a statement as to *what should be*"—what one *wishes* were so—"upon a statement as to *what is*" (358).

Roughly two-thirds of the way through "The Dialectic of Constitutions," Burke remarks that he has sufficiently elaborated "in what way we would equate 'principles' with terms having a volitional element" (373). As the heading of his next subsection, "Principles of the Conflict among Principles," suggests, Burke is now prepared to discuss a second type of principle that structures constitutions, and one that manifests itself without regard for our volitional wills or wishes. "Necessitarian" principles, Burke explains, stand in contradistinction to voluntaristic principles. They refer not to the specific motivational aims or enactments of constitutional clauses, but to the relationships of agreement, overlap, or contradiction that ensue between such constitutional wishes: "There are principles in the sense of wishes, and principles in the sense of interrelationships among wishes. Principles as wishes are voluntary or arbitrary, inasmuch as men can meet in conference and decide how many and what kind of wishes they shall subscribe to. But once you have agreed upon a list of wishes, the interrelationships among those wishes are necessary or inevitable" (375). Considered individually, each ideal or wish expressed within a constitution "is like a sovereign state, proclaiming and maintaining its identity independently of other sovereign states" (344). But when considered in relation to the totality of other such ideals or wishes within a constitution, this illusion of independence and sovereignty vanishes. A group of constitutional framers who wish to guarantee both the right of corporations to pursue their legitimate business interests and the right of individuals to freedom of choice has no power over the fact that, in the event of a monopoly, these two "sovereign" and "independent" wishes are in direct conflict. This principle of opposition between two distinct voluntaristic ideals is a necessitarian principle, one that was not willed into the enactment of this specific constitution but is present therein nonetheless. "In the *volitional* sense, any clause announcing a right or an obligation would be a constitutional 'principle,'" Burke reiterates. "But in the *necessitarian* sense, any statement would be a 'principle' if it signalized a logical or practical conflict between clauses, or defined a procedure for arriving at 'constitutional' judgments despite such conflicts" (374–75).

Contributing even further to this potential for conflict between the collective principles of a constitution is the fact that constitutional principles, "by their very nature as generalizations," are in and of themselves deliberately abstract and ambiguous. They are "expressions which can give no indications as to 'where you draw the line' in specific cases" (384).[12] The constitution of the AFL–CIO, for example, declares that one of its fundamental aims is "to protect and strengthen our democratic institutions . . . and to preserve and perpetuate the cherished traditions of our democracy" (II.6, xxxix). Several articles later, the constitution also declares that the AFL–CIO is devoted to "preserving the independence of the labor movement from political control" (II.12, xxxix). While the relationship, or necessitarian principle, between "democracy" and "independence" might typically be one of agreement, what becomes of this relationship when the "democratic institutions" that participants are admonished to "preserve and perpetuate" would encroach upon the preservation of independence? What happens, for example, when a "democratic" election is dominated by a two-party system of candidates that voters may "freely" choose, yet where both parties oppose the increasing independence of organized labor? How does a would-be adherent to this constitution's voluntaristic principles of democratic preservation and labor independence act both democratically and constitutionally?

The result of such ever-present potential for conflict between voluntaristic and necessitarian aspects of constitutional enactments, combined with the inherent ambiguities of principles themselves, is what Burke describes as the "agon" of constitutionality. "Constitutions are agonistic instruments," he reminds, not merely in the sense that "they involve . . . an enemy" that would threaten the "motivational fixity" a constitution substantiates, but also in the sense of the agon of conflict within constitutions themselves as we apply their generalized principles of substantiation to the "specific cases" of practical life. Faced with situations in which our constitutional wills stand at odds with one another—whether this opposition be "a [necessitarian] function of their construction" or the result of confronting "material conditions . . . beyond our power to alter"—it becomes an ineluctable human task to "draw the lines" of decision that our constitutions cannot. In this sense, as Burke pointedly observes, "every single day has been a day in which the particularities of the scene required some manner of new decision involving motivational ingredients not treated in the Constitutional calculus" (389). And it is within such ambiguities, *A Grammar of Motives* reminds us, that the mergers and divisions of linguistic transformation might transpire. The agonistic center of a constitutionally "circumfered" body of principles, then, given visual form, would be that smoldering "great central moltenness" with which Burke begins his grammatical journey to the center of substance, that ambiguous foundry where the "A" of our wishing becomes the "non-A" of our disenchantment. It is exactly this mercurial dialectic that gives Burke's constitutional theory its titular emphasis—"The *Dialectic* of Constitutions."

Clarifying this productive agonism of voluntaristic wishes and their necessitarian interrelationships does more than illustrate an important feature of Burke's theory of constitutions. Understanding these dialectical workings of constitutional principles also greatly illuminates Burke's references to identity and to the individual generally as "unique 'constitutions.'" In my previous discussion of Burke's various descriptions of "A Symbolic of Motives," I emphasized his language-oriented explanation of the individual as a "set of interrelated terms all conspiring to round out their identity as participants in a common substance of meaning" (RM 21–23). Two aspects of this explanation merit the more detailed explication that my discussion of "The Dialectic of Constitutions" now allows. First, Burke highlights in this passage that the processes through which an individual participates in the formation of identity, like all other acts of language, are grounded in questions of substance. Given his assertion in "The Dialectic of Constitutions" that "a concern with substance is a concern with the problems of constitutionality," Burke himself provides the strongest rationale for examining the substantiation of identity in terms of the constitutional theory and functional concepts he outlines in "The Dialectic of Constitutions." The constitution is, after all, his "representative case" for understanding such acts of substantiation. And if "a thing's substance is that whereof it is constituted," as he states, then exploring "identity constitution" in Burke seems more than just feasible. To more fully engage identity in his work, it seems essential.

Second, aside from justifying a study of identity in terms of a theory of constitutions, Burke's treatment of the dialectics of constitutional functions fills out his piquant, yet vague pronouncement that "identity is like a mutually adjusted set of terms." To speak of the individual and identity in terms of *terms* is, of course, no novel claim, for this language-centered approach, as I have noted previously, defines the very outset of Burke's career. Rather, the novelty lies in investigating this process of "mutual adjustment," the "conspiring" to "round out" that such terms enact *in terms of the interactions of constitutional principles*—in terms of the agon of constitutional enactments that Burke so lucidly elaborates in "The Dialectic of Constitutions." In exchange for the less serviceable, casual idiom of "adjustment" and "rounding out" of the former descriptions, "The Dialectic of Constitutions" provides a nuanced account of the transformative mergers and divisions between a body of wishes and their necessary interrelationships that all attempts to define substance entail. In the case of a legal constitution, as per Burke's example, this substance is the "motivational fixity" that would "shape" the "behavior" of those within its established circumference. In the case of the individual as constitution, this substance is the "common substance of meaning" in which a "set of terms" or principles cooperates in the process of constructing an individual identity.

One chief merit of applying Burke's ideas on constitutional principles to the "adjustment" and "rounding out" of terms that constitute identity is that this application readily lends itself to a reading of conversion narratives. Analyzing their identity transformations as the result of conflicts between the principles that individuals embody—principles that include both the "voluntaristic" wishes of the individual, which can be at conflict, as well as the "necessitarian" principles of interrelationship between such wishes—allows for these narratives to be read as constitutive texts: they are narrative constitutions that would

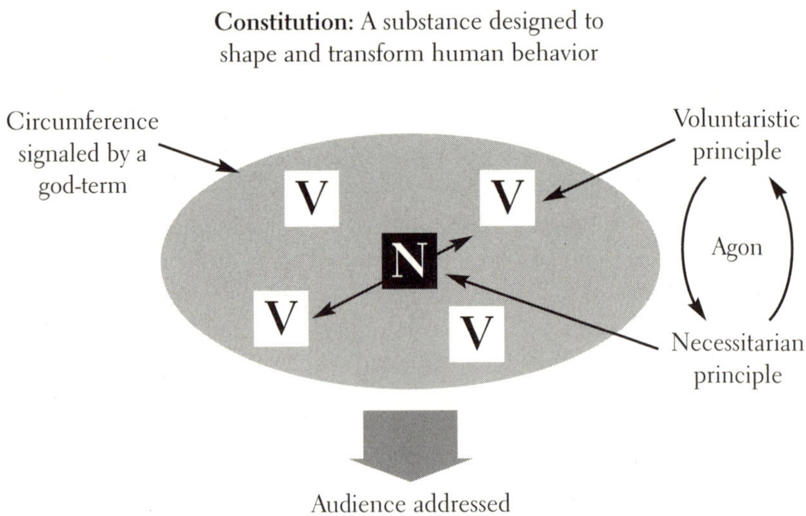

define the substance of the individual's identity in certain ways. These ways of representing an individual's transformed identity, as I have suggested, would serve different strategic, rhetorical ends. Susan Cheever's autobiography, *Note Found in a Bottle: My Life as a Drinker* (1999), for example, illustrates how an author's various changes of identity in a text might be productively explained in terms of Burkean constitutional theory. Indeed, Cheever's opening sentence reads like a constitutional preamble, laying out three foundational principles whose interactions define the text's progression: "My grandmother Cheever taught me how to embroider, how to say the Lord's Prayer, and how to make the perfect dry martini" (15). The story that follows is something of a white-collar *On the Road,* with the author narrating a chain of self-abusive exploits that takes her from eccentric introvert to high-society alcoholic. One particular moment of crisis comes when, at the height of her Holly-Golightliness, Cheever realizes she is pregnant: "I was on the phone with Doctor Buchman's nurse, and she told me the results were positive. I was sitting in the narrow room where I worked in the apartment on Eighty-first Street, and I was suffused with this incredible joy. The walls seemed to be singing with it. Soon enough, pregnancy made me nauseous and cranky. I knew I would have to move. I knew I would gain weight. I knew I would have to stop drinking" (149). Her last pronouncement here is that which proves the hardest for her to realize (as she notes the extent of her addiction in ironic aside, "I had stopped drinking before"). Wanting to truly love and care for the child she is carrying, yet desperate for the fast-paced times that have so long defined her, Cheever finds herself caught in the irreconcilability of these two desires. In more constitutional terms, she suffers at the necessitarian principle of contradiction that obtains between her two conflicting, voluntaristic wishes—the wish not to harm her developing child, and the equally powerful wish for the escapism and shallow jollity of drinking. There is simply no way for Cheever to grant both wishes; there is no "common substance" that these opposing principles share, and consequently, she can articulate no sense of self that might allow both needs to coexist within her. Such conflict of principles is precisely what Burke points to in explaining both the dialectical inner workings and the limited substantiating powers of constitutions, where "to satisfy the promise contained in one clause, you must forego the promise contained in another" (GM 349).

And forego her drinking Cheever does—not immediately, but eventually, over several years. By abandoning alcohol for good, she does not merely assuage or mollify the principle of conflict that arose between her irreconcilable wishes or "clauses": she abolishes this conflict entirely, eradicating drinking from her life and from her identity in a profound act of conversion—of *self-reconstitution.* She realizes that she now has "something to live for," that "someone else existed; someone . . . [whose] welfare was more important than my own." The expansion of circumference in which Cheever now perceives herself and her motives is dramatic, with the old god-term of alcohol being deposed now by family. She copiously attests to this shift of motivation in her narrative, reeling at how her feelings for her daughter "soared above the exhilaration of the perfect flute of champagne or the comfort of a martini shimmering in its glass at the end of a long, dry day" (148). Hers is a transformation of identity just as Burke would define it, as "a change in substance or principle" that produces "a qualitative shift in the nature of motivation" (GM 357). Moreover, it is not simply a transformation of certain principles that "round out" Cheever's identity but rather a total transformation of the "common substance of meaning" in which such principles are rooted. This depth of transformation, as the chapters to follow will bear out, subtends the more discrete fluctuations between principles to which "changes of identity" generally refers. Such depths of transformation effect the total reframing of one's identity, a complete reconstitution of substance and self-understanding that must be reserved for the term *conversion.*

Strategies of Containment: Constitutions as Addressed

One final concept from "The Dialectic of Constitutions" contributes to my reading of identity constitution in Burke: the concept of constitutions as *addressed.* While this concept requires somewhat less explaining than the previous concepts, it is nonetheless central to how identity might be described in terms of Burkean constitutions. Perhaps more important, it is central to discussing identity and first-person constitution in a way that complements the "constitutive turn" of current rhetorical inquiries into identity—inquiries that begin "without the presumption of a fixed origin for identity independent of the process of argument" (Hazen and Williams vi). For argument implies an audience. And in their Burkean function as arguments about substance, so do constitutions.

In sections whose subheadings include "Constitutions and the Opponent" and "Constitutions—Addressed by Agents to Agents," Burke makes clear two obvious and obviously significant facts about constitutions: first, that a constitution addresses some audience toward which it is directed; and second, that a constitution has specific designs on this audience as well. "In actual point of fact, a Constitution is addressed by the first person to the second person," Burke elaborates. "In propounding a Constitution, 'I' or 'we' say what 'you' may or should and may not or should not do. If a Constitution declares a right 'inalienable,' for instance, it is a document signed by men who said in effect, 'Thou shalt not alienate this right'" (GM 360). Recalling again Burke's derivation of the admonitory from the constitutive, a constitution's primary function is to declare what "substantially is" as a justification for what consequently *ought* to be, for what *should* be. Behind all such judgments of ought and should, Burke would remind, "there lies . . . the concept of a constitution that substantiates the judgment" (356). Hence, a constitution, while a "substance," is not a substance in some passive, natural-scientific sense; it is a "substance designed to serve as motives for the shaping or transforming of behavior" (342). And while it can be easy to forget that a constitution, in the "vagueness of [its] address," is "a document addressed by persons to persons," the framers of a given constitution have well in mind that the behaviors their decrees would transform are the behaviors of someone.

Much of what might help to recover this addressed nature of constitutions falls under what Burke discusses generally as "strategy" in symbolic action. In particular, "The Philosophy of Literary Form" takes as one of its primary tasks not just to demonstrate the chart–prayer–dream (or grammatical–rhetorical–symbolic) dimensions of symbolic action, as I discuss in chapter 2, but also to defend Burke's definition of poetry there as "the adopting of various strategies for the encompassing of situations" (PLF 1). Strategy for Burke, simply stated, is that which would move us toward one type of action over another. To "encompass" or "name" a situation strategically, he explains, is to do so in such a way that people "adopt an attitude towards it"—bearing in mind that, in Burkean terms, such "attitudes" are "incipient actions" (PLF 64). Just as an act or agent may be situated in an almost infinite array of different scenes (bound by correspondingly different circumferences), allowing for an equally infinite latitude in interpretation, so the "structure and outstanding ingredients" of a given situation may be characterized in ways as vast as the range of human actions these strategic characterizations would encourage. And lest "poetry" in Burke be read as meaning Dickinson or Keats, he throughout his body of work asserts that poetry is nothing less than the sum total of language use; all human beings, whatever else they might be, are clearly poets as well. From this perspective, his conclusion about the ubiquity of strategy seems fair: "every document bequeathed us by history must be treated as a *strategy for encompassing a situation*" (PLF 109, emphasis in original).

Such documents of historical bequeathment, of course, include constitutions, which Burke sees as especially apt examples of the necessarily strategic aspect of all language use. In fact, in discussing the evolution of the placement of "The Dialectic of Constitutions" in A *Grammar of Motives*, he states that this section, what he had tentatively titled "The Constitutional Wish," was originally "designed as introduction to my material on rhetorical strategies and symbolic acts" (323).[13] And Burke comments on the strategic nature of constitutions well prior to "The Dialectic of Constitutions." Again in "The Philosophy of Literary Form," for example, he notes that "when considering some document like the American Constitution, we shall be automatically warned not to consider it in isolation, but as the *answer* or *rejoinder* to assertions current in the situation in which it arose" (109). Constitutions, then, are like all other "critical and imaginative works" in that they, too, "are answers to questions posed by the situation in which they arose. They are not merely answers, they are *strategic* answers, *stylized* answers" (1, emphasis in original). It would be difficult to utilize Burke's ideas on constitutions without somehow accounting for this essential strategic and addressed nature.

Consequently, Burke's declaration of identity and the individual as "unique 'constitutions'" entails that identity and the individual, too, share this nature as strategic, addressed acts of language. In other words, identity must be considered not merely as a "common substance of meaning" that individuals build in some existential "quest for the self" (Rueckert, *Drama* 44) but rather as a *stylized* substance, a *strategic* sense of self that would influence others. Clarifying both the principled inner workings of constitutions and the explicitly rhetorical aims of their design, Burke's analysis can thus clarify how to appreciate identity likewise, its poetic and rhetorical dimensions as a "substance" and "instrument . . . for the shaping or transforming of behavior" (GM 342). "Naming," "encompassing"—*constituting*—the "outstanding ingredients" of the self so as to move others, persuading them to "adopt an attitude towards it" and toward the situation it addresses (PLF 1, 64): this is identity's strategy.

The Poetic and Rhetorical Substance of Identity

As Burke's representative "text[s] for [understanding] substantiation" (GM 320), constitutions hold an importance in his work that criticism has yet to acknowledge. Connecting "The Dialectic of Constitutions" with his description of identities as "unique 'constitutions'" (RM 21) represents one attempt to harness his remarks on this subject, and one that, as the chapters that follow demonstrate, provides a doubly productive perspective on identity. For in telling us how constitutions decree or "enact" a certain substance, Burke can be made to tell us something about the substance of individual identity, its making and its ends. Like a constitution, this substance can be examined as an agon of voluntaristic and necessitarian principles, of "wishes" and conflicts, circumscribed within the god-term or "ultimate motivation" it strives to realize. And inasmuch as constitutions are patently rhetorical acts for Burke, whatever else this substance of the "unique 'constitution'" of individual identity may be, it is *rhetorical* substance, an *addressed* substance. Like all symbolic action, the expression of identity is a strategy, a way of addressing a situation in order to transform it. The explicitness with which constitutions represent this transformative strategy is ultimately what makes them so important to Burke. This explicitness is also what makes it increasingly difficult to see identities, when viewed through this Burkean constitutional lens, as anything less than a complex and potent means of persuasion.

Applying the poetic and rhetorical perspectives this chapter has developed to conversion narratives illuminates this strategy in first-person constitution at work. In so doing, and as I will now turn to explore, it reveals how narratives about conversion are more than just interesting stories about identities in transformation. They are stories of transformation that would transform us as well.

4

Religious Radicalism Becomes Her

Constituting Conversion in *The Long Loneliness* of Dorothy Day

The fundamental aim of most radical sheets is the conversion of its readers to Radicalism and Atheism. Is it not possible to be radical and not atheist?

Dorothy Day, "To Our Readers," a statement of editorial principles in the premiere issue of the *Catholic Worker* (1933)

When it appeared in 1949, Paul Blanshard's *American Freedom and Catholic Power* gave a rousing voice to already popular criticisms of the Catholic Church: criticisms of its opulence, of its "authoritarian" control of the laity (by which such opulence was maintained), and of its general lack of social concern—a political institution run by the wealthy, for the wealthy. On paper, such claims could be easily countered: papal pronouncements dating as far back as Leo XIII's *Rerum novarum* ("The Condition of the Working Classes" [1891]) and Pius XI's *Quadragesimo anno* ("On Reconstructing the Social Order" [1931]) explicitly declare the Catholic Church's devotion to the needs of working men and women. These and many other papal encyclicals together proclaim Catholic dedication to "the cause of the worker in his struggle for survival" and a determination to remedy the "sprawling city-slums, overwork, and . . . brutal exploitation of the young and the weak" that had become synonymous with modern industrialization (Harte 63; Taft 34). As Pius XII simply, yet eloquently, epitomized the church's prolabor position in 1948, the year before Blanshard's influential critique was published, "The most antihuman and antisocial tactic is to make work hateful" (quoted in Lercaro 71).

But in the closing moments of 1948, 250 grave diggers for the Archdiocese of New York seemed to be proving their church's critics right. Two days after

Christmas, grave diggers for Calvary Cemetery, Local 293 of the United Cemetery Workers, an affiliate of the CIO's International Food, Tobacco, and Agricultural Workers Union, delivered an official proposal for improvements in working conditions to their employers, the trustees of St. Patrick's Cathedral. Chief among these trustees was the Catholic Church's most renowned prelate at the time—the archdiocese's own archbishop, Francis Cardinal Spellman. Auxiliary bishop of Boston until his appointment to cardinal in April 1939, globe-trotting military vicar for the armed forces during World War II, and a personal friend of both FDR and previous pope, Pius XI, Spellman was more than simply the sixth archbishop of one of the nation's largest, most prominent archdioceses. He was "the most publicized figure in the American hierarchy and the best known the world over of all American cardinals" ("Cardinal Brings to End" 2), "a prominent symbol of American Catholic patriotism," a patriotism that he frequently evidenced as a "high profile . . . [and] outspoken foe of communism both home and abroad" (Shelley). Whatever the Catholic Church's venerable social philosophy of "encouraging working men to unionize so that united they may be in a stronger position to protect their rights" (Ehardt 1), few were surprised when Spellman condemned the grave diggers' parent CIO affiliate on the front page of nearly every major New York paper as "a well known Communist-dominated union," or when he then rejected their proposal for improvements outright and refused to negotiate about their conditions ("Cardinal Says" 1).[1] Less than a week later, Local 293 made good on its affirmative vote to strike, picketing at the steps of St. Patrick's on Fiftieth Street, arousing, in the words of Spellman's counselor, Monsignor Edward Gaffney, the "serious concern [of] both priests and laity in the Archdiocese" (Letter to Spellman, 15 February 1949). It was the first documented strike of Catholic laity against Catholic clergy.

One of the few places where the 250 or so strikers found relief over the three months of their picketing was at a nondescript lodging house and breadline on New York's Lower East Side, near the Bowery: 115 Mott Street, the home of the notorious newspaper the *Catholic Worker*, and home as well to this penny-a-copy's equally notorious founders, Dorothy Day and Peter Maurin. Day, the daughter of a racetrack journalist, third-semester dropout from the University of Illinois, Greenwich Village radical, and eventual convert to Catholicism, had met itinerant French peasant-philosopher and fellow Catholic Peter Maurin in late 1932. Together, they set out to "call . . . attention to the fact that the Catholic Church has a social program" ("To Our Readers" 4). Their means of doing so was the *Catholic Worker*, a trenchant monthly paper whose inaugural issue they wrote, printed, and then hawked in Union Square on May Day, 1933.

From its inception, this unlikely journalistic "attempt to popularize and make known the encyclicals of the Popes," this "Catholic paper printed for the unemployed," championed unpopular social causes and often bore the displeasure of the very church whose name it sought to advance ("To Our Readers" 4). The *Catholic Worker*'s response to the grave-diggers strike in 1949 demonstrated both the politics and the tenacity for which it had earned its radical reputation, a reputation that had already cost Day three summonses to the New York Chancery for "correction." Day, Maurin, and the various volunteers at the *Catholic Worker*'s Mott Street headquarters not only doled out two meals a day to the impoverished picketers of Local 293 (whose membership was 100 percent Catholic) but also solicited donations throughout the archdiocese to help pay for the strikers' groceries and medical expenses. And in an even more provocative show of support, Day grappled with Spellman head-on in both a letter to the cardinal and in various published pieces in the *Catholic Worker*, all of which let it be known that the cardinal was "ill-advised" in his knee-jerk reaction against the purportedly Communist cemetery workers' union, a union comprised of picketers that, in Day's observation, "spent as much time in church as they did on the picket line" ("On Pilgrimage," April 1949, 1). In a month the strike spread to nearby Heaven's Gate Cemetery, galvanizing the positions of all parties to the conflict. "I admit to the accusation of strikebreaker and I am proud of it," trumpeted the cardinal in the *New York Times*. "You have been misinformed," countered Day in her impassioned letter to Spellman (4 March 1949). "Is Calvary the Graveyard of Catholic Social Justice?" lamented the sandwich board of a striker. And in a shallow trench behind St. Patrick's Cathedral, more than a thousand unburied coffins huddled beneath a thinning shroud of canvas tarps.

Cardinal Spellman not only survived his limited bad press from the *Catholic Worker* but broke the strike as well. In late March he suspended classes at a nearby Yonkers seminary and then bussed in the priests-in-training there as pro tempore grave diggers. In Spellman's own words, defying this "anti-American, anti-Christian" strike (and forcing the grave diggers to abandon the CIO and reorganize as an AFL affiliate) was "the most important thing I have done in my ten years in New York" (quoted in Miller, *Dorothy Day* 404). For Dorothy Day, however, as she expressed in her monthly column, "On Pilgrimage," it was an "overwhelming show of force against a handful of poor working men" and "a temptation of the devil to that most awful of all wars, the war between clergy and the laity" (April 1949, 2). Remarks such as these brought the *Catholic Worker*'s conflict with the archdiocese and its popular cardinal out of the realm of abstract principle and into the personal, for Day's stance during the strike set in motion what would be her fourth and final summons to the chancery for correction in March 1951. There she met with Monsignor Gaffney, vicar general under Spellman and the same adviser who had counseled the cardinal on behalf of the archdiocese during the strike two years earlier. Much to Day's bewilderment, and to the ire of those who had spent eighteen years nurturing her lay Catholic monthly into a paper with a worldwide circulation of more than sixty thousand copies, Gaffney presented her with a choice: either the *Catholic Worker* must change its name, or it must cease publication entirely.

Such were the conditions in which Day wrote and published *The Long Loneliness* (1952), the third of five autobiographical works she authored before her death at age eighty-three in 1980.[2] Begun in 1948 after the publication of a compilation of her *Catholic Worker* columns, *On Pilgrimage*, and completed by late 1951, *The Long Loneliness* (bearing the subtitle, "The Autobiography of Dorothy Day") was a text through which Day continued a prolific career in writing about what she knew best: herself, and, more specifically, the changes of self that had brought her to her current status as a devout Catholic and an equally devout radical journalist. Not surprisingly, the sheer volume of autobiographical works that she produced in her lifetime has made her a favorite within studies of autobiography and of the conversion narrative, particularly in those studies seeking to map a feminine spiritual-autobiographical tradition in contradistinction to the "representative male tradition" of self-writing (Mason 185). Estelle Jelinek, Patricia Spacks, Mary G. Mason, and, most recently, David J. Leigh have all contributed to this perspective on Day's writing, emphasizing how her various autobiographies enact "a feminine version of the spiritual pilgrimage." In many ways, as Leigh notes, Day is the best exemplar of this feminine tradition of spiritual autobiography, for she "writes her life story from the vantage point of a woman who has discovered and asserted her deeper self far more strongly than most female autobiographers in the first half of the twentieth century" (58).

Seeing Day's writing in this way, as an overall search for a "deeper self," inextricably binds her production of *texts* to the production of her own *identity*. From this perspective, her writing thus becomes a vehicle of her personal "moral and spiritual development," a "drive for self-realization" that "leads [her] out of her partial selves" (Leigh 64). As Sally Cunneen concurs, Day's acts of autobiographical storytelling were her means of unifying the various overlapping, often competing facets of her identity; accordingly, her writing encourages us to "seek to unify ourselves as we become more conscious tellers of our own stories" (293). And Robert Ellsberg has even more forcefully asserted this idea of a unity between what Day wrote and who she was: he argues that "there was absolutely no distinction between what she believed, what she wrote, and the manner in which she lived" (Ellsberg xv).

In this chapter I do not question the shared focus of these claims: that writing for Day was a means of self-discovery, of working through the many "partial selves" and "deeper selves" that readers of her autobiographies continue to identify. Nor do I question the arguable "unity" between what she wrote and how she lived, for in contests of truly practicing what one preaches, Day has few challengers. But I do question how such powerful, almost axiomatic equations of her writing and her identity occlude important dimensions of her autobiographical texts and the constitutions of her changing self that these texts offer. A too-quick acceptance of such claims for the unity between who Day *really* was and what she wrote elides the strategic aspects of self-constitution that she clearly manifests in *The Long Loneliness.*

To bring these strategic aspects to the foreground, I read *The Long Loneliness* through the constitutive perspective on identity I have developed in the previous chapters. In this first of the narratives I consider, I aim to offer what might be considered my own "representative anecdote" for matters of identity and strategy in autobiography: I want to demonstrate poetic concepts that describe how identity is constituted in autobiographical narrative toward illuminating identity as a strategy of influence, a form of rhetorical action upon an audience. If identity is indeed such a rhetorical act, then the identity that Day constitutes for herself in this third autobiographical text cannot simply be a transparent window to some "deeper," ineffable self, as criticism has emphasized. By the same token, this identity cannot merely be a product of Day's time, a reflection of the historical situation in which she produced the text; identity must be understood to *address* this situation as well—engaging it, seeking to transform it in certain ways, as I discuss. Failing to account for such strategic dimensions of her most renowned story of her radical, religious life is a myopia that severs *The Long Loneliness* from problems and potentials of her time to which the story clearly speaks. Such a myopia would see Day's defiant support of striking cemetery workers as nothing more than bread and soup.

Anxiety and Autobiography

The span from 1948 to 1952 in which Day wrote and published *The Long Loneliness* falls squarely within what William D. Miller terms the "anxious years" (1945–1955) of her tenure as chief editor, contributor, and overall matron of the *Catholic Worker.* In part, this anxiety was the result of success: what began in 1933 as a simple monthly Catholic paper had achieved many of its founders' loftiest aspirations and matured into a full-fledged Catholic Worker Movement. *Catholic Worker* cofounder Peter Maurin had come to Day nearly two decades earlier with a truly revolutionary, and, in its time, *radical* vision of Catholic social activism—a "Utopian Christian Communism" in which people of every economic and social stripe contributed to each others' mutual education and spiritual betterment, seeking neither support nor sanction from the American welfare state and without regard for the spirit of self-interest and social positioning that seemed to have become part and parcel of

American Catholicism. As he elaborated throughout the pages of the *Catholic Worker,* Maurin envisioned an activism that challenged people's increasing separation from each other, including the separation implied in such basic ecclesiastical categories as clergy and laity. In its place, he proposed a multifaceted program of "houses of hospitality," where food and lodging could be provided for all, without obligation; of "agronomic universities," where individuals could be taught the value of physical labor and given the skills to make this labor fruitful; and of "roundtable discussions," where all could sit, reason, and develop the art of intellectual give-and-take by which peaceful coexistence could be maintained and the evils of violence rooted out of human interaction. Such a program of "cult, culture, and cultivation" would, as Maurin proclaimed with characteristic candor, "blow the lid off" the Catholic Church, freeing it from the "nice phraseology" of its "hermetic container" and allowing it to become the "dominant social dynamic force" it once had been ("Easy Essays" 1, 8).

By 1952 Day and Maurin had not yet created the society of pacifist, field-tilling, voluntarily impoverished dialecticians-in-Christ that they believed was the true goal of Catholic practice. But the pyrotechnics of their message had at least rattled what they saw as a socially complacent (and thus nominally "Christian") American religious culture. When Harper and Brothers placed the first copies of *The Long Loneliness* on shelves on 19 January 1952 (shortly after the appearance of *Cardinal Spellman*'s *Prayer Book*—advertised as "the finest prayer book in the English language"), the *Catholic Worker* boasted a circulation of nearly sixty thousand copies internationally, a system of twelve communal farms nationwide, and hospices patterned after the original New York house in thirteen metropolitan centers across the nation, including Detroit, Chicago, Cleveland, Memphis, and Portland (with an additional two houses of hospitality in England). Indeed this movement had at least blown the lid off its own hermetic containment within Catholic culture enough that during the February following the publication of *The Long Loneliness*, the *New Yorker* sent feature writer Dwight MacDonald to Catholic Worker headquarters in New York to begin researching what would become a lengthy and laudatory two-part essay on Day's life and influence, "The Foolish Things of the World," published later that October.[3] As MacDonald there observed, whatever the "mis-calculations, cross-purposes, lack of planning and general confusion" that often characterized the movement's daily operations, "the Catholic Workers . . . have accomplished a lot even by worldly standards" (October 4, 1952, 40).

Surely Day found no small measure of anxiety in the sheer logistics of managing these diverse projects. But there was likely even more anxiety for her in the fact that the Catholic Worker Movement's successes no longer seemed to measure up—not by "worldly standards," but, more poignantly, by the standards that the Worker's own brief history had set. Certainly nothing to shrug at was a paper with a monthly circulation of 58,000 copies, an amount "about equal to the combined circulations of the *Nation* and the *New Republic*" (October 11, 1952, 46) and more than triple that of its closest competitor, the fairly progressive Catholic monthly *Commonweal* ("Unmistakable Verdict" 363). But the *Catholic Worker* hadn't come close in the past fifteen years to its all-time high circulation of 190,000 copies in May 1938; in fact, its circulation had steadily, consistently declined over that time to what was presently the paper's record low (a decline that began with its highly unpopular refusal to support Franco as a "champion of religion against infidel Communism" in the Spanish Civil War [MacDonald, 11 October 1952, 54]).[4] The fifteen houses of hospitality that the movement supported in 1952 provided food and shelter for hundreds, the New York house alone aiding more than five hundred people a day; but only twelve years ago, in 1940, there had been thirty such houses. And while the communal farms that the Catholic Worker Movement had managed to maintain provided the hospitality houses with such commodities as fresh produce and wheat bread, they were nothing close to the "agronomic universities" that Maurin had envisioned. The farms were struggling, so much so that in March 1948 Day took a thousand-dollar advance on her Harper and Brothers contract for what would become *The Long Loneliness* in order to purchase a new farm in Staten Island—a replacement for a commune at Maryfarm, New York, whose debacles and general "stagnation" had become so disheartening that she "could think of nothing except to move and begin again" (Miller, *Dorothy Day* 413).

Complicating matters even further for Day were the two summonses to the chancery that the movement had received in a mere four years, the most recent owing in part to the *Catholic Worker*'s confrontation of Spellman during the grave-diggers strike (during which they thanked the cardinal for offering "a classic lesson in how not to deal with a strike" ["Cardinal Brings to End" 1]). And in the heat of these wrangles with the church whose teachings they believed they were advancing, Peter Maurin had died at age seventy-two, functioning in his last five years in the Catholic Worker Movement, from 1944–1949, as cofounder in absentia, suffering the mentally crippling effects of a stroke. Anxious years indeed, for at age fifty-four, a grandmother, yet still a tireless advocate for her unprecedented brand of Catholic liberalism, Dorothy Day found herself the sole custodian of a paper and activist organization whose banner days were literally yesterday's news.[5]

With *The Long Loneliness* Day took full advantage of an opportunity not merely to share her life story (again), but rather to share it in a way that might reassert the radical ambitions of the Catholic Worker Movement, especially in light of the obvious decline it was facing. "I have always been a diarist and a journalist, pure and simple," she self-summarizes in *The Long Loneliness* (11), and her narrative works from both of these poles, interweaving identity and advocacy to argue the continued relevance of the movement's religious radicalism. And just as constitutions, in Kenneth Burke's analysis, are "instrument[s] . . . for the shaping of human relations" (GM 341), so Day's self-constitution in this narrative of her changing identity would shape something of the situation that the text addresses. In short, it urges her readers to see the Catholic Worker Movement as the one sure means of "building a new society in the shell of the old," a society that finds us "living together, working together, sharing together, loving God and loving our brother, and living close to him in community" (LL 170, 243). Anything else, Day will assert, is loneliness.

Writing the Radical Self

At first glance *The Long Loneliness* appears to be one more modern embodiment of the traditional three-part conversion narrative, dividing the story of an author's transformed identity into his or her "early sinful life, the conversion experience, [and] life and works after conversion" (Holte vii). Anne Hunsaker Hawkins has examined how this three-part morphology is perhaps *the* foundational feature of narratives of conversion experiences, as evidenced in the texts that have largely defined the genre—Paul's conversion in the New Testament and Augustine's *Confessions*. The section titles of Day's three-part narrative clearly reveal their indebtedness to this formal tradition. As the text opens, Day is "Searching." What she then finds in part 2 is "Natural Happiness," where the birth of her daughter and the eventual dissolution of her common-law marriage lead her to her baptism as a Catholic. And in part 3 she demonstrates that "Love Is the Measure" of true religious conversion: by far the longest section of the text, this conclusion is a mix of Catholic Worker theory and practice, providing both a detailed outline of the philosophy of the Catholic Worker Movement and a historical review of moments that portray the successes of this philosophy in action.

Within this adherence to structural convention, however, Day yet manages to challenge the expectations associated with the conversion narrative. Moreover, she does so in a way that is particularly relevant to reading conversion narratives as rhetorical constitutions—as stories about identities in transformation that seek discernible persuasive ends. Her challenge comes in the form of a challenge to the idea of autobiography itself. "I have never intended to write an autobiography," she plainly declares in *The Long Loneliness*, in apparent defiance of the subtitle's declaration that the text *is*, in fact, her autobiography (94). Amplifying this defiance is the fact that it comprises a pattern in Day's self-writing: in the very first sentence of her earlier conversion narrative, *From*

Union Square to Rome (1938), she asserts even more directly that "this is not an autobiography"—an assertion she then repeats verbatim in the text's opening chapter (ix). It seems as though she paradoxically would make a career out of writing about herself while simultaneously *refusing* to write about herself as well.[6]

Part of the reason for her refusal to simply wax autobiographical and inscribe "the complete story of the author's life" (ix), as is expected in both texts (whether their subtitles pronounce them official autobiographies or not), is that such a conventional, straightforward narration of lived experiences would hinder Day's more specific persuasive goals in both texts. In *From Union Square to Rome*, for example, she clarifies that the story of her conversion there is addressed specifically to the "many of her relatives and friends, who are Communists, [and who] keep asking with dismay: 'How could you become a Catholic?'" (ix). In light of this declaration of purpose, then, it is not surprising that the text's final two chapters mount, with only the sparsest autobiographical framing, an elaborate apologia for Catholic doctrine over and against Marxist philosophy—an argument so explicit it is addressed to the reader, in the form of a second-person dialogue (for example, "You ask me how I came to reject Communism"; "You say that religion is morbid" [143–52]). In *The Long Loneliness*, Day similarly articulates a more specific purpose for the text than autobiographical recollection: "I have always wanted instead to tell of things that brought me to God and that reminded me of God" (94). One such thing that brings her to God is, of course, her conversion to Catholicism, and the struggle by which this transformation comes about receives due attention in the text. But as she will also make clear, it is the Catholic Worker Movement that truly gives her conversion meaning, through its enactment of desires, of wishes and ideals, that her conversion to Catholicism in and of itself could neither realize nor reconcile. As such, the movement is chief among those things that will bring Day to God in *The Long Loneliness*, bringing her as well to the identity of radical Catholic social activist that this "autobiographical" text constitutes.

Events proceed quickly as the *Long Loneliness* begins: Day moves from her youth in San Francisco and Chicago to her enrollment at the University of Illinois at age sixteen in a slim twenty pages. But these pages prove ample for her to outline three basic, voluntaristic principles whose interrelationships (as Burke describes it) "round out" her identity in the early stages of her narrative ("Curriculum Criticum" 217). The first of these principles is a vague, yet persistent belief in the presence of divinity in her life—sometimes little more than a curiosity about religious things (such as stories about Catholic saints that she hears), but often a compulsion that drives her to obsessive behaviors (such as long periods of prayer and reading of the Psalms). Borrowing the language of Dostoevsky's *The Possessed*, Day characterizes the influence of this presence in her youth as being "haunted by God." This ambivalent status of God in her early life produces contradictions that she carries throughout the text: for example, her impression that when touching the Bible she was "handling something holy," yet her terror that the God who had inspired such a book was a "frightening impersonal . . . Hand stretched out to seize me, His child, and not in love" (20–21).

Second among these defining principles, Day demonstrates that she learned early on to value work. While performing her many chores at home "grew wearisome of course," the consistency of "doing my share" has a formative effect on her outlook: "Without knowing it, I had imbibed a 'philosophy of work,' enjoying the creative aspect of it as well as getting satisfaction from a hard and necessary job well done" (24). She recalls many formative lessons learned in her early years with her family, but few have as determining an impact on how she constitutes herself in the text as this principle of virtue in physical labor. As the text's concluding section will reveal, this principle is just as central to the philosophy of the Catholic Worker Movement, central to the substance of its identity as a vital social intervention.

Third and finally Day articulates a principle whose defining influence in her life might owe something to the cataclysm through which she realized it: the San Francisco Earthquake of 18 April 1906. Eight years old at the time, she lived in Oakland, near the epicenter of the tumult that killed seven hundred and left more than half of the city's population homeless. Rather than recounting the sensational details of the event or her "keen fear of death" during the quake, she instead focuses her narrative on describing the charity and sense of community that ensued in response to the destruction. As she explains, the earthquake jarred her "out of [her] complacent happiness into a world of catastrophe," and she, along with her family, abandoned normal household labors in exchange for "serving the homeless" that the quake had displaced. "Every stitch of available clothes was given away," she relates, and the reality of this cheerful charity in the face of catastrophe is a powerful introduction to "the joy of doing good, of sharing whatever we had with others" (21–22). Beyond introducing her to the merits of selfless service, her experiences following the San Francisco quake—experiences she will draw upon later in the text—instill in her a driving devotion to "the common unity of our humanity." "The longing of the human heart is for this communion," she boldly universalizes, foreshadowing the concluding emphasis of the text and her assertion there of the Catholic Worker Movement as the means by which such longings for unity in humanity might be answered (29).

Initially these three voluntaristic principles that Day establishes as important to her early sense of self seem largely complementary: the dedication to community that she develops after the quake comes as a result of the "philosophy of work" that motivates her to serve others, and both of these principles of community and labor are reinforced by her burgeoning understanding of saints, scriptures, and other things religious. However, the potential for conflict between these overlapping principles of Day' identity becomes clear as she leaves home for the first time to attend the University of Illinois. She left the university after only three semesters, but the changes in her sense of identity that she recounts from this experience begin to establish the conflict between social justice and religious compulsion—between radicalism and religion—that incites both her conversion and her consequent creation of the Catholic Worker Movement.

Among the major changes that university life introduces, Day notes that her reading had begun to be "socially conscious." When she lived at home, she was barely free to read about the plight of the less fortunate, forced to hide such "lurid" texts that "told of the struggles in the labor movement" from her conservative father (36–37). Living on her own, however, she is free not just to read about these struggles but to act upon them as well. One text with which she particularly identifies is Upton Sinclair's *The Jungle*. "*The Jungle* was about Chicago where I lived, whose streets I walked," she explains; living as she did in what was anything but a high-rent district, she could easily relate to this tale of the Chicago stockyards and its embattled protagonist, Lithuanian immigrant Jurgis Rudkus. As she notes, her long walks on the West Side, through the lives of people who were the material counterparts of Sinclair's pathetic fictions, "made me feel that from then on my life was to be linked to theirs, their interests were to be mine; I had received a call, a vocation, *a direction to my life*" (37–38, emphasis added). Whatever Day's various transformations of identity throughout *The Long Loneliness*, this singular sense of "vocation" in being "linked" to the lives of the poverty-stricken does not waiver in its intensity.

Day's literal change of scenery in moving away to school thus has scenic implications for her identity as well. That is, in terms of the poetic perspective I have discussed in the previous chapter, living on her own evokes a redrawing of the *circumference* of her self-understanding. Enlivened by the knowledge and newfound freedoms of student life, she pushes beyond the boundaries that once delineated who she could be, finding in this expansion a new sense of her own potential and capabilities. Coming to see herself in terms of this new "scene" of student life, she comes as well to a correspondingly new interpretation of the *substance* of herself, a new understanding of her nature, her actions, and, ultimately, her purpose in the world.

This significant change in the circumference of the identity she constitutes can be seen as well in the corresponding change of the god-term by which such constitutional boundaries are represented. Day does not clearly articulate what her "ultimate motivation" might have been prior to leaving home. (She seems deliberately to describe herself as lacking any such guiding motivation.) But her narration of her life and reading as a university student makes abundantly clear that she is learning to see herself, above all else, as a potential instrument of social justice. In what seems like a cue from Jurgis Rudkus, who becomes a Socialist after watching the economic violence his family suffers, she herself joins the Socialist Party her second year at Illinois. While Day, writing more than thirty years later in the 1950s, no longer identifies herself with the Socialist Party, nowhere at this point in the text does she question the nobility of what she then sought to accomplish, and nowhere does she disparage the romantic optimism of her youthful desire for "every home to be open to the lame, the halt and the blind, the way it had been after the San Francisco earthquake" (39). What she does lament, however, is the conflict in principles that her newly acquired dedication to social justice brought about. More specifically, she recalls (with the benefit of postconversion hindsight) how the increase in her self-defining devotion to social equality provoked the unfortunate decline of her "religious sense." Her language about this change in herself is pointed: "The radicalism which I absorbed from . . . Jack London, from Upton Sinclair and from the sight of poverty was in conflict with religion, which preached peace and meekness and joy." This upward-looking "happiness," she observes, "seemed to be a disregard of the misery of the world" (42). Such disregard she would not tolerate.

As a result, she engages in what she describes as "a conscious and deliberate process" of "push[ing] religion from me," one that involves purposefully taking the name of God in vain, swearing, and smoking so as to shock her remaining religious sensitivities away. She plies her newfound Socialist idiom in noting that "religion would only impede my work. . . . it was indeed an opiate of the people, and not a very attractive one" (42–43). Could this be the same Day who but a few years earlier had found such peculiar joy in reading the Psalms? With God still haunting her, yet no longer the "tremendous force" he had once been, her notion of a "higher power" takes on a markedly different form: "For me Christ no longer walked the streets of this world. He was two thousand years dead and new prophets had risen in His place. . . . I was in love now with the masses. I do not remember that I was articulate or reasoned about this love, but it warmed and filled my heart. The poor and oppressed were going to rise up, they were collectively the new Messiah, and they would release the captives. Already they had been persecuted, they had been scourged, they had been thrown into prison and put to death, not only in other parts of the world, but right around me in the United States" (46). No longer is she interested in childhood games of playing saints. Now her saints were the "'Molly Maguires' in the coal fields," the Knights of Labor in their crusade for the eight-hour workday, the "unknown women in New England who led the first strike to liberate women and children from the cotton mills," the Haymarket anarchists of Chicago who had been unjustly executed in 1887 for organizing workers. These were more than saints—"they were martyrs!" (46).

"The great mass of workers throughout the country were ground down by poverty and insecurity. What work there was to be done!" Day glories in the fervor of the new direction she is intent on pursuing. A later Dorothy Day would pose a provocative question to the world on the front page of the *Catholic Worker:* "Is it not possible to be radical and not atheist?" At this earlier point in her life, however, in this identity she has constituted, her answer to such a question would be a simple, and likely an indignant, *no.*

Finding Catholicism—and Conflict

From the outset of *The Long Loneliness,* Day, a journalist's daughter, has depicted herself as having always been interested in writing. But as she strikes out on her own in New York to truly make a living at writing—more exactly, to make a living at writing in support of the social causes that continue to compel her—her view of herself as a writer becomes a more central aspect of her identity than it has been previously in the text. In addition to constituting herself around principles or ideals of hard work, community, and social justice, the latter having begun to supplant the innate religious yearnings that have also defined her since her youth, Day now casts herself as a woman for whom the need to write is every bit as foundational and self-defining as these other principles of her self have been.

While she finds work writing for the Socialist daily the *Call,* Day also for the first time finds herself possessed by the loneliness that gives her text its title. "I felt the spell of the long loneliness descend on me," she bitterly recalls. "In all that great city of seven millions, I found no friends. . . . I was separated from my fellows. . . . I wanted to weep my loneliness away." But this permeating loneliness, rather than driving her out of New York and back to the comforts of friends and family, instead drives her deeper into the heart of the city's decay. It thrusts her to the center of the "cheap lodging houses, dingy restaurants, the noise of subways and elevated railways, . . . the smell from the tenements"—a smell that, as she poeticizes, "is not the smell of life, but the smell of the grave." In an observation that will prove important in later sections of her narrative, Day relates that, whatever the putrescence and "damp ooze" of living decay that so horrified her in the city, she nonetheless "wanted to go and live among these surroundings; in some mysterious way I felt that I would never be freed from this burden of loneliness and sorrow until I did" (51).

Day's characterization here of urban destitution as a loneliness that afflicts her is key for reasons other than the book's titular emphasis on loneliness itself. By giving social and economic inequality the form of a "burden of loneliness" that she suffers, the person of Day herself in her autobiography *becomes* her argument against such inequality, and the changes of identity she narrates provide the premises of an incarnate rhetorical proof. Given the praxical goal of the Catholic Worker Movement—to teach and inspire others to live with those who suffer, to "share with them their suffering, too"—her reasons for doing so are clear (LL 214). She wants something much more personal than simply to bring her readers to a rational comprehension of injustice. She wants them to feel this injustice as she did, to "go and live among these surroundings" as she has. Effecting this personal response means she cannot rely on straightforward argument against economic injustice to be sufficiently moving (as in, "We should all fight poverty by living in the heart of it ourselves"). Instead, she herself *embodies* this argument against such injustices. Moving from radical, to religious, to a synthesis of the two through a conversion that finally relieves her loneliness, the progression of her personal experiences adds up to a lived equation for the solution to injustice. This "enactment" of her identity thus tells her life's story, and more: it targets those in her audience who identify with her principles of work, charity, and social change, arguing that the acceptance of these principles entails the same individual response to loneliness on their part that Day here enacts. People who understand Catholic or social positions on economic disparity might attend church and make charitable donations. People who feel poverty's loneliness, however, as Day did, will get their hands dirty and build the communities that dispel it. Anchoring her defense of religious radicalism in the concrete, personal grounds of identity thus grants her a chance of motivating her audience in a way that comparatively abstract arguments about inequality might not. Readers may not want to be lectured about the burdens of injustice. But no one wants to be lonely.

On the whole, however, Day's life in New York could hardly be described as lonely, tempered as it was by her embroilment in the intellectual life of Greenwich Village.[7] She vacillated in her sympathies for many competing causes during this time, but one thing Day remained sure of was that Catholicism topped the list of the socially impotent. "Catholics were a world apart, a people within a people, making little impression on the tremendous non-Catholic population of the country," she notes (62–63). Skeptical of Christianity in general, she didn't doubt that there were "those whose souls glowed with belief, whose hearts were warmed by the love of God, on all sides of us"; nevertheless, she "never met any whose personal morality was matched by a social morality or who tried to make life here a foretaste of the life to come" (71). Adamant in her involvement with radical causes and equally radical friends, such insular and self-centered moralities were simply incompatible with her "ultimate motivation" of radical social change, the god-term and substance-defining circumference of her identity at this time.

A final conflict of principles closes Day's "searching" in part 1 of *The Long Loneliness* and, in so doing, sets the stage for the religious awakening and conversion that are the text's centerpiece. Shortly after the trial for sedition of her friends and editorial coworkers at the *Masses* in the winter of 1917 (a trial for which she was subpoenaed as a state witness),[8] Day experiences a sudden "succession of incidents" whose cumulative effect, as she describes it, is a classical foreshadowing of conversion. "The tragic aspect of life began to overwhelm me," she states; "I could no longer endure the life I was leading" (87). This overpowering through tragedy comes when she decides to volunteer as a probationary nurse at Brooklyn's King's County Hospital. She says little about why she chooses to enact her defining principles of hard work and community-mindedness in this way (other than that the number of women who had signed up with the Red Cross and gone overseas had left "a great need at home"). She is much less reticent, however, about the repugnance of her duties during that year of twelve-hour days—an endless panorama of dressing changes and soiled linens, of administering "hypodermics, enemas, and douches" to patients who clearly ranked among the city's most destitute and disturbed, many of whom had fallen victim to an influenza epidemic that year. One particular afternoon, a patient so offensive that Day had to clean her while holding her breath throws her filled bedpan at her, ruining her shoes and stockings. She flees from the ward, "weeping uncontrollably at the ugliness and misery of life," an ugliness and misery whose rock bottom she seems in tireless quest to fathom. Whatever the joy of labor that Day has constituted as a key principle of her identity throughout the text, her uncharacteristically stark prose lays bare the painful toll of her service: "This ward broke me, the work was so hard." She finds here the same smell that had before attended her long loneliness—"the smell of death" (90).

Perhaps it is this "brokenness," this realization of the limits of her strength in her principles, that inspires a most unanticipated course of events in the final pages of part 1. Soon after she began her service at King's County, Day had discovered that her supervisor, Mary Adams, was Catholic. Adams faithfully attends early Mass every Sunday, and Day, with little explanation, begins to accompany her. Whatever her earlier, deliberate attempts to purge her religious sensibilities, Day was no stranger to houses of worship; she frequently experienced "sudden and unexplainable impulses" that drove her "into any nearby Catholic church" (Forest 41).[9] Similarly, her presence at Mass with the hospital supervisor whose work ethic she admired seems the result of powers she doesn't fully understand: "What were we here for, what were we doing, what was the meaning of our lives?" (LL 93).

"One thing I was sure of," however, Day asserts, "was that these fellow workers and I were performing an act of worship. I felt it was necessary for man to worship, that he was most truly himself when engaged in the act." Her reference to Adams and to the others attending the masses as "fellow workers" is telling, for it reveals how Day is able to begin to mitigate the principle of contradiction between her devotion to social justice—the god-term of her identity—and her conviction that religion, and Catholicism in particular, were anathema to radical devotion. Her reverence for both work and workers is clearly central to her sense of identity at this point in her narrative; thus in seeing her fellow early-morning Mass participants here not as weak-minded dupes in need of otherworldly libation but as *fellow workers*, she is able to similarly reverence the religious inclinations that bring these workers together in community week after week. In this sense, Mass becomes less a matter of *organized religion* than of *organized labor* through this experience. It is a means of reinforcing "the common unity of our humanity," a means of achieving the "communion" that, as Day has previously argued (and will argue again), "is the longing of the human heart" (29).

When seen in light of her central commitments to work, to workers, and to establishing the communities that will be the engines of an improved world, the Catholicism that she once found inimical to such principles begins to coalesce with them—slowly, but perceptibly. "It was the great mass of the poor, the workers, who were the Catholics in this country," she explains, "and this fact in itself drew me to the Church." Her pronouncement of the nobility of worship similarly pronounces the beginning of the dissolution of one principle of her identity: the necessitarian principle of contradiction that once obtained between her ideas of radicalism and religion. While she has yet to understand how specifically these devotions might complement rather than counter each other, she nonetheless realizes that the religious sympathies that persisted in haunting her were no longer something she must purgatively swear, smoke, and shock away from herself. To be sure, Day is no Catholic. But as she concludes the first third of her conversion narrative, this "25 years of floundering" and "searching" has led her to something that she perhaps least of all expected to find: that "Catholicism was something real and rich and fascinating" (106).

God vs. Happiness

Day's segue from her "searching" to an account of her "natural happiness" in part 2 is, mildly put, abrupt and evasive. In the time between her year of nursing in Brooklyn in 1918, her brief return to Chicago in the early 1920s, and her residence in Staten Island with Forster Batterham in 1925, she took in a wealth of experiences that receive little more than passing mention in *The Long Loneliness*. These elisions are curious given that some of these experiences were, in her later accounts, events that most deeply influenced who she was and what she became; much of what she withholds, however, does seem antithetical to her stated purpose here, to "tell of things . . . that reminded me of God."[10] Such omissions rather obviously demonstrate how constituting one's identity is a "strategic" endeavor, a way of "encompassing a situation" by naming certain ingredients as "outstanding" (principles of labor, community, writing, and religious inclination), while naming others not at all (PLF 1). But whatever she withholds, and for whatever reason, Day does narrate events that will drive her to transformation: the beginning and end of her common-law marriage with Forster Batterham in 1924; the birth and baptism of her daughter, Tamar Teresa, in 1927; and her own baptism into the Catholic Church later that same year. Day's allegiances to Batterham and to God, as she elaborates them here, take the form of competing forms of happiness, or "loves." Their eventual resolution in this section of the text requires a transformation of identity so profound that it can only be described as a conversion—as a change that "so completely alters the being of the person that we are inclined to speak of a 'new' person being involved" (Smith, "Concept" 55).

Day moved from Chicago to New York in 1924, taking up residence in a Staten Island fisherman's cottage where she could concentrate on her writing. (She is now buried on the grounds where it once stood, as she requested.) She soon resumed her acquaintances with the "liberal, radical, Bohemian 'set'" that had so influenced her in 1917, acquaintances through whom she met her cottage's eventual co-occupant, Forster Batterham. An erstwhile biology instructor, lover of nature, and self-described "anarchist," Batterham lived with Day for the next two years.[11] Through Batterham's pronounced love of the natural world, his "refusal to do other than live day to day," she as well comes to experience a joy in her idyllic surroundings: "We fished together, we walked every day for miles, we collected and studied together, and an entire new world opened up to me little by little. We did not talk much but 'lived together' in the fullest sense of the phrase" (LL 113–14).

But this shared happiness in the beauty of the natural world cannot outweigh increasingly stark differences between them. Their intrapersonal conflicts begin to become conflicts of identity for Day—conflicts in how she defines herself—when she realizes that she is bearing Batterham's child. Day and Batterham's differences in everything from reading material and talkativeness to ideas of family and love had, in many ways, led her to turn more deliberately to thoughts of religion. She began reading Thomas à Kempis's *Imitation of Christ,* a text she knew well from her youthful penchant for hagiography. She "began to go to Mass regularly on Sunday mornings," as she had with Mary Adams in Brooklyn almost a decade ago. And, as she recalls in amazement, "I was surprised that I found myself beginning to pray daily." When she discovers that she is pregnant, she rightly assumes that Batterham would be opposed to having the child; he "did not believe in bringing children into such a world as we lived in," and "his extreme individualism made him feel that he of all men should not be a father." But regardless of his reaction, Day is certain not only that she will have her child but also about the religious course she will pursue once she does: "I knew that I was going to have my child baptized, cost what it may" (132–36).

"Forster had made the physical world come alive for me and had awakened in my heart a flood of gratitude," Day remembers appreciatively. But what Batterham did not see, refused to see, was that "the final object of this love and gratitude was God" (139). Tamar would be baptized, she explains, so that she too could know that human love was not an end in itself but a means toward God, author of the love and natural beauty that Batterham could not admit. Moreover, baptism might also give Tamar what Day had failed to find earlier in her life: an "order . . . which I felt my own had lacked. If I could have felt that communism was the answer to my desire for a cause, a motive, a way to walk in, I would have remained as I was. But I felt that only faith in Christ could give the answer" (141). The faith that she chooses for Tamar is Catholicism, which she accepts unequivocally. The only reason she provides for this conviction is that the church "claimed and held the allegiance of the masses of people in all the cities where I had lived," again recalling her masses with "fellow workers" in Brooklyn. Day had Tamar baptized in July 1927, four months after her birth. Batterham, deriding the sacrament as "mumbo-jumbo," refused to attend (quoted in Coles, *Dorothy Day* 48).

As Day had fully anticipated, Batterham was more than disapproving of Tamar's baptism and of what had become Day's increasingly disturbing "yearnings toward the life of the spirit," the "morbid escapism" of her "absorption in the super-natural rather than the natural, the unseen rather than the seen" (LL 144). Eventually, the "natural happiness" that Batterham had helped her to see—and thus unwittingly helping her to see God as the author of such happiness—divides them beyond reconciliation. "It was impossible to talk about religion or faith to him," Day relates. "A wall immediately separated us. The very love of nature, and the study of her secrets that was bringing me to faith, cut Forster off from religion" (134). But the resurgence of religious conviction that Tamar's birth and baptism were occasioning for Day was more than simply incompatible with the happiness that she had found with Batterham. She knew that continuing to pursue these convictions would result in the one condition she had spent her life (and this particular narrative embodiment of it) trying to counter: loneliness. If she embraced her innate need for worship, she would be "giving up a mate"; "Tamar and I would be alone, and I did not want to be alone," she again emphasizes. "I did not want to give up human love when it was dearest and tenderest" (140). As Day encapsulates this pivotal conflict here, it was "a simple question of whether I chose God or man" (140). And so she begins the fearful, yet inevitable process of losing Batterham and her bucolic happiness so that she might find the "way to walk in" that both she and her daughter needed. Unable to reconcile this necessitarian either/or between Batterham and religion, she begins the process of delivering the "cruel blow I was going to strike him when I became a Catholic" (147).

Religion, Radicalism, Rapprochement

As I discussed at the beginning of this chapter, Day's refusal to be typically "autobiographical" in *The Long Loneliness* represents a bold rhetorical challenge to the idea of autobiography. Her insistence on instead weaving a purposeful, directed story of herself—a story of the things that have led her to God—demonstrates what I have been examining as the strategic nature of self-constitution. The structural centerpiece of Day's self-constitution in this text is the narration of her baptism into Catholicism, which she now presents. But in the same way that her admitted agenda in her self-storying troubles certain conceptions of autobiography, her narration of her conversion similarly challenges the conventional expectations associated with conversion. Specifically, her ambivalent, near-remorseful presentation of her conversion questions the effects that this profound change has on her identity—and whether it is even a "conversion" at all. As Day's account demonstrates, and as I will shortly consider, the way in which her final acceptance of Catholicism fails to orient her newfound identity, the way in which it fails to bring new value and purpose to her life, is one of the clearest rhetorical strategies of her self-constitution in this text. As such, it is also one of her clearest rhetorical strategies for accomplishing her autobiography's purpose: to depict the religious radicalism she embodies—the same that the Catholic Worker Movement is struggling to advance—as a vital force for social transformation.

In December 1927 Day was baptized in the same chapel where her daughter had been baptized five months earlier. She now officially embraced the principle of religious need that had pervaded her sense of self since childhood. But rather than comforting her, this formal baptism, penance, and communion instead seems only to exacerbate her confusion. As she tells, "I had no particular joy in partaking of these three sacraments. . . . I proceeded about my own active participation in them grimly, coldly, making acts of faith, and certainly with no consolation whatever. One part of my mind stood at one side and kept saying, 'What are you doing? Are you sure of yourself? What kind of an affectation is this? What act is this you are going through? Are you trying to induce emotion, induce faith, partake of an opiate, the opiate of the people?' I felt like a hypocrite if I got down on my knees, and shuddered at the thought of anyone seeing me." Part of this confusing absence of joy, of any "consolation whatever" in becoming Catholic, owes to what she refers to as "the misery of leaving one love"—the loss of the happiness she had known with Batterham, albeit a happiness that introduced serious conflicts in her self-understanding (149).

As Day then reveals, however, her ambivalence about her new religious commitment stems from another loss as well, the absence of "another love" she had been forced to abandon—"the life I had led in the radical movement" (149). Her love for Batterham, as she has characterized it, was in such clear contradiction to her "yearnings for the life of the spirit" that it presented her with a clear-cut decision: "a simple question of . . . God or man." But no such clear-cut relationship exists between the radical and religious devotions that continue to be central to her self-understanding. As a result, she continues to struggle with the ambiguities between these principles of her identity as she has constituted it. In rationalizing her attendance of Mass during her year of nursing, she had been able to reconcile her defining love for social causes (the god-term of her identity at this time) with her obsession with worship by virtue of the fact that such worship had the power to generate communities: it organized diverse people around a common cause in a way that seemed to her the essence of radical social change. Now, however, having committed herself well beyond her general respect for worship by becoming a baptized Catholic, Day finds herself again besieged by seeming contradictions between her religious and radical principles. In practice the Catholic Church had seemed to her "the church of the poor" (107). But ideologically on the other hand, "of course the Church was lined up with property, with the wealthy, with the state, with capitalism." Thus while she proclaims her love for the church because of how it had brought her to understand Christ, she simultaneously bemoans how she "was going over to the opposition" in becoming Catholic, "betraying the class to which I belonged, the workers, the poor of the world, with whom Christ spent his life" (149). In this sense the conflict that she describes between these two crucial principles of her identity perfectly demonstrates Burke's observation that "constitutional principles or ideas, by their very nature as generalizations, are expressions which can give no indications as to 'where you draw the line' in specific cases" (GM 384).

Thus while the "conversion" that Day's acceptance of Catholicism supposedly represents in the text certainly does change her, it does so in a way that appears to have negative consequences for the identity she constitutes here. Rather than *resolving* pervasive conflicts of self, her baptism instead *heightens* the conflict between her religious needs and radical devotions. Worse still, this baptism has cost her the companionship of both her lover and the father of her child. And rather than "pointing [her] life in a particular direction" (Rambo 31), her new religious identity instead has rendered her truly directionless, a Catholic in creed and a radical in action, knowing that each pole of her allegiance in some way means the undoing of the other. Unable to find any rapprochement between these principles of her identity, Day faces what appears to be yet another either/or decision regarding which of these principles might remain within its circumference. When identity is considered as "a unified, mutually adjusted set of terms," as Burke describes, her dilemma can be seen as a failure of these apparently contradictory principles to "adjust" adequately, to round each other out in establishing some "common substance of meaning" that these principles might share (RM 22–23). Given then that this substance of meaning enables a certain "calculus" of motives, a set of "future acts" that are compatible with it (GM 368), Day is consequently conflicted about the acts she feels she can or should now perform. How can she act on behalf of social causes, yet act as a Catholic? How might Catholicism be something more than "an opiate of the people," and, conversely, how might radical action against wealth and property—against capitalism and the state—not be heretical?

The events that draw 1932 to a close, however, with Day's baptism a full five years in the past, set the stage for the resolution—in her words, the "synthesis"—of these principles that she has sought throughout the entire text. Day had been making regular contributions to two widely read Catholic magazines, *Commonweal* and *America*, and in November she was jointly dispatched to cover a Communist-organized hunger march on Washington, D.C. There, she watched as approximately six hundred unemployed marchers departed from Union Square, arriving at the Capitol on December 8 after a week of abuse from both protestors and police alike. Just prior to her narration of this march in *The Long Loneliness*, she emphasizes the shocking economic decline of the Depression and, just as lamentable to her, the equally shocking decline of Catholic involvement in efforts to assuage the Depression's effects. This "was a time for pressure groups, for direct action," she states, "and radicalism was thriving among all groups except the Catholics" (159). As she notes, there were many groups striving to help the needy and to correct the causes of their hardship. But while "there was Catholic membership in all these groups of course," there disappointingly was "no Catholic leadership." This lack of Catholic presence in what Day considered to be causes that any and all faith-professing organizations should be advancing—especially her own *church of the poor*—leaves her bewildered, depressed, and distant. "I felt out of it all," she mourns, terse in her disillusionment (159–65).

This feeling of disenchantment, of paralysis in her inability to act in consistency with her conflicting sympathies, returns to Day in force as the marching entourage triumphantly enters the Capitol. "I stood on the curb and watched them," she reports with pride in their courageous affront, yet with "bitterness too that since I was now a Catholic, with *fundamental philosophical differences*, I could not be out there with them" (165, emphasis added). Her resentment of her inability to participate—not for lack of will, but for her failure to negotiate around the prohibitive "fundamental philosophical differences" of her Catholicism—culminates in a powerful interjection: "How little, how puny my work had been since becoming a Catholic, I thought. How self-centered, how ingrown, how lacking in sense of community!" Having been a Catholic for the past five years and having formalized her faith through her confirmation apparently is not enough to quell the conflict that has defined her identity throughout the narrative. More disturbing yet, Day finds that after all this time and struggle, she still has failed to realize the one ambition she has sought: to increase the *sense of community* in society, to help others to see the "common unity in our humanity" (29).

The conclusion of the hunger march on December 8 happened to coincide with an important occasion of worship for Day and her fellow Catholics: the Feast of the Immaculate Conception. After drafting her story on the hunger march, she walked alone to the National Shrine at nearby Catholic University in observance of the feast. Descending into the basement of the shrine (the upstairs not yet completed), Day there offers up a prayer for the reconciliation of radical and religious motivations she had failed to achieve on her own, despite five years of trying—"a special prayer, a prayer which came with tears and with anguish, that some way would open up for me to use what talents I possessed for my fellow workers, for the poor" (166). She has prayed many times before this incident in her narrative: prayers as a child in imitation of her kindly neighbor; prayers while in jail for picketing the White House with a group of suffragists, when she "prayed and did not know that I prayed"; prayers with Mary Adams during masses she attended without knowing why; prayers after her baptism that were "an act of the will," forcing herself to feel prayerful. But Day has not yet prayed in *The Long Loneliness* as she does now at the shrine, pleading that she be changed, directed, shown how she might serve her faith while also serving the "fellow workers" whose lives were inseparably bound to her own. It is a plea for transformation—for a dissolution of contradiction between key principles of her identity without dissolving the principles themselves. The subtext of this passionate prayer is the selfsame question that has surfaced throughout Day's life: *is it not, after all, possible to be radical and not an atheist?*

"When I returned to New York," Day concludes part 2 and her account of this prayer, "I found Peter Maurin . . . whose spirit and ideas will dominate the rest of this book as they will dominate the rest of my life" (166). Her proof of the above radical, religious possibility is underfoot.

Conversion to the Catholic Worker Movement

Meeting Maurin later in December 1932 after her plea on the Feast of the Immaculate Conception was quite literally, as Day often remarked, "an answer to my prayers." In finding Peter Maurin, she also found the philosophical inspiration for what would become the *Catholic Worker* and its attempt "to protest, to expose, to complain, to point out abuses and demand reforms without desiring the overthrow of religion" ("To Our Readers" 4). Thus in agreement with her concluding words in the previous section, the "spirit and ideas" of Maurin do dominate the remaining half of *The Long Loneliness* and its review of two decades of Catholic Worker Movement theory and practice. This final section breaks dramatically with the text's previous two sections: unlike their emphasis on how specific events have influenced Day's identity, such "exploration and consideration of her inner 'self' is almost entirely absent" as *The Long Loneliness* works toward its conclusion. Instead, the text shifts "from telling [Day's] own story to telling the story of the Catholic Worker community," offering a "mosaic account" of the efforts of this community whose focus is not the historical past but instead is "located very much in the here and now" (Valenta 273–74).

This shift of emphasis from Day's own autobiographical past to the Catholic Worker Movement's *here and now*—from Day's changing identity to the current identity of the movement—also marks an important shift in the argument of *The Long Loneliness*. As I have already noted, Day defines a specific purpose for this autobiography at the outset of the text: to narrate the "things that have brought me to God." At the opening of the third and final section of her narrative, however, she forcefully articulates a more specific purpose within this spiritual-autobiographical focus. After briefly explaining how Maurin helped her to see the compatibility between radical social activism and religious faith that she had long sought, she plainly asserts, "Now I can see clearly what he was talking about, *but I am faced with the problem of making others see it*" (171, emphasis added).

This "problem" in the here and now aptly summarizes Day's exigence in writing *The Long Loneliness*—the problem of clarifying the radical, religious synthesis of the Catholic Worker Movement that, in the two decades since the movement's inception, either had faded from public interest or had failed to be understood. In fact, an experience such as the 1949 grave-diggers strike against the New York Archdiocese perfectly demonstrates the extent of this problem for Day; for not only did it seem that the general public might not understand how religious devotion could inform progressive social change (as evidenced by the movement's declining programs), it seemed that Day's own church might not understand it either. As she had indicated from the very first issue of the *Catholic Worker*, her goal was to promote a Catholic religious direction for changes in personal and social practices. Rather than challenging the authority of the church through such changes, she instead sought to advance it, to *popularize* the church and the social teachings that had already been a part of its papal canon since well before her baptism in 1927.[12] The front page of the paper's premier issue plainly evidences this aim: it copiously cites the previously mentioned encyclicals of Leo XIII and Pius XI as justification for everything from supporting the NAACP on behalf of the nine "Scottsboro boys" to decreasing electricity usage as a way of protesting inadequate wages for utility workers ("For Gentle Sabotage, Style and Economy, Dine by Candle Light"). Supporting striking grave diggers in need of food and financial support, as Day saw it, was an imperative of Christian love and a logical entailment of the biblical concept of community. On what doctrinal grounds, then, could the archdiocese fault the Catholic Worker Movement for reaching out to fellow Catholics in an obvious time of need? Moreover, how could the archdiocese later present the movement with the ultimatum that the *Catholic Worker* drop its titular reference to the church that structured its social advocacies or else cease publication?

Addressing this "situation" of the Catholic Worker Movement at midcentury, Day crafts *The Long Loneliness* to reassert the movement's synthesis of radical and religious aims through an autobiographical narrative of personal transformation. Inasmuch as the paramount event of this narrative is Day's experience of conversion, her treatment of this conversion in *The Long Loneliness* provides some of the clearest demonstration of her self-strategizing at work. As I noted earlier, one pronounced strategy of self-constitution in the text is the way in which the anticipated conversion event, her Catholic baptism, fails to perform for her the unifying and life-directing functions that define religious conversion. As Mel Piehl summarizes, Day's decision to become a Catholic "settled some of the issues that had dominated her youth, but left others unresolved. It . . . gave little indication of where her new religious identity would take her" (*Breaking Bread* 19). In other words, the "new religious identity" that she assumes in becoming Catholic seems new in name only, for it fails to prescribe any remedy for the conflict of radical and religious devotions that will continue to define her identity for another five years. This pronounced state of conflict and confusion provides essential preparation for the true persuasive centerpiece of Day's self-constitution in *The Long Loneliness*, the creation of the Catholic Worker Movement that her prayer at the National Shrine sets in motion. The strategic nature of this preparation can best be highlighted by reading it against Day's markedly different and prior account of her conversion to Catholicism in *From Union Square to Rome*.

Despite the thirteen years that separate the two texts, *From Union Square to Rome* and *The Long Loneliness* are strikingly similar, so similar at times that long passages appear verbatim in both autobiographical accounts. Up to this point in Day's story of her life, both texts present largely the same conflicted vision of her having become Catholic. As she states in "New Life," the last narrative section of *From Union Square to Rome* prior to her concluding apologia for Catholic doctrine, "I had no sense of peace, no joy, no conviction even that what I was doing was right. It was a thing that I had to do, a task to be gotten through. . . . I was a Catholic at last though at the moment I never felt less the joy and peace and consolation which I know from my own later experiences religion can bring" (141–42). Similarly, in the conclusion of part 2 of *The Long Loneliness*, and the last section prior to her extended discussion of the Catholic Worker Movement, she confesses that "I never regretted for one minute the step which I had taken in becoming a Catholic, but I repeat that for a year there was little joy for me as the struggle continued" (LL 151). As both texts concur, receiving the Catholic sacraments, while an event that she later celebrates, does little more than to aggravate her apparently contradictory religious and radical sympathies at the time. And as both texts also make clear, the event that begins to reassure her in her identity as a Catholic is her confirmation at Pentecost the following year. It is in the reassuring and optimistic tones of this confirmation that Day concludes the account of her conversion in *From Union Square to Rome:* "A year later my confirmation was indeed joyful and Pentecost never passes without a renewed sense of happiness and thanksgiving. It was only then that the feeling of uncertainty finally left me, never to return, praise God!" (142).

But neither the tenor nor the time frame of *From Union Square to Rome*'s narrative conclusion correspond with Day's account in *The Long Loneliness*. Rather than ending her story by singing praises to the certainty that her later confirmation brings, she instead appends her account of the 1932 hunger march, an event that she does not cover in any of her previous autobiographies. In language that rarely if ever approaches "happiness" or "thanksgiving," she demonstrates how her initial five years as a Catholic neophyte are plagued specifically by "feeling[s] of uncertainty" regarding her equal fervor for both religion and radicalism—feelings that *From Union Square to Rome* disavows. In fact, this uncertainty in effect depicts her baptism as the exact *opposite* of a conversion experience; it is anything but an experience "by which a self hitherto divided, and consciously wrong inferior and unhappy, becomes unified and consciously right superior and happy, in consequence of its firmer hold upon religious realities" (James 186). Not only is Day clearly still unhappy as she observes the hunger marchers from the sidelines, she is unhappy precisely *because of* the "firmer hold upon religious realities" that her baptism has brought: as she states, what separates her from the strikers she praises are the "fundamental philosophical differences" that her Catholicism embodies. The regretful interjection in *The Long Loneliness* that recapitulates her "self-centered" and "puny" efforts since embracing Catholicism—"how lacking in sense of community!"—is therefore quite unlike her concluding interjection upon embracing Catholicism in *From Union Square to Rome*: "Praise God!"

By emphasizing the ongoing conflict between her religious and radical principles following her baptism in *The Long Loneliness*, Day consequently directs attention away from this baptism and highlights the later events surrounding her prayer at the National Shrine as the central moment of identity transformation in the text. This shift in emphasis between *From Union Square to Rome* and *The Long Loneliness* illustrates how different self-constitutions allow her to attempt strikingly different rhetorical projects within these obviously similar autobiographies. As I have already noted, her stated purpose in *From Union Square to Rome* is to justify her Catholicism to "dismayed" Communist "relatives and friends" (ix); her account in this text therefore emphasizes changes of self in relation to the act of accepting the church—an emphasis that leads her into the Catholic argument against Communism that concludes the text. *The Long Loneliness*, however, depicts a Dorothy Day in search not of religious faith but rather of a *synthesis* of religious faith and radical social action: "How I longed for a synthesis reconciling body and soul, this world and the next," she proclaims shortly after the account of her baptism in the text (LL 146). Inasmuch as this baptism clearly does not provide her with such a synthesis, focusing on how this sacramental acceptance of the church changes her identity would prove inadequate to the argumentative task. The identity-transformative center of *The Long Loneliness* must therefore be an event with the potential to somehow convert this conflict between religion and radicalism into the synthesis that the text would argue, an event where the incongruence between these principles of her identity is at its apex.

Day's plea at the National Shrine is just such an event. Itself an enactment of the synthesis of principles that Day seeks—a prayer (religion) that her faith and talents be directed toward improving the lives of the poor (social action or radicalism), and on a day that conjoins a religious feast and a hunger march—this plea performs a vital rhetorical function. For while the prayer itself provides Day with no immediate relief to her identity-defining conflict (there is no "conversion" at the shrine), it does, as part 2 concludes, focus attention on the text's final section as the place where this conversion will be presented. In this way, the creation of the Catholic Worker Movement and its corresponding newspaper become the anticipated experience that will orient, unify, and provide "ultimate value" to her identity (Rambo 6). What might otherwise have seemed little more than a straightforward review of Day's involvement with the movement (a section that, like her concluding apologia in *From Union Square to Rome*, does nothing to develop her identity in that text and is therefore easily skipped)—instead becomes the crux of her self-constitution here. It becomes the transformation that, in its synthesis of her social concern and religious need, finally forges in her "a coherent center from which to conduct one's life" (Rambo 31).

In meeting Peter Maurin and embracing his theory of a green revolution through Catholicism, Day finds the synthesis of religious and radical ambitions that profoundly transforms her sense of self. Moreover, this transforming synthesis provides her with something else she has long sought: the remedy for isolation, for indifference to the world's inequalities, for despair—for *the long loneliness*. This remedy is *community*, something that she has long valued but only now understands in both its religious and radical importance. As she pronounces, "The only answer to this life, to the loneliness we are all bound to feel, is community. The living together, working together, sharing together, loving God and loving our brother, and living close to him in community so we can show our love for Him" (LL 243). In the context of neither social action nor Catholicism does such community-building seem radical. The basis of both, after all, is a call to "unite," whether as a body of workers or as members of the body of Christ. But the truly "radical" aspect of the movement's community-building agenda lay in the means that it advocated for fostering such communities: the training of a laity skilled both in means of material production (farming, building, cooking) and in the Catholic "works of mercy"—basic practices of individual worship, ranging from instructing the ignorant to feeding the hungry.[13] Such "independent lay initiatives" like that which Day and Maurin proposed in this combination of spiritual and material education "were almost unheard of in an era when the accepted role of lay Catholics was to 'pray, pay, and obey'" (Piehl, *Bread* 138). Thus the creation of such lay communities through Maurin's program of "cult, culture, and cultivation" could be radical indeed—a way of enacting real social change without subverting either doctrine or church authority. What could possibly be more orthodox than encouraging fellow Catholics to more fully incorporate the most basic practices of Christlike conduct into their daily lives?

Moreover this "vision of a lay Christianity transforming the world" was potentially radical from a social standpoint as well (Piehl, "Catholic Worker" 266). As Day explains, communities that thoroughly practiced the works of mercy would "combat the taking over by the state of all those services which could be built up by mutual aid." Caring for one's neighbor, she explains, is first and foremost an act of individual "charity"; it is "personal," and, as she quotes Maurin, "it is not the function of the state to enter into these realms" (LL 179). Thus in place of the burgeoning philosophy of the welfare state, Catholic Workers would nurture a "philosophy of work," a Catholicized version of the same sense of virtue in labor, of bearing the burdens of others, that Day has constituted as central to her identity since her youth (226).

Such communities, anchored in the praxis of the works of mercy, could thus be both faith promoting and world changing. As Day comes to understand these microcosmic syntheses of "body and soul, this world and the next," she also begins to forge a merger between religious and radical principles of herself that once seemed flatly contradictory. "Going to the people is the purest and best act *in Christian tradition and revolutionary tradition* and is the beginning of world brotherhood," she is now able to declare (216, emphasis added). As a result, the either/or dilemma she once faced concerning how these two principles might coexist finally abates. In its place she is able to articulate a summarizing aim for her identity, the unity of an "ultimate motivation" where before there had only been division and dilemma. Speaking as someone who is neither religious nor radical, but both, Day pronounces the dialectical merger of these terms into the god-term that reciprocally pronounces her the product of their synthesis—a *Catholic social activist.*

Conclusion: Conversion as Self-Reconstitution

Unlike other changes of self that Day has experienced throughout *The Long Loneliness,* this transformation in the text's final section can be described as a conversion because of the depth of change it effects in her identity. Her shifting allegiances to different radical organizations, her vacillating resentment and reverence for acts of worship, her changing feelings of love and estrangement from Batterham: all of these changes, while clearly vital to Day's self in the text, might be described in terms of the back-and-forth of the agon of constitutional principles—the competition between wishes and ideals that cannot always be satisfied. As Burke notes in explaining the ambiguities of constitutions, "to satisfy the promise contained in one clause, you must forego the promise contained in another"; moreover, "the law that frustrates one wish in the Constitution will, by the same token, gratify another" (GM 378). As a result, any attempt to act "on principle" is also contrary to principle in some sense at the same time. Every act, then, is ultimately an act of hierarchizing or prioritizing; every act is also an act of determining which principle reigns at any given time, for no single act can honor all that is willed in a constitution's concept of substance.

Identity, as a "unique 'constitution,'" enacts the same agonistic scenario. Inasmuch as an identity in this Burkean perspective is composed of an individual's wishes or ideals, acting on behalf of any one principle of the self inevitably foregoes some other principle, placing it beneath another in importance. For example, Day's decision to attend Mass in Brooklyn (a clear change in her life at the time) privileges her religious leanings above her principled, radical rejection of religion as a weakling's crutch. This act does not *dissolve* or *abolish* her radical sentiments; nor does it elevate her spirituality to some summit of preeminence from which it cannot be toppled, re-hierarchized by future acts.

Such changes of self or of identity are simply the result of the fact that identities, like constitutions, are complex and ambiguous "generalizations": they are substances capable of enacting many different motives, even contradictory motives, at different times (GM 384).

But the change of conversion is different. A change not simply in any individual wish or principle of identity, a conversion instead signals a transformation in the overall *substance* that a constitution would decree—the "common substance of meaning" that the principles within the circumference of that constitution share. As the shared grounding of these constitutional principles changes, so the relationships between them change as well, and along with them, the "ultimate motivation" that these principles would cooperate in achieving. One may persist in being religious, or radical, or anything else both before and after a conversion. After conversion, however, one is differently religious, differently radical—perhaps differently everything, depending on the conversion narrative in question. In this sense, conversion can also be called a "reconstitution" of identity: its change yields a transformed concept of substance and, within it, a correspondingly transformed complex of voluntaristic or "willed" principles and necessitarian relationships between them. The "converted" identity is *a new constitution.*[14]

Day clearly undergoes such a reconstitutive transformation of identity in *The Long Loneliness*, a narrative of the struggle through which religion and radicalism eventually coalesce to redefine her sense of self and her actions. But, again, this is not to say that the "reconstituted" Day of the Catholic Worker Movement is therefore somehow entirely different from the unregenerate Day of the past: in fact, the same principles that she has constituted in her identity at the outset of the text are every bit as present after her conversion—principles of virtue in labor (her "philosophy of work"), caring through community, religious passion, and writing. What has changed in the converted Day, however, is the overall aim toward which these principles now aspire, the "ultimate motivation" that her redefined radical-religious substance now provides. She still maintains a philosophy of work, but a philosophy that is now concretized in the specific practices of the Catholic works of mercy. She still seeks to perform charitable, community-building service for others, as she did after the San Francisco earthquake; now, however, that service has an overtly religious significance for her that her earlier charitable acts did not express—the ends of charity now being not merely *material* betterment but *spiritual* strengthening as well. And Day clearly retains her pervasive religious sensibility after her conversion, that same spiritual yearning she foregrounds in her narrative of her youth. But now that yearning is different, too: it is less an ambiguous "haunting by God" than it is a deliberate concentration on the divine around her, a focused awareness of God that is not spiritualistic, but *spiritual.*

Thus while Day maintains foundational principles of her identity throughout this narrative of her changed self, her experiences with the Catholic Worker Movement redefine the relationships between these central principles in a way that can accurately be termed a *conversion*—a "total personal revolution" (Haughton 23). This *reconstitution* of her identity, of the "common substance of meaning" that grounds it, is just the type of change that John E. Smith reserves for the idea of conversion: it is a change that "seems not to be a difference in this or that feature of the person's life, but a change *of* person as if a new being now dwelt where another had lived before"—a change so thorough that its roots are "difficult to locate or determine" (55). The result of this profound change is a Dorothy Day quite unlike the university student and radical Greenwich Villager of her "searching," a Day bearing little resemblance to the woman who once prayed at the National Shrine, realizing that she had been a Catholic for three years yet, in her isolation, "still did not know personally one Catholic layman." The result is a Day who, though once proclaiming herself "in love with the masses," now counters in her newfound focus on lay involvement that "it is people who are important, not the masses." Finally, and most significant, the result is that a woman who once lamented how "ingrown" and "lacking in sense of community" she had become instead is transformed into the veritable embodiment of the answer to this lack: "We have all known the long loneliness and we have learned that the only solution is love and that love comes with community" (LL 166–286).

Epilogue: Identity—"A Power and a Possibility"

Shortly after her appearance at the Chancery for correction on 3 March 1951, Day sent a letter to Monsignor Edward Gaffney, responding to his ultimatum that the *Catholic Worker* change its name or cease publication. "I will admit that I personally am at fault in not being more careful an editor and censor," she humbly acknowledged. "I confess I have not given sufficient time to the matter of the paper, being occupied with so many other cares." Granting that "of course we would change the name rather than cease publication," she nonetheless asserted her stance unflinchingly: "the *Catholic Worker* has been in existence for eighteen years . . . under that name, and . . . this is no time to change it so late in the day" (quoted in Miller, *Harsh* 427–28).

Gaffney, bothered with complaints within the archdiocese about the paper's views, yet unable to document a clear instance when these views had demonstrably contradicted church doctrine, indirectly nullified his own ultimatum by deciding not to act on it at all. The *Catholic Worker* would continue, and still continues, to publish with reference to the church whose teachings underpin its community-building efforts, a reference that Day was loathe to drop for reasons other than the simple consistency of title that she cites in her letter.

"Many times we have been asked why we spoke of *Catholic* workers [rather than "workers" generally] and so named the paper," she explains in *The Long Loneliness*. "Of course it was not only because we who were in charge of the work, who edited the paper, were all Catholics, but also because we wished to influence Catholics. They were our own, and we reacted sharply to the accusation that when it came to private morality the Catholics shone but when it came to social and political morality, they were often conscienceless" (210). The movement's proudly stated allegiance with Catholicism, then, more than a theological marker of its staff (and more than a sign of "visible piety" to placate the archdiocese), defined the paper's audience in important ways (Piehl, "Catholic Worker" 264): it called to those already in the fold to exercise the "social and political morality" that their church's encyclicals had outlined since before the turn of the century. Putting these teachings into practice would not only foster the changes that Day and her movement sought but also would provide the clearest counter-witness to criticisms of Catholic social disregard, criticisms that texts such as Blanshard's *American Freedom and Catholic Power* had so powerfully rallied.

And more than defining its audience, the paper's titular emphasis on Catholicism served to define the movement's *identity* in important ways as well. It indicated the movement's acknowledgment of church authority (albeit an authority open to critique); it credited the source of the papal social teachings that grounded its philosophy of work; and, most significant, it signaled the unique synthesis of aims—of "body and soul, of this world and the next"—that distinguished the movement's singular *religious* radicalism from other social agendas that embraced either one side of this conjunction or the other. Given these vital audience- and identity-defining functions—*rhetorical* functions—of the "Catholic" in *Catholic Worker*, the "choice" between ceasing publication or a seemingly simple changing of name that Gaffney presented to Day was really no choice at all. Both options would yield the same result: rending the identity of the *Catholic Worker* in this way was as good as Day agreeing to terminate the paper that she had it in her heart to publish, the paper that, according to *The Long Loneliness*, had itself been the vehicle of her conversion.

This understanding of identity's rhetorical potential defines *The Long Loneliness*, where Day's own transformed identity becomes the locus of her argument for her Catholic Worker Movement and, through it, for a transformed social order. Overall, her identity in this narrative of her changing self can be described in words that she once used to describe the masses: her identity is "a power and a possibility" (LL 97). It is a potential for persuasion whose power lay in the many possible ways of presenting her changing self. Considering this strategic nature of self-constitution through the poetic and rhetorical framework I have here demonstrated begins to account for how Day melds autobiography and argument in this text; it begins to account for how she addresses the problem of "helping others see" the social–religious praxis that illuminated her own life, "tell[ing] of the things that have brought me to God" in a way that might, in the telling, bring others along with her.

In this sense, the transformed identity Day constitutes in this conversion narrative performs the same function that constitutions do by definition in Burke's analysis. "What a Constitution would do primarily is to *substantiate an ought* . . . to base a statement as to *what should be* upon a statement as to *what is*," Burke asserts (GM 358). In its concern with narrating who Day *is* in her conversion to Catholic social activism, *The Long Loneliness* is similarly concerned with declaring what *ought* and *should be* in the world at large because of such Catholic social activism. We ought to bear one another's burdens. We ought to mourn with those who mourn. We ought to cultivate in ourselves the skills and spirituality that would answer the deeper human needs no "state solution" could address. And we ought to bind together in the "common unity of our humanity" that such truly radical collaboration would reveal to us, workers of mercy all who, in losing the insularity of ourselves, would find the community of each other. We ought not be lonely.

5

Ethos, Identity, Lies

The Questionable Conversion of David Brock's *Blinded by the Right*

Even from the depths of depravity and desolation, a conversion of politics, morals, and ultimately of spirit is possible.

David Brock, preface to *Blinded by the Right*

How can you be believed?

Matt Lauer to David Brock on *The Today Show*

To talk about self-representation in language is to invoke *ethos*, one of the most basic concepts of rhetorical theory since Aristotle first codified it in the *Rhetoric*. Ethos has a rich and varied history, evolving through more than two-and-a-half millennia of rhetorical practice, but its contemporary rhetorical usage can generally be summarized in the single word to which ethos is most often translated: *character*. When President George W. Bush dons a flight suit for an aircraft carrier photo op to exude military competence, that's ethos. When a college instructor addresses her students with an openness and respect she hopes that they will likewise enact in their discourse, that's ethos. And when clothier the Gap moves an impressive quantity of pants with an ad featuring an iconic 1954 shot of James Dean strolling down Times Square, its only text the simple declarative sentence, "James Dean wore Khakis," surely that is ethos as well. Inasmuch as our impressions of the character of a speaker, writer, or human object of language matter to our understanding of how language persuades us, *ethos* is the word for how these impressions matter, and why.[1]

If there is room in rhetorical theory for a concept such as identity—and not merely room, but a need for such a concept as well—then this space and necessity must both be negotiated in relation to ethos, "the inclusion of the speaker's character *as an aspect of discourse*, the representation of that character in discourse, and the role of that character in persuasion" (Baumlin, "Introduction" xvii). This chapter aims to accomplish just such a negotiation, and, in so doing, to provide a clearer sense of the complementary, yet distinct rhetorical functions of *ethos* (which I leave generally defined for now) as the linguistic presentation of character and *identity* as the strategic constitution of the self. Given how broadly productive ethos has proven to be in its application to everything from issues of student voice in first-year composition (Keller) to gender and self-fashioning in Renaissance English letters (T. Baumlin) to the "prophetic" discourse of charismatic leaders such as Louis Farrakhan (Pauley) to how online stockbrokers create the impression of reliability (Mulvey and Stech), it is temptingly practical to regard *ethos* as *the* term for how the person of the rhetor factors into that rhetor's attempts to teach, to delight, and even to move us toward specific beliefs and behaviors.

My argument, while acknowledging the centrality of ethos in matters of self and persuasion, is contrary. As I discussed in chapter 1, the doxastic or commonsense "given" that people can possess a certain sense of self-understanding underwrites our ability to share those self-understandings with others, and to share them toward persuasive ends. Such expression of self-understanding or self-definition cannot be subsumed within the concept of ethos. Despite the great similarities that prevail between *identity* and the ethotic referent of *character*, in rhetorical as much as in common cultural usage, failing to account for identity and ethos as distinct forms of persuasive self-presentation means failing to fully appreciate the complexities—the strategies, the risks—of making oneself rhetorical.

To illustrate I turn to one of the most controversial political memoirs of the past quarter century, David Brock's *Blinded by the Right: The Conscience of an Ex-Conservative* (2002). As the hardback's jacket flap touts, Brock, "the original right-wing scandal reporter," was a pioneer of 1980s neoconservatism and an influential journalistic cog of its muckraking machine for more than a decade.[2] Even those whose interests never stray near the Beltway will know—and will have felt the consequences—of political changes that his articles and books fomented. Brock helped to clear the way for the 1993 appointment of Clarence Thomas to the Supreme Court by successfully attacking in print the one obstacle between Thomas and the bench, Anita Hill. Brock advanced the "dirty tricks operation of the Gingrich era" by working to turn a two-party war into a holy war. And he even helped set into motion one of the only three presidential impeachment hearings in U.S. history, authoring the "Troopergate" story (1994) that would eventually inspire the Kenneth Starr hearings to probe President Clinton's personal life for moral weaknesses—hearings without which Monica Lewinsky would likely still dwell in anonymity. But after "a series of revelations great and small" about the "corrosive partisanship, visceral hatreds, and unfathomable hypocrisy" that stained his hands, about how he had been battling "on the wrong side of a culture war that divided our country and poisoned our politics" (BR xi), Brock publicly renounced his position of prominence in the "vast right-wing conspiracy" that Hillary Clinton famously indicted. *Blinded by the Right* is the story of Brock's "conversion of politics, morals, and ultimately of spirit," a memoir he pens "to hold accountable for their hypocrisies those who sought the destruction of others for partisan ends" (336), as well as to show that he has "reset [his] own moral compass" ("Unliving" 75)

Since the book's appearance in March 2002, innumerable politicians, journalists, talking heads, and bloggers have passed judgment on Brock's narrative of his self-termed conversion away from a conservative movement that "plotted in the shadows, disregarded the law, and abused power to win even greater power" (BR xi). Not surprisingly the responses have been as partisan as the scheming and culture warring that his memoir unearths. The party celebrating *Blinded by the Right*'s appearance in paperback in April 2003 was cohosted by then Senate Minority Leader Tom Daschle; Brock has been a regular commentator on Air America's *Al Franken Show* (where Franken has hailed him as "my hero"); and his highest-profile former target, Bill Clinton himself, has given the book his imprimatur, urging others in his own recent autobiography (*My Life*) to ponder Brock's "brave memoir" for themselves (565). Brock's former friends on the Right, however, have countered such accolades note for note, lambasting this "book written in bad faith [that] disqualifies itself," as his former editor at the *American Spectator* has proclaimed (Pleszczynski 82). Rush Limbaugh made a practice in the 1990s of reading entire sections of Brock's work on the air on his radio show, driving into the mainstream Brock's caricature of Anita Hill as "a little bit nutty and a little bit slutty"; now Limbaugh frequently lampoons Brock's believability on both his broadcasts and his Excellence in Broadcasting website. And Adam Bellow, Brock's former editor at Random House for *The Real Anita Hill* and other works (and son of Saul Bellow), has entirely dismissed his conversion in the *New York Review of Books* as a convenient literary trope, not a reality. Brock's recantation of works on which Bellow collaborated "should not be taken too seriously," he admonishes, for his rejection of his past "is simply necessary to conform to the Pauline conversion narrative he has constructed. As Brock's former editor, I know a good deal about the construction of such narratives" (23).

Responses that do not so predictably walk a party line in their wholesale dismissal or embrace of Brock's ethical about-face, however, together suggest a more relevant—if much more difficult—criterion than partisanship for gauging the reality of Brock's conversion: the present-day character of its convert author. Brock has written his narrative well aware of what *Newsweek*'s Jonathan Alter calls the "obvious question" that this deceiver's memoir raises: "why should we trust anything Brock says, including his own confession?" (36). How can Brock, an admitted career liar, credibly convey that he is truly converted—that he has (in William James's fitting phrase) established "a complete division . . . between the old life and the new" (178)? How can he detail his past dangerous liaisons and, at the same time, believably show that he has "reset" his "moral compass" today?

Forging such trustworthiness of character after years of actions that belie it becomes, in Brock's words, the daunting task of "unliving a lie." Whatever personal therapeutic goals he has met in writing *Blinded by the Right,* his broader public aim of regaining credibility depends entirely on his narrative persuading that he has indeed begun to unlive the lie of his past, that he is a transformed man worthy once more—or perhaps for the first time—of credence. These aims of securing public trust and of restoring one's credibility are, to be sure, issues of ethos. But as the story of Brock's conversion illustrates, they are also issues of identity.

Identity and Ethos as Companion Rhetorical Concepts

Identity—our sense of who a person is, or how one defines oneself—and *character*—our sense of how a person acts, or one's nature as a moral agent—are both powerful, and powerfully connected, terms in contemporary culture. Different enough not to be synonyms, yet ambiguously intertwined, they share defining similarities that thwart any attempt to easily disentangle them. Beyond the simple fact that both are typically regarded as features of persons, both identity and character share an intangibility that sets them apart from other basic features of personhood. That is, when we speak of people as "having" an identity or character, we do not mean that they have them in the same way that they have physical stature or genealogies. Unlike such attributes of person that seem equally accessible to pretty much any qualified observer, identity and character do not so readily lend themselves to objective observation.[3] Our inability to directly apprehend—and our consequent liability to misjudge—these chimerical, yet foundational qualities of persons is a given fact of daily life.

This nebulous intangibility or interiority that identity and character share allows for a wide latitude of mutual inference between them as well. Back and forth, identity and character: our observations about one readily draw in the other, blurring any precise dividing lines between our perception of who people are and how they act. A person's expression of identity can and often does lead us to infer something of that person's character from it. For example, if you tell me you are Muslim, I anticipate that you will probably make preparations for fasting as Ramadan approaches. If you proclaim that you are an environmentalist, I expect that the plastic water bottle you are holding will likely find its way to a recycle bin when you are finished. In this way, identity implicates character: articulations of *who* you are create expectations about *how* you act. Such inferences can also move in the other direction, with character seeming to tell us something about a person's identity. If in a discussion on tort reform you demonstrate formidable argumentative prowess and an uncommon grasp of precedent, I might surmise that you are a lawyer or some other legal professional. If I see you fasting at Ramadan, and doing so with particular presence of mind (reciting the prescribed daily prayers and spending your day in contemplation of the Koran), I might conclude not just that you are Muslim, as you have expressed, but that you are devoutly so; your faith seems not just a part of who you are but at the very heart of your self-understanding. Whether you actually define yourself in these ways is, of course, a matter apart from my perceptions, and something you could clarify by expressing your self-understanding to me, should you so choose. But regardless of my conclusions, and as this inferential dynamic illustrates, the ways in which character and identity reveal each other are many. The interpenetration of action and self-definition makes these two foundational dimensions of personhood hard to separate. Depending on one's philosophy of human existence, they may never have been separable in the first place.

Perhaps it is because of this intertwinement or overlap between identity and character in common understanding that rhetorical usage of these terms so overlaps as well. "We look at questions of identity, voice, self, and authenticity as intrinsic to *ethos*," Jan Swearingen has observed (115). And surely there is something "intrinsic" about identity to ethos in rhetorical analysis, just as much as identity and character pull at each other in general usage: it is counterintuitive indeed to take an interest in a "speaker's character *as an aspect of discourse*" (Baumlin, "Introduction" xiii) or "the process by which character becomes persuasive" (Kinneavy and Warshauer 183) without somehow implicating the character of *someone*, a person, a *who* with an identity. But this intrinsic relationship that identity and ethos exhibit in rhetorical theory, left at that, too readily collapses into a muddled synonymy; and the persuasive functions of ethos can no more be circumscribed wholly within the province of identity than identity can be circumscribed within ethos. Exactly what should stand in the place of such a loose interchangeability between identity and ethos is what I want to demonstrate in this chapter. Accordingly, my aim is not to offer a nuanced theory of ethos but rather to suggest how ethos should be conceptualized, especially in order to clarify a place for acknowledging the persuasive function of identity as strategic self-constitution. The sense of ethos and its relationship to identity that I will outline and apply to Brock's narrative, then, is offered in terms specific enough to support that analysis, but general enough that I hope to invite further consideration and clarification.

As both James Baumlin and Nan Johnson demonstrate, the history of ethos is a history of conflict, of rival conceptualizations of the nature and place of a rhetor's character in discourse. This struggle is at least as old as the familiar contention between Platonic and Sophistic ideas of virtue. One reason why ethos has assumed many different "competing, even contradictory meanings" in the history of rhetoric, as Baumlin illustrates, is that its referent of *character* is part of a broader nexus of coevolving terms and concepts for describing the human organism; a society's idea of character derives its meaning in the confluence of various other attributes of personhood, including "the nature of the human psyche" and culturally and historically specific models of "selfhood," among others ("Ethos" 263).[4] Marshall Alcorn Jr. has followed this line in arguing that the coevolution of ethos in relation to culturally and historically specific ideas of selfhood is not just a historical trend but, more important, a contemporary necessity as well. "A theory of ethos needs to be grounded in a relatively clear, but also a relatively complex, understanding of the self," he asserts. When ethos is thus formulated in light of a culture's understanding of selfhood—an understanding I have treated as doxa in chapter 1—ethos becomes something more ambitious and useful than "trustworthiness" or "character" alone: it becomes a rhetorical tool to help "describe relationships between differing ideas of the self and differing abilities of selves to act rhetorically in society" (12).

Such a conception of ethos that Alcorn calls for is precisely what I want to pursue here, an ethos informed by a contemporary cultural understanding of selfhood, enabling a more refined assessment of the rhetorical potentials of selves within that culture. An important aspect of how selves act rhetorically in society, as I have been arguing, is in the expression of identity or self-understanding, a rhetorical ability made possible by identity's doxastic status as a culturally assumed feature of persons. Inasmuch as identity is central to a society's understanding of what a person is, identity should be equally central to how we approach ethos—to the relatively clear, yet relatively complex idea of selfhood that grounds our understanding of the term. To conceptualize ethos and identity in this way is thus not to compartmentalize them but rather to better understand how they come together, to refine their observed interpenetration, overlap, and "intrinsicness" toward a refined sense of the contributions that ethos and identity can together make in analyzing self-representation in language. Clarified and connected in this way, identity and ethos form a conceptual tandem better equipped than either term alone to account for the complex ways in which the person of the rhetor becomes itself a means of persuasion.

A necessary starting point for clarifying the interconnectedness of ethos and identity, however, is clarifying how they differ, especially where these differences impact their respective rhetorical potentials and limitations. Within the contemporary cultural "understanding of the self" that both Alcorn and Baumlin reference as essential context for theorizing ethos, salient distinctions about the "realness" of the characters and identities that rhetors express in discourse bear directly on how they persuade. Simply stated, the identity or self-understanding a rhetor portrays evokes much more powerful expectations about realness and authenticity than the character or agential nature a rhetor may depict. Identity draws on—and often depends upon—these cultural expectations of realness in persuasion in a way that character does not.

In fact, character's *independence* from reality in its ability to persuade seems exactly what the concept of ethos was intended to highlight in the first place. George Kennedy clarifies this independence in differentiating two senses of ethos in Aristotle's *Rhetoric:* ethos as one's "'moral character,' as reflected in deliberate choice of actions and as developed into a habit of mind"; and ethos as a mode of persuasion, as "the trustworthy character of a speaker as artistically created in speech" (Kennedy, *Aristotle* 163). As Aristotle asserts, where persuasion is concerned, what matters more than the actual virtue or vice of a speaker's character is that the speaker "construct a view of himself as a certain kind of person"; "it makes much difference in regard to persuasion," he continues, "that the speaker seem to be a certain kind of person and that his hearers suppose him to be disposed toward them in a certain way" (1377b). This ethos that persuades—technic or artistic ethos, or what Johnson calls "strategically presented" ethos (244)—bears no necessary connection to the actual character of the rhetor. Eugene Garver soundly demonstrates this in his masterful reading of Aristotle's *Rhetoric* as *An Art of Character*, summarizing that "the *ethos* which the audience trusts, then, is the artificial *ethos* identified with argument. It is not some real *ethos* the speaker may or may not possess. It is an *ethos* not necessarily tied to past experiences of the speaker . . . [an] *ethos* as exercised in some particular argument" (196). This age-old distinction between the "real" or inherent character a person may possess and the discursive character of ethos that persuades in language continues to define rhetorical practice.[5] Rhetorically as much as culturally, we are keenly aware of the persuasive potential of characters that rhetors "invent" for certain occasions and purposes. We understand all too well that the discursive ethos an individual "exercise[s] in some particular argument" permits no easy assumptions about the inherent ethos of that individual; by the same token, we also know that what we esteem to be the virtuous or admirable "real" character of individuals in no way guarantees that their discourse displays this character, or even that their discourse is persuasive at all. To state this distinction between inherent and discursive ethos in a vitiation of Quintilian's ideal rhetor—the *vir bonus dicendi peritus*, the "good man speaking well"—the well-spoken may not be good, and, perhaps more unfortunately, the good may not be well-spoken. Any inference between "real" and "discursive" character is often precarious, and always specious—a fact that Aristotle's rhetorical coinage of *ethos* highlights and that rightly "directs our attention away from an understanding of *ethos* as a person's well-lived existence and toward an understanding of *ethos* as an artistic accomplishment" (Hyde xvi).[6]

Another way of phrasing cultural expectations about the reality of character in discourse, then, is that the reality of some kind of character within an individual may be assumed, but *appropriateness* of character to a given situation is what is expected. In fact, we often may not care if the ethos one displays is real or an "artistic accomplishment," provided it suits the situation in which it is displayed, a rhetorical situation that includes both the audience for whom it is presented and the purpose for which it is designed. Depending on the situation, it may need to be *unreal* in order to persuade, so much so that it is perhaps better termed a *persona*.[7] Often it is comforting, reassuring to see something more than this appropriateness in the character one displays, to infer a rhetor's real character from the character they present in discourse; we may want—and hope—the world leader to be as competent a military commander as his borrowed flight suit makes him seem. But despite what we may want, we most likely recognize that this character is a discursive, "strategically presented" ethos. Not a manifestation of any necessary interior source, it is donned like loaned military vestments because it is "likely to produce in the addressees an impression befitting the circumstances" (Amossy, "*Ethos*" 6). As displays of character go, it is what we would expect.

This audience- and purpose-driven "appropriateness" that attends our reception of character, however, is quite the opposite of what we expect of identity. Let me not misstate this difference in expectations *about* reality as a difference *in* reality: from a rhetorical standpoint, the identity that one communicates is every bit as much an artistic accomplishment of discourse as ethos. Indeed, this is just what I have been arguing in the preceding chapters—that the first-person constitution of identity is *strategic*, a declaration of the substance of one's self, formed in response to some situation this constitution addresses (the decline of a radical–religious social program, as in the previous chapter; the medical community's misunderstanding of gender, as in the next; and so on). But while both identity and character are equally discursive creations, identity is more limited than character in its ability to shape itself to these situations, constrained by our cultural expectations about the realness of identity. Taken as a reflection of the personal truths of an individual's experience, identity articulates that which we regard as "accepted by individuals to be true of themselves independent of time and location" (Williams 7). A less ontically or ethically freighted way of saying that we expect identities to be real or true, then, is that we expect them to be trans-situational. Unlike displays of character, we expect the claims people make about who they are to be true regardless of why they are making them or whom they are addressing. You may enact antitheses of character in different rhetorical situations, wrathfully indignant in one yet patiently forgiving in another; but antitheses of identity are not so amicably received by one's audiences. Are you a father, a Croat, a Christian, or aren't you? When ethos fails to meet the expectations that underlie its persuasiveness, it is inappropriate. When identity fails, it is a lie.

But such expectation of "truth" or trans-situationality in identity does not mean that identity cannot shape itself to situations. Expressing one's identity in discourse is hardly an all-or-nothing proposition, and this selectivity in self-representation grants identity a strategic situatedness akin to that of character, albeit to a reduced extent. Depending on the different principles that compose our identities (*principles* meant here in the Burkean sense, as components of the substance of our self-understanding), any of these principles may strike us as more important to a certain expression of our identity or, conversely, as unimportant—or inappropriate—to this expression. David Brock's speaking gigs for the Christian Coalition's annual Road to Victory conference, or his many gatherings at the homes of "well-financed right-wing operatives," seem the wrong places for him to reveal to his conservative cohort, as he later will to their chagrin, that he is gay. His evenings on D.C.'s Dupont Circle strip with other closeted conservative "laissez fairies" like himself, however, seem much better opportunities for him to express his homosexuality and to discuss it with others who are similarly trying to reconcile their sexual identity with the "transparently antigay GOP" their labor supports (BR 37, 40).

Brock clearly frames his portrayal of who he is in relation to these and other situations: He strategizes the expression of his identity to accomplish specific effects relative to these specific situations. But changes of situation are insufficient to change the principles themselves by which he defines who he is. Although he opts not to proclaim it at the time, Brock *is* gay when he appears on *The 700 Club* to promote "traditional values," and neither the irony nor the antipathy are lost on him. We may find ourselves in situations where we similarly feel ourselves to be, as he describes, "Jew[s] in Hitler's army," forced to downplay or deny aspects of who we are in order to appease the powers that be (BR 162). But we do not, Zelig-like, *become* Nazis; the personal realities of our self-understanding persist regardless of their (in)appropriateness to the changing scenes we occupy. That is, until a self-transformation such as a conversion comes along to change them. This key distinction between identity and character in cultural expectation, between trans-situational reality and situation-driven appropriateness, is implicit in Michael Halloran's observation that, "in contrast to modern notions of the person or the self, *ethos* emphasizes the conventional rather than the idiosyncratic, the public rather than the private" (60). For if *ethos* is rhetoric's term for that which can be called conventional about self-representation, then some other term or "notion" about selfhood must, by implication, function to contrastively name that which is *unconventional* about self-representation—that which is more personal than public, more "idiosyncratic" and trans-situational than malleable according to audience, purpose, or other situational imperatives. That term is *identity*.

Identity and ethos merit distinction in rhetorical practice. For in arousing and channeling these different expectations in those to whom they are addressed they license different possibilities for persuasion as well. This fact is easily lost when *identity* is jettisoned outright from rhetoric's vocabulary of the person as a myopic humanism, or, more frequently, when what we commonly would understand and refer to as *identity* is subsumed within *ethos* in rhetorical practice. When *identity* makes an appearance in rhetorical analysis at all, *ethos* is usually not far behind, often as close as the other end of a conjunction ("identity and ethos," and vice versa). While this may just be further evidence of their "intrinsicness," this move also seems like hedging one's bet, an effort to justify the use of *identity*, a term with largely nonexistent rhetorical-theoretical backing, by linking it to a related term with a robust critical literature (where everything from Playboy.com to Ultimate Frisbee has an ethos [Frobish; Robbins]).[8] The motion by which ethos subsumes identity can be subtler still. A recent analysis of Augustine's *Confessions*, for example, illuminates "the rhetoric through which [Augustine] was converted to his new belief, to a better idea of God, and, ultimately, to a new *ethos* and a new Christian life" (Olmstead 65). I do not think the claim here is that the "new ethos" Augustine's conversion "ultimately" yielded is simply a new way of presenting his character in language (although, as the analysis shows, it did grant him that). Maybe this new ethos refers not just to discursive character, as it typically does, but rather to inherent character as well, asserting that Augustine's conversion transformed the very nature of his intentions and actions (which, in his account, it most certainly did). But isn't the "new Christian life" he goes on to enact as much a matter of new self-understanding and new self-definition as new actions and new character? In other words, don't Augustine's ponderous descriptions of how he understands himself now as a servant of the Word instead of as a word merchant indicate that what his conversion ultimately yields might be not just a new ethos but also, along with it, what we would call a new *identity?*

One benefit of seeing *ethos* and *identity* as distinct, companion terms is the possibility of thus seeing interrelationships between them in attempts to persuade through self-presentation. Rarely do identity and character stand apart in our evaluation of others, a broad interpenetration of agential nature and self-definition that rhetoric might more thoroughly explore as a *topos* of persuasion. One such relationship I have already discussed, and that which I will focus on here, is the relationship of mutual inference between identity and character. How can a rhetor's depictions of identity lead a given audience toward certain conclusions about that rhetor's character, and conversely, how can such impressions of a rhetor's character, intentionally created by the rhetor or not, lead an audience toward certain conclusions about the rhetor's identity? Stated in the terms I will employ in exploring these questions of mutual inference, representations of identity can have *ethos effects* and representations of character can have *identity effects*. Attending to ethos and identity in this way helps rhetoric account for a dynamic that character and identity prominently manifest in culture. More important, as an analysis of Brock's narrative illustrates, it also highlights an intuitive, and therefore subtle, rhetorical strategy of self-representation.

Conversion from Conservatism: A Tale of Three *Ēthē*

Blinded by the Right, as Brock declares in the preface, is the fruit of his "attempt to find a sense of peace, emotional balance, and personal integrity," one that, as he indicates, "eluded me during my dozen years in the right wing." But this memoir of his conversion from conservatism has much broader ambitions than interior harmony: "I wrote this book as an act of conscience," he exclaims, "to illuminate for others the dangers that I see in an empowered conservative movement." This purpose is truly an exigent one, for "the wounds on the body politic from this era are still open." And lest readers turn away from these wounds, supposing that our attention is better spent on matters more vital to our current "war on terror," Brock adjures that "the need to shine light on the operations and agenda of the right wing has not abated in the wake of September 11." *Blinded by the Right* presents his fullest confession of his own part in these still-looming, still-dangerous operations and agendas, a confession that he offers in what he describes as "a spirit of both full disclosure and reconciliation" (xii–xv). Even in this prefatory couching of his story, he knows that the former is going to be much easier for him to accomplish than the latter.

Brock's narrative of his conversion, then, is a confession that serves these two interrelated purposes: He excoriates the still-functioning "vast right-wing conspiracy" by disclosing his complicity in its lies; and, just as important, he seeks to do so in a way that might reconcile him to his audience by convincing readers that he is truly changed, not just in who he is, but in how he acts as well. His strategy for achieving these two interrelated aims of disclosure and reconciliation is itself dual, a strategy where identity and character work together in an inferential relationship such as I have just described. Brock recognizes the challenge of addressing the character question on its own terms: is merely demonstrating a better character enough for him to persuade that he has changed, especially when he is an admitted character assassin and dissembler, trained in making actions, his own as easily as others', appear as something they are not? He instead attempts to render a credible change of character by drawing on how we infer character from identity, forming our expectations about how one acts based upon our impression of who one is. That is, Brock depicts the flawed character whose convincing reversal he hopes to accomplish as an extension of deeper flaws in identity. These preeminent identity conflicts are eventually resolved in his memoir through a profound personal transformation. When the identity that motivates this character is transformed through the conversion he describes, so presumably is the character that springs from it. Shifting the terrain to identity in this way, Brock thus saddles the question of his credible change of character to a much deeper, much more personal change in the very nature of who he is—a transformation of self that is as much easier to sympathize with as it is more difficult to dispute. This manipulation of inference between identity and character, however, is as double-edged as it is sharp. As the speculation about the believability of his conversion demonstrates, these inferences can work in the reverse of Brock's strategy as well, from character back to identity: when one's character becomes questionable, so, too do the identity claims behind it, including claims of conversion. The rhetorical aims of his conversion narrative and the debatable extent of their achievement can thus both be explained by analyzing the interaction of identity and three character impressions, or *ēthē*, in his memoir. Cooperating in the analysis of Brock's self-representation, ethos and identity together illuminate both the means and the complications of his attempt to condemn those with whom he "plotted in the shadows" without overshadowing the possibility of his own redemption.

Blinded by Identity: Brock's Preconversion Ethos

From the outset of his narrative, Brock asserts that the troubled character he displays before his conversion is driven by an equally troubled identity that subtends it. He is only eight as his memoir begins, yet the same realities of self-understanding that define his youth will also define his identity as a young adult, a sense of self that all but guarantees his eventual co-optation by some group or another that will all too easily blind him. As the title of the first chapter indicates, in plotting out the main components or principles of this identity, Brock is plotting out the tangle of misaligned devotions and personal truths that enable "The Making of a Conservative." The chapter opens by depicting the interest—the passion—that is central to his identity before, during, and even after his conversion: politics. He underscores his youthful political aspirations by quoting a much earlier autobiographical piece he authored, an elementary school essay titled "All about David," which articulates his master plan to become a "lawyer as a way of going into politics." He further relates how, at fourteen, he audiotaped Jimmy Carter's presidential campaign ads from the TV and replayed them incessantly in his room, singing along. (Hinting at the irony to come, he notes that "what cinched my vote for Jimmy Carter was his post-Watergate promise to never tell a lie to the American people.") Brock will have ample opportunity to put this longstanding political passion into action as he wends his unlikely way from social liberal to "right-wing attack dog"—from interning at the Memorial Foundation of Robert F. Kennedy (Brock's "first political hero"), to editing Berkeley's student paper, the *Daily Cal,* to reporting for the then-fledgling *Washington Times* (which "Reagan said . . . was his favorite paper") and then for the bombastically conservative *American Spectator* (11–21). Illustrating how some factors of one's identity withstand even the seismic upheaval of a conversion, Brock still enacts this political passion today, writing articles and a book since *Blinded by the Right* and founding the online media watchdog group Media Matters for America.

But this early passion for politics, Brock discloses, seems in part an outgrowth of another equally self-defining personal reality—his implacable need for attention and approval, a need epitomized in his lifelong yearning for a close relationship with his emotionally absent father. "Talking politics helped me relate to my otherwise remote dad," he relates. "It was the only way I felt I could attract his attention and evoke his affection" (9). Complicating this need for fatherly approval—or, as Brock's story unfolds, for *any* kind of approval—is his knowledge that he and his sister are both adopted. As one would expect, this fact renders him that much less sure not just about where approval can be found but also about where it should be sought in the first place.[9] In talking politics to win the attention of his adoptive father, a man at the double distance of emotional and biological remove, Brock enacts in microcosm the drama that is *Blinded By the Right,* a drama wherein "anyone who gave me attention could dictate my beliefs" (8). These two interrelated principles of political interest and the desire for personal validation powerfully define his sense of self at this point of his youth, and this equation between the two drives the development of his memoir. A reversal of an ERA slogan of his early political inspirations summarizes their commingling well: for Brock *the political is personal.*

Exacerbating this already painful, undirected need for acceptance is a principle that Brock's mother anxiously inculcates in his self-understanding. Ashamed of her child's adopted status in a way that he never comes to understand, she teaches him that he must protect the secret of his adoption at all costs. By his account, her need to keep this hidden is almost pathological. So are the results for Brock, who, as he summarizes, "acquired an unusual ability to block out and avoid the truth and to live my life with no inner questioning." Interestingly, the actual fact of being adopted is itself a much less formative or self-defining personal reality for him (he downplays the "confusion about . . . identity" it yields as "typical") than his mother's paranoid response to this reality. As a result of her schooling in duplicity, "living with . . . secrecy and lies" becomes a subconscious—and anti-conscientious—daily reality for Brock. Uprooting the "inner questioning" of conscience, it implants in its stead a complex system of "avoidance strategies" for eschewing self-scrutiny (12, 330). Whatever the extent to which one's adult lies can be believably traced back to childhood conditioning in self-deceit, the ring of truth attends Brock's description of this principle's influence upon him when he confides that "so ingrained was the lesson that I never told even my closest friends about my adoption until my father passed away when I was thirty-seven years old" (12).

One personal truth about which Brock must be vigilantly secretive also functions as the final principle of the identity he constitutes in beginning his memoir. "At the age of eleven," he relates, "I became powerfully aroused during a game of touch football with the neighborhood boys at a nearby park. When I got home, thinking about one of the players, I had my first orgasm. I didn't know the terms 'homosexual' or 'gay,' but from that moment on, I knew I was sexually interested in men." His discovery of his homosexuality is an unwelcome one, for it even further complicates his overwhelming desire for fatherly attention and acceptance. "As I came to understand what homosexuality was, I feared that both of my parents, and especially my religiously devout father, would reject me all the more if they knew this truth," he states (13). This irreconcilable conflict between his homosexuality and his need for approval represents what Burke describes as a "necessitarian principle" in the agon of the identity Brock has constituted, an "interrelationship" among principles of his identity that is "necessary or inevitable" (GM 375). Unable to conceive of some way in which he might openly acknowledge and act on both of these aspects of himself, Brock portrays himself as forced to flatly choose one over the other. As a result, he heels to his need for approval and pushes his homosexuality even deeper into secrecy, "conceal[ing] what was at that age the most important thing I knew for sure about myself" (BR 13). His need to keep this fact hidden is one he can easily meet, of course, given the artistry in self-deceit and secrecy that his mother has already taught him; the "avoidance strategies" that sit in the place of his conscience all too easily reduce the personal truth of his homosexuality to just "another reason to fear and avoid self-evaluation" (12). Ensuring the persistence of these crippling conflicts, his ingrained fear of self-scrutiny prevents the contemplation that might bring any coherence or direction to his sense of self—and this is just the point. His identity constituted as a profile in self-defeat, Brock intimates that if he is unable to provide any guiding ultimate motivation for himself, then something else will.

Perhaps the autobiographical form of the conversion narrative mandates that Brock spend the beginning chapters of *Blinded by the Right* as he has, detailing the identity that will be transformed in the course of his story. But this focus on the principles and conflicts that define him also establishes his memoir's strategy for disclosing his past without precluding his redemption in the present. In emphasizing his pervasive identity confusions, stretching all the way from childhood touch football to the adulthood of the "anti-Clinton Jihad" (226), he argues that his reprehensible actions in the neoconservative cause originated in something other than reason or personal conviction. They originated in identity. More accurately, they originated in what he calls the "sick sense of my own identity," in the confounded self-understanding that consequently confounds his actions. And his actions are truly, perplexingly vacillating. This Berkeley student who once "decorated [his] dorm room with postcards portraying the Reagans as victims of a nuclear holocaust" would in a few semesters be run off of the editorial staff of the student paper for his vituperative support of Reagan and the war in Grenada. And why? Most definitely *not* because he had come to comprehend the logic and humanity of the Reagan Doctrine in foreign policy. Rather, in his thirst for personal approval, Brock had "f[allen] easily under the spell of . . . surrogate father figures," an attentive cadre of wizened conservative professors who provided him with "the critical affirmation and acceptance, and the firm sense of who I was that my fragile psyche yearned for." Glad to finally find some source of validation, and, along with it, a more concrete and motivating sense of self, he explains that "I slapped the label of the entire conservative movement on my lapel, gave it authority over my being, without even understanding what it meant." By the time he graduates from Berkeley, conservatism will have become, as he describes, "*the defining aspect of my life* . . . provid[ing] me with everything—a way of making sense of the world, of fitting in, even a self-image that I would not question for years to come" (8, emphasis added). Eagerly gaining momentum in this "conservative trajectory that would cause me to live my life along a certain but wrong course for the next fifteen years" (20), he demonstrates that he has found the "circumference" and "ultimate motivation" to define and guide both who and why he is.

Just as Brock has led readers to expect, he has found this "defining aspect" of his life not through introspection but through surrender, yielding to something that assuages identity needs even deeper than those of the conscience he has labored, successfully, to subdue. And its god-term is neoconservatism.

Focusing on the principles and conflicts of his identity thus equips Brock to cast as an extension of this maladjusted identity the maladjusted character of his preconversion self. Or, in the term I have suggested, he utilizes the identity he narrates as a means for creating specific ethos effects: identity provides the grounds from which he leads readers to derive his character as an unscrupulous conservative "journalist," one motivated by the notoriety of scandalmongering rather than the accuracy of fact-based reporting. This character, by Brock's own frequent acknowledgment, is truly reproachable. But it is the dupe's reproach that he merits; his character is that of a man blinded to the consequences of his actions by identity conflicts as old as (and concomitant with) his first political memories. As he summarizes, "The sad reality is that I was trying to fill my unmet, private emotional needs through my professional life." Acting upon his confused need for approval, and finally finding that approval in others who seem to be as devoid of conscience as he has been trained to be, he becomes, as he confesses, "a perfect—and perfectly willing—instrument for the wishes of others for agendas I didn't share" (102–3). In this passivity of his instrumentality, Brock's actions on behalf of these agendas are only "actions" in an impoverished sense, lacking the conviction or reasoned motivation that are action's hallmarks. His horrors are instead the machinations of a "right-wing robot," an automaton wound up and released upon the world, its honed propagandistic armaments sighted on targets not of its own choosing. "I was content to think what everybody else was thinking," he elaborates on the programmed nature of his actions. "Unlike the Berkeley profs who recruited me into conservatism, I had no deep understanding of conservative ideology." Had he been asked about his adherence to the ideology he advanced at the *Times* and later at the *American Spectator*, this clockwork Brock "would have spouted the party-line sound bites, but there would have been no real conviction behind them" (33).

Because this character stems from identity issues much deeper than rational belief, it is perhaps more pitiable, and perhaps thus more forgivable as well. As an ethos effect of the preconversion identity he constitutes, this blinded character and the confessed evils that issue from it garner something that the reasoned actions of a true believer might not: a measure of sympathy for their author. Brock reveals that his first sexual experience is with his high school journalism teacher (yet another instance of politics becoming personal, and intimately so) in a mall parking lot when he is fourteen—a tearful encounter with a woman, and well after he knows with certainty he is homosexual. Do we not expect him to experience a lifetime of similar missteps until he finally comes to terms with who he is? If the character that results from these and other such *hamartiae* is something short of admirable, is it not at least *understandable?* With this modicum of understanding on the part of his audience Brock also gains an increased ability to depict his misdeeds without painting himself too far into a corner of culpability. And depict them he does, vividly detailing this character of a print assassin acting out his "identity . . . as a radical right-wing outlaw." He becomes fast friends with future conservative luminaries such as Ann Coulter, Laura Ingraham, and Dinesh D'Souza ("Distort D'Newsa" in Brock's parody). He writes a lauding interview of Allan Bloom and publishes his first op-ed in the *Wall Street Journal* on "Combating Those Campus Marxists." He receives the blessing of Henry Kissinger, who, upon meeting Brock at a dinner party, proclaims, "'Oh, you're David Brock. I've read your work'" (119–20). And he even cossets the Chilean ambassador in Washington in order to earn a "world exclusive" on Augusto Pinochet, whom he interviews while wearing a bullet-proof vest aboard "the Chilean equivalent of Air Force One, joining Pinochet and his generals on a campaign swing to Easter Island." (As Brock swaggers in heightening the extremism of this preconversion ethos, "supporting the Contras was one thing, but defending Pinochet? You couldn't get any more hard core than that" [29].)

"Monstrous moral wrongs," he now admits, but ones that, blinded by his identity, he "paper[ed] over . . . with little awareness of what I was doing" (29).[10] As Brock keeps the focus on his identity and its problems as the source of his regrettable character, his actions in that character become the "acting out [of] my personal drama"—the acting out of a troubled *identity* (102). A review in the *New Yorker* indirectly attests to the effectiveness of Brock's strategy of anchoring his conduct not in consciousness but in the comparatively shadowy interiority of his struggle for self-understanding: while other political conversion narratives such as Arthur Koestler's or Richard Wright's in *The God That Failed* describe transformations that are "the product of intellectual reflection," Brock's, on the contrary, "was the result of harrowing experience . . . the story of a change of heart, not of mind" (Hertzberg 85). Making identity the source from which we infer his ethos as the "right-wing hit man," this strategy enables Brock to narrate his character failings in the detailed "spirit of full disclosure" he promises while simultaneously creating the possibility for his own exculpation, his "reconciliation" to the reader. This possibility lies not in reason but rather in the place of his character's origin, the place of its pending transformation—the place of identity.

From Blindness to Insight: Brock's Postconversion Ethos

Brock's strategy of leading his audience to see his character defects as an extension of identity issues—that is, encouraging readers to infer this ethos from an identity that grounds or motivates it—is implicit in his very choice of genre. *Blinded by the Right* is a memoir, a text we naturally expect to deal in the expression of self-understanding, and hardly the most accommodating genre to some of his aims—"to correct the public record," "to illuminate [the] dangers . . . in an empowered conservative movement" (BR xii). (Brock's most recent book, *The Republican Noise Machine: Right-Wing Media and How It Corrupts Democracy*, tackles just such purposes without autobiographical emphasis.) His explicitness in tracing the correspondence of his character back to his identity reinforces the expectation that readers most likely already formed upon encountering the word *conversion* in his memoir's preface: that a dramatic change in his identity should also yield an equally dramatic change in the character that radiates from it.

Meeting this expectation is exactly Brock's purpose in relating this foreshadowed conversion. This promised self-transformation has a more distinct ending point than a beginning in his narrative. But some time during his reporting on Anita Hill for the *American Spectator* in 1992, Brock becomes aware of a "palpable anger [that] imbued my prose in a way that it never had before" (103). He has already elaborated the deep disconnect between his actions and any reasoned personal belief, a disconnect that defines the robotic neoconservatism of his preconversion ethos. "My own support of [Clarence] Thomas was as unrooted in ideological belief as my support of Judge Bork had been," he explains in underscoring this point. But what angers him is something that threatens this segregation of belief and action: his sense that Hill is actually telling the truth about Thomas's sexual impropriety, an impression that, were he to heed it, would make his present course of action impossible. But yielding as he always has to the matriarchal indoctrination of his childhood—"to fear and avoid self-evaluation," "to defer to what others did and to tailor my behavior accordingly" (11)—Brock not only publishes his *Spectator* article but also parlays it into his first six-figure book contract. As he sees in hindsight, trashing Hill in his article and then in *The Real Anita Hill* was nothing more than an expression of his own trashed, incoherent identity as a closeted homosexual in an increasingly antigay conservative movement. "At the bottom of my rage there must have been a loathing, not of liberals, but of myself," he posits. "By giving voice to their hatred of Anita Hill, I was trying to force the conservatives to love a faggot whether they liked it or not" (104).

Brock eventually sheds this "monkey of [his] sexuality" by coming out to a reporter for the *Washington Post*—importantly, less because he finally decides to be honest about who he is than because the reporter threatens to out him regardless. In that moment he begins to forsake his conservative trajectory for a new course toward conversion. His next book deal (seven figures this time) to write what will become *The Seduction of Hillary Rodham* (1996) catalyzes his process of "breaking ranks" by inadvertently alienating him from his "friends" on the Right: what readers expected to be a hit job at least as salacious as his attack on Anita Hill ultimately offers a fairly sympathetic portrait of the first lady. Brock becomes a pariah in the eyes of the movement within months of the book's appearance, all but finalizing a separation that he had set in motion with his coming out (despite his best efforts to be "the Gingrich Revolution's openly gay dancing bear" [232]). Recording the "personal toll" of his rejection, he publishes his formal resignation from neoconservatism in *Esquire* as "Confessions of a Right-Wing Hit Man" (1997). These and many other "rather difficult and uneven steps on a path of self-discovery" eventually lead him through a process of "arduous self-examination" that he has never before dared to hazard. No longer defined by a movement as fed up with him as he is with it, he strikes out alone to "find a separate sense of self" from that which he so eagerly, blindly, slapped upon his lapel and gave "authority over [his] being" a decade earlier (BR 8–13).

What ultimately grants Brock this separate sense of self and clinches his mounting conversion away from conservatism is an act through which he finally reconciles the identity conflicts that have determined his self-understanding since childhood. "The defining moment" that accomplishes this transformation, "the point of no return . . . my Kronshtadt," he pronounces, comes as he beholds the frenzy with which the "Republican sleaze machine" latches onto the Monica Lewinsky scandal. Tooling it into the crowbar they have long sought to pry Clinton from office, they exhibit a blind rapacity that repels Brock, especially because he sees in their character a mirror on his own (242). But rather than pity or berate himself, he decides to take action: "I decided to disclose what I knew about the anti-Clinton plot while it was still politically relevant. . . . I wanted to do what I could to redeem myself, inform the public, and hopefully move events onto a more just course" (311). He does so by speaking his mind to reporters that call him for comment on the Right's tactics (even pointing to the manipulations in his own book on Hill to illustrate) and by divulging what he knows to Clinton White House aide Sydney Blumenthal. "I spilled my guts," he states, and "this unpremeditated purging was its own reward" (316). This candor also informs Brock's second piece for *Esquire*, what he calls "the second installment of my confessions"—an apology to President Clinton in which, for the first time, he inscribes a written admission of his own misdeeds as part of the sleaze machine he now denounces. Where the old Brock acted politically as a means of winning personal approval, this new Brock has done just the opposite, acting politically in a way that can only yield increased disapproval—from his old cohort, of course, but also from the much broader audience of anyone who expected honesty and objectivism from him as a journalist in the first place.

In this self-indicting sacrifice of "help[ing] the White House pull back the curtain and reveal the machinery behind the Lewinsky scandal," Brock finds the first signs of the new sense of self he has been pursuing. With it comes as well some much feared, yet much needed insight into the "sick sense of [his] own identity" that had been motivating his actions all along (150). Up until this moment, his politics had been a means for meeting his "tortured need for friendship and affection and acceptance." Now, however, finally seeing these "misdirected desires for validation" for the handicaps they are, he realizes that "I didn't need a surrogate father or love and acceptance from a political movement after all" (312, 333). With this realization, he severs the destructive connection between political passion and personal validation that has anchored his identity and driven his resultant character. Moreover his disclosure to the press and to Blumenthal defies perhaps the most self-defeating of those principles that has mired his preconversion identity: the "unusual ability to block out and avoid the truth and to live [his] life with no inner questioning" that enabled his blindness in the first place, delivering him bound to the "surrogate fathers" that dictated his beliefs. As Brock summarizes this process of transformation from blindness to insight, "Only as I gave up my cherished place in the movement, which allowed me to confront the false right-wing ideology of exclusion, intolerance, prejudice, and hate that I had advanced so blindly, did I find my conscience and principles underneath. Now I was free to follow them. . . . I had no allegiance to a political platform, I was a member of no party or movement, and I was on no one's team. I was following only the facts of my personal experience, and my interior convictions" (311–12).

Honest about his homosexuality, in touch with and able to direct his need for approval, and politically active as a matter of personal interest rather than unmet personal need, Brock has realized the "conversion of politics, morals, and ultimately of spirit" that his preface portended. His youth-ingrained "emptiness inside me" now filled with "interior convictions" all his own, his conversion is perhaps less a reshaping of self-understanding than it is coming to know himself for the first time. As if to provide the god-term for this newly constituted identity, a "title of titles" for this transformed sense of self, the memoir's epilogue shows Brock registering to vote as the one thing he has never before been in his life: Independent.

Just as Brock has encouraged readers to expect, achieving this transformed identity also leads him to realize a correspondingly transformed character. As he states, clearing away his debilitating identity conflicts through his conversion enables him to find beneath their tangle his long-effaced conscience, the capacity to evaluate and control his own actions that has been slowly emerging since his work on Anita Hill. This conscience—"the conscience of an ex-conservative," as the memoir's title emphasizes—can now govern his new postconversion character, the ethos of a man who, once blind to the morality of his actions, now sees, and clearly. Like the reprehensible preconversion ethos it overturns, this character impression of the wide-eyed and ethical Brock is an ethos effect of the identity he constitutes. It is an impression of *how he acts* as a moral agent that he wants his audience to derive or infer as an extension of *who he is,* as an outgrowth of his postconversion identity.

Needless to say, there are other available means by which Brock could try to convey this rational, independent, trustworthy ethos; impressions of character in discourse can be built of many things other than articulations of one's self-interpretation. There may always be potential implications for ethos in expressing identity, but ethos is more than simply talk about oneself. As both Garver and Wisse discuss, one such contributing factor in the classical understanding of ethos is the decision-making ability that one's discourse manifests, the process of reasoning that one exhibits in language. Amossy notes that one's "style of speaking" or writing contributes to ethos, which is "built on the level of the enunciation process as well as on that of the utterance." (Amossy further qualifies that "it is often not good to talk about oneself" in achieving a rhetorically effective ethos for certain situations ["Crossroads" 8].) And one might also draw on one's reputation in creating ethos—just the strategy of the Gap's James Dean ad, letting their audience's prior collective knowledge of his iconic coolness sell their khakis for them.

Brock does take advantage of some of these options to help in creating his postconversion, present-day ethos (although reputation is obviously not among them). For example, he attempts to communicate his fair-mindedness in relating that, even in the midst of his rising repugnance of the Right, he yet "had no doubt that countless conservatives outside the Beltway were people of decent will, and strong convictions, people who lived the values they preached" (207). Similarly, anticipating an audience from across our bipolar political spectrum, he emphasizes his commitments to general political values he assumes readers of all stripe will reverence—the sanctity of the Constitution, for instance.[11] But these means of character construction are not the foundations of Brock's postconversion ethos, and for good reason. Such quasi-Aristotelian demonstrations of newfound prudence, goodwill, and civic virtue are likely insufficient to persuade that he has truly mended his ways, especially considering his memoir's emphasis on how he successfully, lucratively pretended such character traits in the "chameleonlike career" of his reporting (Rich 36). The radical transformation of self that is conversion, however, might just be profound enough to convince his audience that his equally radical transformation of character is possible.

More than just the subject of his memoir, Brock's identity is thus a tool for accomplishing specific ethos effects. His use of identity in this way, as the grounds from which readers should infer the characters that correspond to his pre- and postconversion selves, well demonstrates a Burkean point about constitutions I mentioned briefly in chapter 4. In describing the relationship between substance and action in constitutions, Burke observes that, by decreeing substance, a constitution delineates an "'environment' for future acts" (GM 362). And this is what identity does for Brock: constituted a certain way, his identity substantiates the grounds from which a corresponding kind of action follows. Before his conversion, his actions mirror the conflicts of his self-understanding; after conversion, as he encourages readers to infer, his actions reflect, and will continue to reflect, psychological health and rationality. They will continue to bespeak the man who, on the other side of transformation, proclaims, "I was happy, finally, to be in the right place, both morally and emotionally, . . . surrounded by friends who didn't want me to say or be anything but myself" (BR 328). In fact, given his stated mission to unlive the lie of his past, Brock is perhaps most concerned that his "future acts" beyond his memoir continue to be perceived as an extension of the converted identity he constitutes therein.

And in what kind of future course does Brock seek to be this new person and to enact the new character that has come with it? At first he seems unsure: "I had turned thirty-nine, and I didn't have much of a game plan for the rest of my life beyond publishing this book," he pauses. But as the memoir's last line hints, "since I planned to stay in Washington for a while, I took Harry Truman's advice and adopted an amazing dog" (335–36). Independent, possessed of "interior convictions" to ward off future blindings, and rational enough to accept a Democrat's counsel about a subject as personal as one's choice of pet, a new David Brock has begun to live, and to unlive the past. Looking away from that past toward the horizon of opportunity that dawns at his Washington doorstep, both Brock and his shingle are out.

"Brock Delivers Deep Dish": The Complicating Ethos of the Tell-All Insider

One merit of Brock's strategy, as I have suggested, is how well it plays to the expectations of his audience. Readers would most likely intuit the correspondence he creates between his blinded character and the blinded identity responsible for it without the guidance toward this inference he provides. An additional benefit of this strategic use of identity is that it moves the battle over his credibility to a grounds where he has the home court advantage. Whether because of our predisposition to regard others as authorities in matters of their self-interpretation, or because we might feel ourselves better qualified as judges of character than of identity, identity claims meet with an acceptance that character rarely evokes. If identity claims are not met with acceptance, they yet invite a much different kind of scrutiny than do claims or impressions of character. I do not mean that people's expressions of how they define and interpret themselves, claims about "who they are," fly under the radar of our inquiry, evading detection as potential exaggerations, as persuasive fictions, as lies. They do, however, fly lower than impressions of character. Brock's revelation that he is plagued into adulthood by an irrational need for approval, for example, elicits a different kind and extent of judgment than his claim that he "drifted along" with the conservative movement's "holy war" against the Equal Rights Amendment (which, in the words of Pat Robertson, "would encourage women to leave their husbands, kill their children, practice witchcraft, destroy capitalism, and become lesbians"; BR 121–23). Perhaps because "we cannot judge the truth of a writer's sense of his or her own lived experience" (Spigelman 81), our default becomes that of accepting people's claims about the realities of their self-understanding. As Brock states, his conversion is a "fact . . . of [his] personal experience." And what evidence does one leverage against such facts—against the personal truths of identity?[12]

But identity's inscrutability can also be a liability. If some claims about who one is cannot be evidenced, they can at least be doubted, and doubted indefinitely. Such doubt seems to arise when the self-knowledge one claims is unorthodox—literally, in conflict with common understanding. This frequently doesn't bode well for experiences as mysterious as conversions, especially the more Pauline their proportions. (See, for example, David Jacobs's analysis of the conversion experiences of alien abductees, many of whom also heard voices and saw blinding lights.) And beyond unorthodoxy, identity also incites speculation when, despite the fact that we typically can't disprove people's claims about who they are, we yet feel we have some kind of evidence for questioning those claims. Often this evidence is character. If you tell me you're a devout Muslim, but you act as though *Ramadan* means little more than *October*; If you claim to be an amusement park enthusiast, but you don't know Kennywood from Dollywood: as such instances suggest, the relationship of inference between ethos and identity is mutual and bi-directional. Just as the identity one expresses can have ethos effects, the character one conveys in discourse can have identity effects. Our impressions of a person's character can support our sense of who that person is, and they can undermine and question that identity as well.

Doubt about the reality of Brock's conversion manifests just such an identity effect of character. Thus far I have discussed two *ēthē* in *Blinded by the Right* that cooperate in his strategy to persuade that a profound transformation of his identity has produced an equally transformed character. An emergent third ethos in the text, however, complicates this rhetorical effect. In its perceived incongruence with the redeeming postconversion ethos that Brock depicts, this third character renders suspect his claims of total personal transformation. In other words, this character impression has the identity effect of calling into question the self-understanding he articulates, inadvertently leading many to wonder if he has changed as completely as he claims. As the title of one review encapsulates this identity effect, the debate that ensues over his believability becomes a debate over who "the real David Brock" is (Graves 1).

The elements of the memoir that foment this questioning of Brock's identity are hardly subtle. On the contrary, they are trumpeted on the jacket flap. Given his neck-deep involvement with all things (neo)conservative, he is uniquely qualified to do just what his marketing blurb entices: to "name names" with "stunning candor," publicly calling out transgressors from this "dangerous and deeply disturbing period of American politics." On this promise of insider knowledge, he delivers. Much of what he narrates are events in which he himself played a key role. In such cases, he relies on his conversion to dissuade readers from impeaching the Brock of today: the buck of those treacheries stops with old Brock, the slate wiped clean with the transformation that wiped away their author. Other lies and hypocrisies he relates as a mere witness; given this safe remove of spectatorship, and because much of what he has witnessed is wrong by any rational standard, he can narrate these events without tarnishing his own character as the reformed narrator of the present. For example, he tells how as the Starr hearings strove to substantiate President Clinton's infidelities, "Newt Gingrich vowed to say the word 'Monica' in every speech," even though Gingrich himself "was conducting his own illicit affair with a congressional aide" (302). Similarly, Brock reveals that Clarence Thomas did, in fact, have a demonstrated history of renting pornographic videos, even though Brock lied to the contrary, aided in the coverup by Theodore Olson—as in current U.S. solicitor general Theodore Olson.

A hit, a hit, they must confess't. But other slices of behind-the-scenes "deep dish" (Goldstein 45) are not so cleanly delivered by their messenger. Several of Brock's observations seem more than just out of place in a memoir that bills itself as a repentant "act of conscience"; to some, they bespeak a character—an agential disposition—that seriously threatens the believability of his post-conversion ethos. As a result, this contradictory, competing ethos of the tell-all insider complicates the clean break of conversion Brock asserts and the transformation of his identity it supposedly accomplished. One such potential self-incrimination is his sharp-toothed assault on William Bennett, *New York Times* best-selling "morality czar" who, as Brock impugns, "knew from decadence." "The hulking Bennett got very rich in the virtue industry while doing little but bloviating," he accuses. The sententious "Bennett's only self-confessed vices were eating red meat, drinking martinis, and casino gambling, yet other virtues that Bennett preached, hard work and humility among them, clearly eluded him" (BR 304–5). A biting critique, yes, but not entirely out of line with Brock's aim of unmasking "unfathomable hypocrisy," one might argue. But his name-naming candor claims other victims in tones less resonant with this errand. With only "ambiguous relevance to the narrative at hand," some of what he shares about erstwhile colleagues "undeniably holds the reader's interest . . . [but] is disconcerting in unintended ways" (Bruni 14). Conservative columnist Christopher Hitchens, for example, is "a misshapen, unkempt, and seemingly unshowered man," as well as "a deadbeat," sticking Brock with a dinner bill (BR 297); and Brock's former confidante and news media darling Laura Ingraham is a violent drunk who lobs death threats and who also snorts cat tranquilizers. In bathroom stalls. Even greater support for this complicating tell-all ethos comes from Brock's harangue against internet gossip and conservative author Matt Drudge. After deriding Drudge's unlikely rise from dumpster diving for confidential tidbits to having his own show on Fox News, he relates an "amusing interlude" at a Hollywood dance club where he intuits that "Drudge and I had even more in common than I thought": revealing a suggestive private email from Drudge for corroboration, Brock outs him as a homosexual (282–83).[13] This move has puzzling implications at best for the present character—and, consequently, for the claims of transformation—of an author who suffered at the threat of just such an outing himself, and who has narrated that suffering just pages earlier.

All of what Brock says about these and other sordid sundries may be true. But as many responses to the text affirm, it is not the truth or falsehood of these claims but their presence alone that has serious implications for the credibility of his conversion. One reviewer indicts Brock's misplaced flair for the tawdry, noting how the memoir's "often-breathless prose style has tabloid overtones" (Cooper 1186)—a style unsettlingly reminiscent of Brock's writing at the *American Spectator.* Another similarly wonders at how character traits a true conversion should have exorcized yet remain in full force in the text: *Blinded by the Right* proves that Brock has "lost none of his ability to insult and belittle people, a talent he uses with relish" in his "scathing memoir" (Hoover E8). Such comments together target an element of the text that makes reading it a "creepy experience" (Goldstein 45), a sense of misgiving about both tone and content that seem not entirely unlike the Right's moral attacks against the Clintons—or, worse, not entirely unlike the supposedly entombed old Brock's attacks on Anita Hill. Why would a Brock so grateful to really, truly now walk a morally and politically higher road even sully his hands in scooping such ordure from the gutters of his past? Does his stooping to do so suggest that his conversion, as has been alleged, is more trope than truth? The post-fig-tree chapters of Augustine's *Confessions* pontificate on the divine nature of time and space; one wonders if he would have rendered his conversion similarly dubious had he instead spent these pages dissing the Manicheans.

In thus conveying the impression of a questionable postconversion character, Brock also creates an opportunity for readers to question the identity behind it. This identity effect of his tell-all, tabloid ethos, provoking readers to infer something of who he is from this character impression, hardly seems intentional, for it jeopardizes half of his rhetorical goal. The particular "disclosures" that convey this ethos, true or not, ultimately undercut the "reconciliation" he seeks in his text, for they question the reality of the conversion that makes him worthy of that reconciliation. This panting, "vengeful" element (Bozell 10) could be an oversight, something Brock never intended to articulate in the text. Perhaps he knew some "scathing" would be entertaining to many in his audience (only the already alienated or scathe-worthy would object), and so he plays the smarmy gossip, hoping that readers understand this as a simple matter of discursive character, not real or inherent character. Indeed, perhaps he assumes readers will regard it as a voice or mask appropriate to the situation with no potential moral implications for any "real" Brock outside the text; that is, he assumes it will be seen as a persona.[14] But segregating *how Brock acts* from *who he is* flies in the face of every cue he provides in the text: readers are at every turn encouraged to *connect* character to identity, not to sever it. It feels natural, then, almost inevitable, to trace this complicating tell-all character back to the *real* Brock somehow, to perceive this ethos as in some way reflective of his identity.

The benign reading sees this complication for Brock as a matter of genre violation. As Kerry Lauerman comments, "a mea culpa doesn't necessarily mix well with a tell-all." Brock's problem, then, is merely a breach of decorum. Surely he has some license to share salacious and potentially hurtful anecdotes from his past. There is a time, a place—back at the bars, perhaps, where maybe he and his companions might catch a glance of Laura Ingraham crawling on the floor and drunkenly berating patrons again. He has simply misjudged the rhetorical situation of his own memoir as an appropriate setting for doing so, sharing these vignettes in a way that violates expectation and thus jeopardizes his overall persuasive aims. But the extent to which much stronger conclusions about Brock have been drawn manifests something more at work than formal propriety. Those who read in his memoir's complications of character a consequent complication in determining who he really is manifest that, however risky the leap from the discursive to the real, sometimes "*ethos* is ontological" in its effects: it "leaves a trail that reveals moral fiber and standing" (Smith, "*Ethos*" 15). In *Blinded by the Right*, that trail of character's ontological effect, a trail to realness, leads directly to Brock's identity and to the conversion that may or may not have transformed it. As Howard Schwartz summarizes the unwelcome implications of this identity effect, "Brock switched sides when he moved from smearing Anita Hill to smearing his friends on the right, but he remained identically David Brock" (82). To readers of similar inference and persuasion, Brock's redemption—the "reconciliation" of restored credibility he seeks—requires something he has yet to deliver.

Self-Centered Rhetoric: Considering the Source

Sometimes it's hard to be a convert. This seems especially true when what you've converted away from has left a string of high-profile casualties and an extensive (and falsified) public record of its sins. In Brock's case, the much-welcome "sense of peace, emotional balance, and personal integrity" that comes with his conversion brings with it a heavy burden as well—the onus of conscience and its apportioned task of unliving the lies that are his past. Unliving those lies requires that his confession and correction of them in his memoir be believable, no small feat when his own honesty is the first of the casualties he narrates.

One essential part of thus regaining the credibility he seeks is demonstrating a change in his nature as a moral agent, a change in character. But as both his personal experience and his effort to credibly, persuasively narrate that experience indicate, character is not enough. Brock's character cannot change, and its change cannot be made believable, without him changing who he is as well: he must also change the self-understanding that subtends that character, a change in identity. Whether his depiction of his character as an effect of the identity he constitutes in his memoir is true to his experience, or savvy rhetorical strategy, or both, this tandem of character and identity working together stands as his surest hope of an unliving that is both personally and rhetorically successful. To sever this interrelationship of character and identity is to see but half of what he claims his conversion is, and but half of what it rhetorically attempts toward obtaining the restored credibility he seeks.

Examining this dynamic at work in Brock's narrative should move rhetorical theory in general to the same conclusion. That is, in the analysis of persuasive self-presentation, neither character nor identity alone is enough. And though they should be recognized as distinct both in their referents and in the cultural expectations that attend them, identity and character enact relationships that can be as much about connection as separation. Everywhere they implicate each other, self-definition and agential nature. The rhetorical equipment for analyzing the persuasive potential of identity and character in discourse should thus uphold a dual charge: it should account for how these important dimensions of self-presentation differ, while being able to account as well for their interpenetration and overlap—their "intrinsicness" (Swearingen 115).

Such a charge finds support across rhetorical theory, especially from those who have argued for the necessity of viewing ethos, rhetoric's reigning metric of character in discourse, as evolving in significance. Comprehensible only within the broader nexus of terms by which a culture understands and defines selfhood, a workable concept of ethos must shift as does this doxastic body of givens about the human person. Thomas Benson articulates just such an objective in arguing that ethos be extended "beyond 'credibility' . . . to take in its role as central to place, community, identity, and moral action." Doing so, he acknowledges, may "require a readjustment of some of our settled teachings about the concept" (ix). Part of that readjustment, as I have argued, is the more precise, more deliberate consideration of identity in relation to ethos—not as a (near) synonym nor as a subsumed tangent of inquiry but as a rhetorical companion and equal in assessing the persuasive functions of self-presentation. Their confluence and effects are at least as complex as the rhetor in whose person both identity and character coalesce. However ethos and identity are conceptualized, they need to be employed in analysis with an eye toward this complexity, toward highlighting their interweavings rather than flattening them through a reductionism or misguided practicality that would subsume one term within another. Such a task, like self-representation itself, is complex. But it seems well worth the effort if it indeed helps us to more fully "grasp the self as a rhetorical entity" (Alcorn 13). In our person as much as in our words, we are persuasive, and heterogeneously so.

I strain to provide closure here in my commentary on Brock's conversion when its reality is yet actively disputed. But I might offer something along those lines by referring to a standard trope of conversion—the idea that the surest proof of these self-transformations lies in the "fruits" that they bear. Brock's current project of working to keep the political media honest has done much to earn him public trust, bringing to fruition some of the seeds he claims his conversion planted. While satisfying the skeptics is clearly a question of time, works such as this might eventually achieve the end of moving his presently questionable conversion beyond question.

But perhaps the speculation about who "the real David Brock" is has as much to do with conventional wisdom regarding character and identity as it does with Brock himself. Are there some actions that ultimately have no credible recantation, some things a person can be that just seem too formidable to change, no matter what kind of conversion comes along? Burke's "problem of identity" suggests that what makes identity interesting is its ever-present potential for change and transformation. But surely part of what makes identity interesting is its intransigence, too—its resilience, its reassertion of personal realities that even we ourselves believed we had overwritten. Such questions of limits, however, of what may or may not be within our power to change about ourselves, are more properly the questions of the next chapter.

6

Identity beyond Agency

Imprudent Gender in Deirdre McCloskey's *Crossing*

An identity is both made and not made. —Deirdre McCloskey, *Crossing*

How, and where, do gender and sexuality fit in identity? Few topics in identity studies have received more attention. Judith Butler, for example, has examined with profound impact how the materiality of sex—the "biological intractability" of the male or female sexed body—constrains gender, "the cultural meanings that the sexed body assumes" (*Bodies* 28; *Gender* 12, 6). Challenging the commonplace conviction that gender somehow inheres within the body itself, Butler contends that gender is much less a matter of bodily nature than of discourse and social practice. "The appearance of an abiding substance or gendered self," she asserts, is a "fictive production"; our identity categories of "male" and "female," rather than "natural fact[s]" of biological inheritance, are *performances*, the effects of "acts and gestures, articulated and enacted desires [that] create the illusion of an interior and organizing gender core" (*Gender* 136). This orientation to gender and identity—as "performatively constituted by the very 'expressions' that are said to be [their] results"—might be summarized in a single iconoclastic claim from Butler: "There is no gender identity behind the expressions of gender" (25).[1]

Not exactly. At least, not in the case of Deirdre McCloskey, professor of economics and history, whose notoriety began with works she published as a *he*, as *Donald* McCloskey (*The Rhetoric of Economics*, *Knowledge and Persuasion in Economics*, and others). In her 1999 narrative of her transgender becoming, *Crossing: A Memoir*, McCloskey depicts her gradual, anxious, and often painful evolution from male to female—from "macho, tough guy economist," family man, and closeted "heterosexual cross-dresser" to fifty-five-year-old divorced postoperative transsexual, a "full-time gender crosser" whose losses in family and public esteem are countered by gains in her own sense of identity.[2] Addressing an audience she assumes is largely unfamiliar with transsexuality, McCloskey constructs a memoir of her transformation that is equal parts personal narrative and public service, an exercise in what she terms *gender education*. The subject of this education is something that she herself learned from the conversion experience that is her text's centerpiece, a lesson in the nature of gender identity. This "nature," as she elaborates, is at once thoroughly enmeshed in the performance of gendered social practices while yet transcending matters of performance; "gender must be enacted daily," she concedes, "but [it] must be felt, too" (CM 84). As the experiences she relates in the text argue, there is, in fact, something of a "gender identity" beneath an individual's gendered practices, beneath the behavioral norms that our actions either reify or subvert. "An identity," she insists, "is both made and not made" (177).

Crossing is McCloskey's memoir of more than forty years of struggle against the "not made" of her own gender identity, a narrative of failed resistance to the "unpleasant truth" she knew from age eleven—that Donald was a she (8). In the conversion experience through which she finally realizes and accepts her own femaleness, McCloskey also realizes the limitations of human agency in identity. Phrasing this lesson as she does in the language of economics, she realizes that we are always more than the sum of our *prudence*—that there is more to identity than our conscious deliberations and decisions about costs and benefits. "In our culture the rhetoric of the very word 'decision' suggests cost and benefit," she explains. But in this sense, McCloskey never did "decide" to be transsexual; "my gender crossing was motivated by identity," she corrects, "not by a balance sheet of utility." To be sure innumerable such costs and benefits follow McCloskey's converting acceptance of the reality of that part of Donald's identity that, for four decades, proclaimed itself female. But "calculating pleasures and pains was not the point," she reminds. The point was *identity*; "the point was *who I am*" (xiii, emphasis added).

The "epiphany" through which McCloskey achieves this resolve about her gender identity holds obvious personal significance. But it plays an equally significant public, rhetorical function in her memoir as well, for it anchors her overall effort to transform her audience's thinking about gender and identity. If gender identity does, at some level, transcend agency, as her conversion demonstrates, then we must rethink those social and medical perceptions that regard transsexuality as something chosen and, therefore, as something changeable—treatable—about transgendered people. If there is a "not made" to identity that even the most prudent deliberation and choice might not sway, then we must rethink how we esteem the identity "decisions" of those imprudent individuals who would practically and physiologically, *permanently*, cross the seemingly unassailable lines of gender.

Between Choice and Compulsion: The Ambiguities of Action

McCloskey is plainspoken in revealing her designs upon the readership she addresses—what she calls the "politics" of her memoir. "I want the medical models of gender crossing . . . to fall," she exclaims; "I want the courtesy and the safety of a whyless treatment extended to gender crossers" (CM xiv). In this proclamation of purpose, she illustrates Burke's claim in *The Philosophy of Literary Form* that texts (autobiographical and otherwise) are "answer[s] or rejoinder[s] to assertions current in the situation[s]" from which they arise (109). McCloskey's rejoinder, in memoir form, to the "medical model" of gender crossing and to the question of *why* that transsexuals constantly face is a refutation of the assumption that they both bespeak: that transsexuality is a choice of some kind, and a choice whose reasoning can be clearly articulated. But as McCloskey will respond, "gender crossing is a matter of identity," not of choice; the question of *why*, therefore, "does not make sense, because it asks a prudential answer when the matter is identity" (177). Even worse than requiring explanations for decisions that were never made, the "demand for an answer to why carries with it . . . an agenda of treatment"; thus if transsexuality is a choice about identity, and one that can be explained, then it can also be corrected.

But texts offer more than answers or rejoinders to such aspects of their situations. They assert *strategic* answers, *stylized* responses to these situations, to the specific beliefs and actions within them that they would transform (PLF 1). McCloskey's primary strategic response to the erroneous economy of choice and prudence in gender, as I have already noted, is her own conversion in the text. Transpiring in the ambiguity between choice and compulsion—between "made and not made"—it is the narrative center around which she constitutes her identity.

The opening chapter immediately introduces this ambiguity about gender and agency in identity that will define both the development of McCloskey's argument and the role of her conversion experience within it. The chapter begins with Donald's unusually "sharp memory" of using a ladies room in Harvard Square with his mother when he was five; it ends with him in his fifties, married, a father of two, and an active professor at the University of Iowa, "a tough-guy economist, as tough as professors get." But whatever his bulldog masculinity, his "ferocious professional reputation . . . developed in a dozen years of harsh seminars," McCloskey reveals that the man Donald had become was more facade than true expression of who he was. Looking back from her present-day perspective and speaking about herself in the third person (as she does throughout the text, whether she is speaking of Donald or Deirdre),[3] she reveals that Donald "had a mild sense of straining at the tough-guy role, as though reading lines from a script he could not see distinctly, worrying he might accidentally say a woman's lines" (10). In McCloskey's own metaphor, Donald's "tough-guy role" was exactly that—a dramatic *performance*, a part he played not because it pleased him (as surely it did other male academics, "anxious in America about their masculinity," she suggests), but because of what he needed to conceal behind his masculine histrionics.

What Donald must hide is that from age eleven to age fifty-three, from "Boy to Man," as the chapter is titled, he has been a cross-dresser, and one whose interest in being cast in a part with "a woman's lines" has been growing over time. In his childhood Donald had been a "normal boy, though never a thrusting, macho one," McCloskey relates (5). Yet his adolescence brought with it feelings that seemed anything but typical for such "normal" boys. At age eleven, for example, he "was having the first wet dreams of maleness," as normal boys do. Quite unlike most other boys, however, his dreams were not of females but "of *femaleness*, of having it, of being" (5, emphasis added). Like normal boys, Donald was curious about women's bodies and undergarments. But unlike normal boys, he frequently tried on his mother's intimates—not to fantasize about accessing "what lay underneath women's clothing" but instead to imagine *having* what lay underneath, to dream about *being* what nature had not made him. Perhaps many normal boys, religious or not, prayed for providential favor in relation to the opposite sex. Donald prayed as well—"*Please, God, please. . . . Tomorrow when I wake up . . . I'll be a girl*" (6).

More than a passing interest, Donald's curiosity about female being and female dress continues throughout his teens. In fact, as the narrative progresses, "curiosity" clearly understates the obsession with female being that comes to define McCloskey's young adulthood. By age fifteen he had made a regular habit of wearing his mother's underclothes, sometimes stealing them from the hamper or the garbage, and sometimes even wearing them when he wasn't alone in the house. Eventually he is no longer content with clandestinely donning his mother's appropriated throwaways, and his longings lead him into actions that are dangerous by any standard, let alone those of the 1950s. "As a teenager Donald broke into neighboring houses to wear the crinolines, and shoes that fit, and garter belts and all the equipment of a 1950s girl," McCloskey admits. But he was careful, stealing nothing, disturbing nothing, and so "the crossdressing never became an issue" (7). That is, it never became an issue for anyone other than Donald, forced to explore and make sense of his peculiar inclinations behind closed doors—and not just those of his own suburban home.

McCloskey's narration of Donald's early cross-dressing vividly establishes his ambivalence and insecurity as his gender, rather than a biologically determined nonissue, becomes a subject of daily contestation. Moreover, this tug-of-war between Donald's male biology and the allure of female being achieves one of the most important rhetorical effects of McCloskey's memoir: it calls into question the extent to which Donald has any conscious control over his desires to embrace femaleness, the desires that compel his habitual cross-dressing. In other words, it questions the limits of Donald's agency in the narrative—his ability to deliberate or decide concerning matters of gender in his developing identity. Agency, as Charles Taylor explains, might be simply defined as "the power to *evaluate* our desires, to regard some as desirable and others [as] undesirable." This ability to deliberate is the "minimum degree of reflectiveness which we associate with a human agent," he asserts, comprising the very center of "what we describe as the exercise of free will" (*Human Agency* 16, 28). Yet it is precisely this evaluative power concerning his gender desires that Donald appears to lack in McCloskey's depiction of his teenage cross-dressing. His repeated, "heart-thumping expeditions" into neighbors' homes—again, not for more typical motives of theft or vandalism, but rather to wear women's clothes that fit him (his mother's no longer did)—would clearly seem to be an "undesirable" course of action in light of its potential consequences. Even though these covert opportunities to explore femaleness provide Donald with pleasure, the risks inherent to breaking and entering in one's own neighborhood, and doing so in order to cross-dress, no less, would surely cause even the most intrepid youth to recoil at the peril. After all, as McCloskey interjects, these *were* the 1950s, the psychiatric "dark ages," where "they gave electroshock treatment for homosexuality, to say nothing of gender crossing." But still Donald continues, sometimes narrowly "escaping out back doors as families came in the front" (7). Why not keep his cross-dressing within the walls of his own room, as he had in the past? Yet even home wasn't completely safe anymore; his father had already caught him once in his mother's underwear. So why do it at all? Why take such chances? Neither Donald in the moment of transgression nor Deirdre in her present-day recollection offers any answers.

By thus questioning Donald's ability to deliberate concerning matters of gender, *Crossing* lays the foundation for the text's argument against any clear sense of choice behind the behaviors and desires that define gender. This inability to act as an agent in relation to his own gender defines Donald's adolescent identity in the text, defying any sense that he consciously chooses when, where, how, or even *if* to cross-dress at all. This ambiguity concerning his power to decide about his gender and its role in his overall identity also marks the circumference of his identity at this stage of the narrative, the boundary of his power of self-definition. The "ultimate motivation" associated with this identity-defining circumference, then (while it lacks any concrete god-term to summarize it), is his persistent struggle to figure out the place of his "curiosity about [female] being" and his resultant cross-dressing in his identity, and, moreover, to figure out what power he has to decide about such matters of gender at all.

Constituting Donald's identity around this defining ambiguity between agency and gender, McCloskey manages to interrogate the limits of choice in gender and simultaneously to invoke sympathy in her audience for Donald's actions. Rather than rebellious trespassings of both the boundaries of private property and the much more punitively transgressed boundaries of normative gender, his actions are instead pitiable: it is as though he *knows* to act differently but simply *cannot*. This continual gender crossing, as McCloskey depicts it, is not a deliberate foray into the taboo but rather an uncontrollable compulsion that Donald must assent to as he strives to make sense of his own conflicted gender. (What other than predeliberative compulsion could motivate him to wear his mother's girdle beneath a bathrobe as she serves him breakfast, for no reason other than "curiosity about being"?) Consequently, the reader is left with little grounds for judging or criticizing Donald's actions; instead, we can only hope that such ambiguous compulsions are not our own to navigate in matters of our own gender identities. We can only hope that our own imprudent and potentially transgressive behaviors might be graced with the same serendipity in remaining, despite all odds, unpunished.

"Just Sex. Not Identity."

Donald's powers of choice in relation to gender are purposefully ambiguous in McCloskey's account of his early feminine curiosities. He does, however, manage to make several clear, reasoned decisions about his gender. For example, while he had once pleaded with God for a miraculous overnight transformation of his maleness into femaleness, he reluctantly "decided not to wish to be a girl" anymore. He also decides to capitalize on his quintessentially masculine, big-boned, and six-foot-something physique, becoming co-captain of his Cambridge private school's football team, "which meant he could not possibly be a girl." But whatever such decisions he is able to make, some underlying desire cannot consciously be rooted out, a "dull ache" that permeates his masculine performance. Despite repeated efforts to "purge" his yearning and his collection of women's clothing along with it, "he kept on crossdressing when he could" (7). McCloskey describes the mounting pressure of this stalemate between Donald's conscious gender decisions and the compulsions that undo them in an apt "hydraulic metaphor": "the river of his life [was] pouring and pouring into a lake behind a dam, from age eleven to age fifty-three" (9). It is a dam that must, of course, break.

These and other experiences from Donald's youth soundly establish the ambiguity of choice in gender that, in defining the overall substance of his self, demarcates the circumference of his identity at this point in the text. And while this fundamental ambiguity about his agency in relation to his gender is difficult to summarize in a single corresponding god-term, Donald does encapsulate this conflict in a mantra he recites to console himself throughout the text: his persistent cross-dressing, as he sees it, is "just sex. Not identity." In other words, placing cross-dressing in the realm of "sex"—of behaviors that people freely choose to enact because they find them more or less pleasurable—allows him to attenuate the depths of this interest in cross-dressing; if his obsession with female being is a matter of "sex," as he wants to believe it is, then it is simply something he *does*, not something he *is*. Whatever his cross-dressing is, it is *not identity*; it is *not* at the core of who he is, despite whatever pleasures or pains it produces for him. As Donald explains, he's "*just a guy who gets off dressing occasionally as a woman.*" (Or, as he jokes in an aside for Monty Python fans, he is "*not a transsexual. . . . 'I'm a lumberjack, and I'm OK.*'" [20]).

Donald's actions as *Crossing* moves into his adulthood appear to back up this assessment—that his transgender interests are acceptable matters of male *sex*, not female *self*. For example, in 1965, during his first year of graduate school in economics at Harvard, he decides to get married. This marriage, McCloskey clarifies, "had nothing to do with crossdressing or gender crossing. It was not a cover-up." Donald married his wife because he did, in fact, love her, and it was "for the sake of [this] finer love" that he decides to limit his cross-dressing, keeping it to himself. Perhaps this isn't the youthful Donald of crimes-for-crinolines days. Perhaps his graduate education's emphasis on costs and benefits has made him a more prudent arbiter of his gender desires. Even when he breaks down and confesses to his wife three months after their marriage that he cross-dresses regularly in private, it still seems as though he has resolved the old ambiguity of cross-dressing and gender identity, normalizing it as a peculiar expression of male heterosexuality. "No big deal, we decided. Lots of men have this or that sexual peculiarity. Relax, we said" (xiii). In short, maybe it is, as he insists, "Just sex. Not identity." He had, after all, *decided* to reveal his cross-dressing to his wife, and once she was convinced that he hadn't married her because their shoe sizes were the same, all seemed well between them. He also quite prudently decides that, with the birth of his son and daughter a few years later, his wife is correct in pleading that he "put the cross-dressing further back in the closet" (14–15). Such deliberate actions wholly contradict the compulsively, perilously cross-dressing Donald prior to marriage and fatherhood. They evince a man who, perhaps in finding love, has also found some foothold of gender certainty that allows him to see his curiosity about female being for what it really is—"*a minor matter. I'm just a heterosexual crossdresser. . . . Nothing serious*" (16, 22).

Yet McCloskey undermines these impressions of certainty almost as quickly as she offers them in her narrative, these "self deceptions" about Donald's gender identity that both he and his wife clung to (13). Yes, Donald had agreed with his wife that it was best to hide his cross-dressing from their children. But rather than curb his dressing, or not dress at home at all, he instead begins to do it at home even more frequently, "cunning at hiding [it], so that his wife formed a low estimate of how much he dressed" (a figure that he estimates was "about five thousand episodes" over four decades; 14–15). And yes, Donald had decided to be open and reveal his cross-dressing to his wife, who "never liked the crossdressing . . . [and] never discussed it." But even though the fact that they "never mixed the two lives" is what grants him his limited freedom to cross-dress at all, he still pushes the limits of their tacit contract, "persuad[ing] her to buy him a girdle" when the threat of discovery bars him from doing so (13). Through this continual conflict of choice and compulsion, McCloskey heightens both the ambiguity between gender and agency that defines Donald's actions and the reader's need for this ambiguity to be resolved. Is it sex, or is it identity? The persistence of this question as McCloskey constructs her conflicted past demonstrates how such ambiguities, in Burke's estimation, "afford . . . a major resource for rhetoric" (GM 51): that is, they are central to how texts strategically, *rhetorically*, "encompass a situation" in a way that moves readers to "adopt an attitude toward it" (PLF 1).

As I have already noted, the ambiguity of agency in gender is one such rhetorical resource in McCloskey's memoir. In marking the circumference of the identity that she constitutes, this ambiguity establishes Donald's identity as a site of perpetual contestation. Consequently, with no clear sense of the substance of himself that is constituted within this circumference, the various principles or "wills" Donald enacts within it lack a defining aim to guide their interaction. Inasmuch as his constituted identity is "a substance, and hence a set of motives" (GM 342), his confusion as to the substance of his gender identity creates corresponding confusion as to the motives of his actions in relation to gender. Is his devotion to the role of happily married man the result of male gender identity? If so, is he heterosexual enough in this role that his devotion to cross-dressing is really just a practice of sex rather than a manifestation of some deeper transgender "identity"? Doesn't his decision to keep his cross-dressing from his children prove that he does, in fact, have some agency in matters of his own gender, and, moreover, that he is able to act prudently, in favor of the greater good of his family?

To consistently interrogate this interplay of gender and will is exactly McCloskey's aim, for it evokes a very specific attitude toward Donald's evolving "situation"—an attitude of impatience for resolution, yet of tolerance and sympathy for the struggle that seems neither wholly forced upon him nor wholly within his power to control. Ultimately, this question of his ability to control his own gender presents the reader with only two possible responses to his struggle: either dismiss this ambiguity outright as something Donald willfully perpetuates—a conscious (not to mention imprudent) decision to live in confusion about his gender identity; or sympathize with his efforts to act the part of a gender identity that he has yet to realize and is striving to define. In addition, this ambiguity of agency in gender lays the groundwork for the conversion experience that is the crux of the memoir's challenge to assumptions of choice in gender, assumptions beneath the social and medical perspectives on transsexuality McCloskey seeks to overturn.

"It's Identity, Stupid"

"For forty-one years Donald dressed when he could and otherwise lived a normal male life," McCloskey summarizes (15). Aside from in hotel rooms when he traveled to conferences, most of this cross-dressing occurred at home. This dressing is mostly hidden from his wife, whose acceptance of Donald's behavior seems to strain over time. From his son and daughter (and from his siblings and mother as well), it is hidden entirely. "A *mistake*," McCloskey interjects in hindsight, wishing that Donald and his wife had dared to be more open with their family about his behavior. At the time, however, this tension between his desires to cross-dress and to be a father is something he cannot resolve. That is, this tension presents itself as a necessitarian principle of conflict between his incongruous wills for fatherhood and for full family acceptance of his cross-dressing, something he is as afraid to solicit as he is certain he will not receive. "As young parents in 1969, the McCloskeys were not equipped for taking such a course [of openness]. . . . They were of the closeted decade, the decade of those state secrets, the decade so attractive to the authoritarian personality." Consequently, Donald places his status as father above his desire to cross-dress freely, a hierarchizing of principles that thus places Donald "firmly in the closet" (15).

But his daughter's departure for college in 1994 allows him to readdress this conflict, and, consequently, to further explore the "dull ache" of femaleness that he has been damming up since adolescence. "For the first time in twenty-five years no kids made the house safe for cross-dressing," he realizes, and he strikes an agreement with his wife that permits him to cross-dress openly at home on odd days. Discovering a wealth of information about transgendered life on the Internet, he also begins to spend many hours posting to related bulletin boards and participating in online chats with other cross-dressers (through the alias "Jane Austen"). Among other eye-opening discoveries, he learns about the specific procedures by which male physiology can be feminized, procedures that were proving effective even for tall and big-boned men like himself.

Donald also begins to participate actively in Tri Ess, the national sorority of cross-dressers, an involvement that proves far more educational than secretly reading the handful of published texts by and about transsexuals in the library (17–21).

As a result of this new openness about cross-dressing, made possible by the absence of his children, Donald is finally comfortable enough to "accept . . . crossdressing as part of who he was." He is not a deviant nor a transsexual. He is simply a male heterosexual cross-dresser. His cross-dressing is not symptomatic of some deeper gender identity conflict, he believes; rather, it is just one of the many different devotions that defines him, a voluntaristic or willed principle of his identity like any other role he chooses to enact, be it husband, father, professor of economics and history, or model train collector. As he puts it, it's "*Just a hobby. Relax*" (49). Whether he is bowling a few rounds with other men in female dress (a "mixed league," he jokes) or camping up an impromptu Karaoke rendition of "Lipstick on Your Collar" in the Cincinnati Tri Ess Convention hotel bar, Donald has never seemed more sure of himself. "A heterosexual crossdresser," nothing more (16).

This increased openness does more than just make Donald comfortable with cross-dressing as "part of who he was," however. For while there is contentment in his acceptance of cross-dressing as part of his identity—that is, his gender identity as a male, heterosexual cross-dresser—there is renewed struggle as well, for it begins to turn his thoughts again toward the total transformation of gender he had prayed for as a young boy. Of course, Donald as a teenager had "decided not to wish to be a girl" anymore, no matter what his feelings to the contrary. He had even taken up quintessentially masculine activities to seal this decision (7). As an adult who cross-dressed much more frequently than in his adolescent past, he found similar ways to reassure himself that his cross-dressing was simply a matter of "affectual preference"; it was "just sex. Not identity" (31, 13). And even if he had now, at fifty-three, fully accepted cross-dressing as part of his identity, that certainly didn't mean he was one of that minuscule minority who pursued their interest in another gender beyond these matters of dress, of performance. "*I am a fifty-three-year-old heterosexual crossdresser, married thirty years, two grown children, a professor of economics and history*," he declares in a moment of self-inventory. "*I don't want to be a woman*" (49). It is a decision about his gender identity he has made at many different points throughout his life, as McCloskey has narrated it. Such a decision, as Donald is about to realize, is not in his power to make.

Driving home to Iowa City one August night from a friend's pajama party in Illinois, Donald experiences a conversion that resolves once and for all the ambiguity of gender and agency around which McCloskey has constituted Donald's identity in *Crossing*. Moreover, this central event of the memoir will prove the foundation of the argument about choice and gender identity that follows in the text. As I mentioned earlier, McCloskey often discusses the nature of gender and identity in *Crossing* in the vocabulary of her academic profession: economics. More specifically, she draws on the idea that might be considered a god-term of economics—prudence—as a way of questioning the limits of choice in matters of gender identity. Prudence, as defined in the Aristotelian tradition that McCloskey references (appearing there as *phronesis*), refers to the "ability for *actions* concerning what is good or bad for man." Aristotle's "prudent man," then, is "one who is able to deliberate well concerning what is good and expedient for himself,"—or, in the language of economics, one whose actions are guided by a careful surmise of *cost* and *benefit* (*Nicomachean Ethics* 1140b 5–6; 1140a 27–28).

Frequently modeling this economy of cost and benefit, McCloskey's memoir is often as much a lesson in prudent deliberation as it is a lesson in the nature of gender. Consider, for instance, Donald's precision in evaluating his purchase of certain wigs from a shop in Philadelphia, where he had been attending a conference: "Donald tried on dozens of wigs, and they agreed on five, each for about $80. They were good wigs, at that price not human hair, though unless you are going to buy an expensive human-hair wig, as Deirdre did later in Holland, the synthetics are fine. One of them became Deirdre's standby when she went full time, before the human hair fitting, and she amortized the investment in the six synthetic wigs (with one from the Los Angeles shop) over six months of daily wear. Still an economist: the expenditure on the synthetic wigs was about $2.70 a day of full-time wear. Not imprudent" (26). Donald later enacts a similar calculus (immediate expense versus long-term payout) in determining how much electrolysis he will require before his thick beard is no longer an obstacle to his passing for a woman. In these and other instances, McCloskey demonstrates quite clearly not just Donald's ability to act but also his ability to use his agency prudently—to deliberate about his wants with an eye toward gains and losses. More than professional digressions, these periodic demonstrations of prudent deliberation provide crucial context for McCloskey's argument through her conversion. By clearly demonstrating what prudence looks like, she can then more effectively argue how her ultimate realization of her identity as a woman is anything *but* prudent. Becoming a woman isn't a decision carefully weighed on the scales of cost and benefit, she will assert. It isn't even a decision for Donald at all.

Somewhere outside of Chicago on the East-West Tollway, recalling his evening of bar-hopping and dancing with fellow cross-dressers, Donald diverts himself with a "mental experiment": "*Just try it on . . . How would it feel to actually* be *a woman?*" At first, he is quick to qualify the extent of his curiosity about transsexuality, just as he has in the past: "I'm not transsexual. I don't want to cross permanently, be a woman. . . . Me still Tarzan, not Jane" (50). Twenty miles later, however, his mental experiment inadvertently leads him to the self-termed "epiphany" that fundamentally changes his understanding of his gender identity and, consequently, the course of his future actions.

> *Wait:*
> *Good Lord.*
> I can *become a woman.*
> *I have always wanted to. I have learned by accident that I can.*
> *I am not a heterosexual crossdresser. All this time.* I am *a transsexual.*
> *I can be a woman,* he said. And he wept in relief, as the car drove itself. *I am a woman,* he said. *Yes!*
> She said again, *I am a woman,* and wept. (50–51)

This realization of who he is—or, as the shift of pronouns indicates, who *she* is—finally puts the gender conflicts of Donald's past in perspective, his losing battle to convince himself that he is "just a heterosexual crossdresser": "He knew himself. Herself. *That's it,* she said. *I am a woman.* . . . the old uneasiness dropped away. The question since age eleven was answered. He knew: another life" (51–52).

In describing what this transformative epiphany of self-understanding was for Donald, McCloskey also makes sure to clarify exactly what it was *not:* it is not the result of personal choice or will. Donald's conversion to the fact that he is actually a woman rather than a heterosexual cross-dresser is not the product of deliberation about his desires, not the product of *agency.*[4] In sum, it is *not* a decision. "He [Donald] and then she [Deirdre] didn't 'decide'" to be a transsexual, McCloskey clarifies, "though an economist would like to think this way, in terms of cost and benefit and decision" (51). Donald's frequent illustrations of the prudent intellect at work underscore the nonrational nature of this conversion experience; his sudden, almost accidental, on-the-road realization of his female gender identity bears no resemblance to his numerous moments of pensive deliberation in the text, be they about his career, his family, or beard electrolysis. "Silly," Donald mocks the thought of explaining the reality of his gender through such calculations. "*It's identity, stupid. Not cost and benefit*" (52).

Noting the drama inherent in her use of the religious term *epiphany* to describe this experience (how the word cannot help but evoke "Saul on the road to Damascus"), McCloskey derides the comparative banality of her own moment of transformation—of Donald "on the toll road near De Kalb." Yet however much she demurs, the life-altering significance of the Damascan road for Saul-become-Paul seems an appropriate parallel for how this "moment of personal insight" will transform Donald-soon-to-become-Deirdre. Indeed, the profound certainty in Donald's realization of his female gender identity shares much with another equally foundational conversion experience—that of Augustine. Overwhelmed by very different revelations in their respective moments of personal transformation, these two converts could yet rejoice together in the same rhapsodic tones of the *Confessions:* "it was as though my heart was filled with a light of confidence and all the shadows of my doubt were swept away" (*Confessions* 183).

As I have discussed in chapter 3, *conversion* within my approach to identity as a "unique 'constitution'" refers to a change in the circumference of an identity, a change signaled by a corresponding alteration of the god-term or "ultimate motivation" that this constituted identity seeks to realize. Such a transformation of circumference effects a transformation in the overall *substance* that this constitution attempts to decree as well—the "common substance of meaning" that the diverse individual principles of an identity together define (RM 23). The "epiphany" that McCloskey narrates here is just such a moment of identity reconstitution, for it replaces the gender *ambiguity* that had marked the circumference of her identity with a gender *certainty*: "*I* am *a transsexual*" (51). What is also certain in this moment of insight, as McCloskey depicts it, is the complete absence of agency in the moment that Donald's gender conviction comes to be. It is not a conclusion that he induces from the collective details of his gender-ambiguous past and then decides to act upon; rather, it is a new understanding about himself that he realizes and to which he then submits. Such submission is a typical feature of religious conversion experiences, what William James has called the "crisis of self-surrender" in conversion (207). And while Donald's epiphany may not be, in the Christian or Pauline tradition, a submission to "the irresistible power of God's will" (Dorsey 34),[5] it is most certainly a submission to a higher power: the power of his gender identity, a power that, despite his best efforts to either mask it or alter it over the past forty years, is simply beyond his ability to change. This lesson about her identity has required nothing short of the power of a conversion experience to communicate, and this experience now becomes McCloskey's most persuasive evidence in her argument against the "treatment" of transsexuality.

"*Why Are You Doing This?*": Refuting the "Medical Model"

Before Donald—now Deirdre—is able to make her new conviction of her transsexuality known to her peers at the University of Iowa, she is "outed" by a gossiping member of the university's philanthropic arm. Responding to the rumors in an open letter to her colleagues, Deirdre reveals that the man they knew as Donald had been "deceiving [himself] about [his] gender identity." She goes on to state that she will be pursuing "The Operation" to bring physical appearance into agreement with this identity, asking for their tolerance and understanding. (She would later reveal her "decision" to the economics community in particular in an article for the *Eastern Economic Journal,* titled "Some News That at Least Will Not Bore You.")[6] To her surprise Deirdre will find that the inevitable challenge to her transgenderedness she anticipates does not come from her profession. In time she is not only accepted by the majority of her colleagues but supported and defended by them as well—a welcome fact, especially in light of her backup plan to "move to Spokane and get a job as a secretary in a grain elevator" (*Crossing* 89).

The expected opposition to Deirdre's transsexuality instead comes from the very medical establishment she is beholden to—at least, if she ever hopes to physically acquire the female gender identity she realized in her moment of conversion. The "medical model" of gender identity she confronts in this pursuit, as McCloskey characterizes it, is as invasive as it is stigmatizing: it "enslaves" otherwise free adults to psychologists and psychiatrists who, by professional decree, approach transsexuality not as a legitimate gender identity but as a pathology—as a treatable "gender identity disorder." It is this medical model that McCloskey takes as the addressed of her argument through identity in *Crossing,* the specific aspect of "human behavior" that the "unique 'constitution'" of her transformed identity would likewise "shape . . . or transform" (RM 21; GM 341–42). "Constitutions are agonistic instruments," Burke explains in *A Grammar of Motives;* they are decrees of substance that "establish a motivational fixity of some sort, in opposition to something that is thought liable to endanger this fixity" (GM 357). The identity that McCloskey constitutes through her conversion experience functions in just this agonistic way: in characterizing the motives of her quest to become materially transgendered as a mix of conscious choice and inevitable reality of who she is, she articulates a new understanding of the nature of transsexuality, one that recognizes the limits of choice in gender, the "made and not made" of identity. In more constitutional terms, she accomplishes a reconstitution of the substance of transgenderedness itself, one that might challenge the extreme "fixity" of the medical model that very literally "endangers" the well-being of transsexuals.

In her foundational study of male-to-female transsexuality, *In Search of Eve,* anthropologist Anne Bolin scrutinizes the practices of the two major groups that determine a man's success in becoming a transgendered woman: the medical community (psychiatrists, surgeons, endocrinologists, and others) and the mental health professions (including psychologists, counselors, and social workers, for example). Together, these groups diagnose potential gender identity disorders and then determine whether patients are viable candidates ("good risks") for the hormone therapy and the various surgeries that comprise gender reassignment (48). While "gender identity disorder" did not become an official psychiatric diagnosis until 1996, the first general guidelines for handling issues of gender dysphoria (literally, discomfort with one's gender) were established in 1979 by what is still the primary organization for the study of the treatment of transsexuality, the Harry Benjamin International Gender Dysphoria Association. Published as *Standards of Care: The Hormonal and Surgical Sex Reassignment of Gender Dysphoric Persons*, and more commonly known as the *Standards of Care*, or "Benjamin Standards," these guidelines seek to ensure that transsexuals achieve "lasting personal comfort with the gendered self in order to maximize [their] overall psychological well-being and self-fulfillment" (Harry Benjamin). Within this long-term concern for "overall . . . well-being," however, the more immediate purpose of the *Standards of Care* is simple: they work to discern whether individuals are transsexual enough and competent enough to undergo a physiological transformation as painful and expensive as it is irreversible.[7]

The strict requirements of these standards will twice be levied against Deirdre in *Crossing*, causing her to endure both arrest and civil commitment to a mental ward (not to mention prejudice and abuse from her medical insurance providers) before she finally obtains the bodily appearance that corresponds with her transgendered identity. And while she acknowledges that the Benjamin standards are "well intentioned" in their effort to normalize the treatment of gender dysphoria, she nonetheless faults them for the "contemptible, unfair, unconstitutional, inconsistent, crossphobic, terrifying, cruel, illiberal, lawyer-driven, [and] psychologist-enriching" handling of transsexuality they perpetuate (71).[8] In *Crossing*'s effort both to reveal this pervasive mistreatment and to counter the medical misconceptions about gender identity that encourage it, McCloskey draws on the most powerful evidence about the real nature of gender that she has: her own conversion.

The most obvious injustice of the medical handling of transsexuality that McCloskey addresses is how it empowers caregivers and disempowers preoperative transsexuals. More specifically the Benjamin Standards' requirement that transsexuals receive a "psychological evaluation" prior to hormonal and surgical reassignment places transsexuals entirely at the mercy of psychiatric "gatekeepers" who wield an authority in their "care" that is virtually unimpeachable (*Crossing* 70–71). As Bolin explains, "inherent in the *Standards of Care* and in the policy relations of caretaker to client is an inequity in power relations such that the recommendation for surgery is completely dependent on the caretaker's evaluation." This dependence "results in a situation in which the psychological evaluation may be, and often is, wielded like a club over the head of the transsexual who so desperately wants the surgery" (51). Because of this inherent imbalance of power, the deeply personal "decision" to materially complete one's transgender identity is subjugated to, and often nullified by, the comparatively impersonal decisions of mental health professionals whose permission stands between the preoperative transsexual and gender reassignment. "*That the crossers are free adults,*" McCloskey scoffs, "*is not deemed pertinent*" (71).

But even more problematic within this de facto imbalance of power, as McCloskey's experience illustrates, is that these irreproachable gatekeepers are "so often ignorant about crossgendered people"; "they know nothing about [transgenderedness] and are not interested in learning" (70, 145). In the absence of real understanding of the nature of transsexuality, subjective opinion (and typically prejudicial opinion) fills the void, so much so that, as Viviane K. Namaste argues, it is ultimately "the attitudes of service providers [that] determine the extent to which transsexuals will obtain services" (188). Chief among such attitudes that Deirdre confronts in seeking gender reassignment is the opinion that transsexuality is a personal choice, something she has decided about her identity—a misconception that her conversion in *Crossing* directly refutes.

Some time following Deirdre's first civil commitment to the University of Iowa hospital, a legal hearing about her competency rules that she must submit to additional psychiatric evaluation before her eligibility for reassignment can be determined. Conducting the evaluation is none other than the hospital's chair of the Department of Psychiatry, and the reach of his authority in that capacity renders the depth of his ignorance about transsexuality all the more offensive in McCloskey's account. "Are you a homosexual?," he tersely begins his evaluation, a line of questioning that quickly conveys both his misinformed stance and his disdain for Deirdre's situation. "*Doesn't he know the difference between homosexuality and transsexuality,*" Deirdre shrinks, "*who you love and who you are?*" His persistence in this misguided inquiry—"Have you ever had a homosexual experience? . . . Do you wish to become one?"—reveals to Deirdre exactly the kind of malpractice she is in for: "*Holy Mary, he's got a category Them in his mind, containing all sorts of threats to maleness. . . . I might as well be 'diagnosed' by the average homophobe drinking boilermakers at the American Legion*" (111). The telltale question comes as Deirdre's puzzled evaluator, denied homosexuality as a possible explanation, begs of her the rationale of her insistence on becoming a transsexual: "Well, then, *Why are you doing this?*"

Deirdre offers him no such explanation at the time. (Any response that is not what such evaluators want to hear, McCloskey has already learned, only counts as further evidence of your mental illness.) In her memoir, however, she takes the time to express her shock at the implications of his question: "*Good God in heaven. Can it possibly be true that the chair of psychiatry has the religious right's theory of homosexuality, as something you decide like style in clothing? That gender crossing is that sort of thing too? It looks worse: he appears to think that homosexuality and gender crossing are the same thing—that homosexuals want to be women and that gender crossers are in it for the sex"* (111). McCloskey's dismay here centers on her inquisitor's clear inability to distinguish homosexuality from transsexuality. Ironically, this erroneous lumping together would favor Deirdre if her evaluator understood his profession's perspective on homosexuality. As a legitimate "sexual orientation," homosexuality is not a mental illness and therefore not an object of psychiatric treatment (American Psychiatric Association, "COPP Position Statement"). In agreement with this position, the American Psychological Association further clarifies, "psychologists do not consider sexual orientation to be a *conscious choice* that can be voluntarily changed"; thus if "human beings cannot choose to be either gay or straight," then there is no faulty decision-making behind homosexuality to be reversed and "cured" (through treatments often referred to as "conversion therapies" [American Psychological Association, "Answers," emphasis added;] "Resolution"). The appropriate psychiatric and psychological attitude toward homosexuality, then, is simple. There is no "treatment." There is no asking "why." Just accept it.[9]

But as her evaluator's exasperated inquiry indicates, there is no such "courtesy of a whyless treatment extended to gender crossing" (CM xiv). The very possibility of his asking Deirdre *why* entails that, in contradiction to how his profession understands homosexuality, there must be some element of choice in her transsexuality to be explained; it entails that beneath Deirdre's choice to pursue gender reassignment is another choice as well—her conscious decision that her gender identity is a woman's, not a man's. But as McCloskey's conversion argues, and as *Crossing* has reiterated from that conversion experience onward, no such agency or decision-making accompanied Donald's life-changing declaration, "*I* am *a transsexual*" (50). And while, as Deirdre, she would go on to make many important choices about her gender (some of her most prudent decisions being those about where, when, and from whom to obtain her various surgical transformations), none of this careful decision making about the material reality of her gender identity contradicts the "singular truth" she realized "on the toll-road near De Kalb": "He and then she didn't 'decide'" to be transsexual (51).

The overall message of Deirdre's competency evaluation is clear: for the general public to erroneously believe that transsexuality is indeed a choice, in much the same way that many still think of homosexuality, is one thing; but for this misconception to flourish at the uppermost levels of mental health professionals who, according to the *Standards of Care*, are enjoined "to educate family members, employers, and institutions about gender identity disorders," is quite another (Harry Benjamin).[10] McCloskey's account of the chair's ignorance to the realities of gender identity thus benefits her argument doubly, for devaluing the supposed competence of the mental health professionals that guard the way to her gender reassignment consequently validates the authority of Deirdre's firsthand understanding of transsexuality. Given her personal experience with gender and transformation, a practical understanding that no one else in the text possesses, she becomes, by default, the true voice of reason in matters of gender identity. As a result, her frequent generalizations about the inadequacy of the medical model of transsexuality—that psychiatrists "don't know now, and never have" known about cross-gendered people, that they "satisf[y] the gender anxieties of society, not the good of the 'patient'"—manage to stand credibly without the more specific proof they seem to beg (70–71).

McCloskey thus challenges both the authority and the prejudices of the "gender police" who must rubber-stamp Deirdre's passport to gender reassignment, particularly the all-too-common assumption that transsexuality is a lifestyle *choice*. Going even further, and higher up, she targets the prejudice inherent in the very medical model itself, as it is codified in the veritable bible of psychiatric practice, the *Diagnostic and Statistical Manual* (DSM): its pronouncement that transsexuality, rather than a legitimate gender identity, is instead a "gender identity disorder," "a profound disturbance of the individual's sense of identity with regard to maleness or femaleness" (508). If the medical model goes unchallenged in this definition of transsexuality as a pathology—as a mental illness to be treated, as homosexuality once was—then the attitudes and prejudices of particular caregivers are ultimately a smaller part of a much larger problem. The perspectives of individual psychologists or psychiatrists matter little, be they more or less informed about transsexuality, more or less sympathetic, when the diagnostic criteria by which these psychiatrists must all conduct their evaluations are inherently biased against those who seek gender reassignment.

As the DSM clarifies, transsexuality is, by definition, a disorder: it involves "fantasies, sexual urges, or behaviors [that] cause clinically significant distress or impairment in social, occupational, or other important areas of functioning" (576). But McCloskey's depiction of Deirdre's resolve in her postconversion quest for gender reassignment disputes any presumption that her actions are the product of disorder or illness. Quite the reverse, Deirdre's patience and prudence as she works toward permission for reassignment argue that, since her converting acceptance of her transsexuality, she has never been less in need of psychiatric assistance; she has never been less "disturbed" and more certain of who she is. Following her conversion, Deirdre had "watched for signs of doubt" about her transsexuality, McCloskey relates. "She could recognize doubt. Donald couldn't sleep for doubt when he was chair of economics at Iowa. He knew from the experience that he should not go into administration." But the turmoil of self-doubting that plagued McCloskey's past "never did [come], and she slept better as Deirdre than as Donald" (148). Even as

Deirdre's own sister, a professor of psychology at the University of Arizona, orchestrates innumerable legal and medical obstacles to her gender reassignment, the Deirdre that McCloskey narrates is more single-minded and composed than at any other point in her narrative. If anyone in her memoir is mentally ill, McCloskey implies, it is Donald, the man who had denied rather than embraced his gender identity, the man whose tumultuous gender ambiguity has become, for the postconversion Deirdre, a reassuring gender *certainty.* As she pithily summarizes in the 1996 *Chronicle of Higher Education* story that brought word of her transformation to the academy, "the fact is I am not crazy, I am transsexual" (quoted in Wilson, "Leading").

McCloskey's presentation of Deirdre's professional successes further refutes the "significant distress or impairment in . . . important areas of functioning" that she is supposed to be suffering in her gender identity disorder. In fact, "tough-guy economist" Donald was never more on top of his academic game than "professional girl economist" Deirdre is now. While Deirdre's life had been difficult in the past (as *Donald,* that is), it is especially fraught with conflict following her conversion and coming out: she is at once struggling to maintain her relationship with her wife and children, to jump through the often degrading hoops of the *Standards of Care* in pursuit of surgery, and to stay out of her sister's crosshairs. At the same time, however, as McCloskey details, she is publishing in her field, presenting at the conferences of the Social Science History Association and the Speech Communications Association,[11] serving on the board of the American Economics Association (to which she had been elected as Don), and preparing for her upcoming appointment as Tinbergen Visiting Professor of Economics, Philosophy, and Art and Cultural Studies at Erasmus University in Rotterdam. In fact, when Deirdre's sister manages to have her arrested a second time in Chicago, it is right before her appearance at a Social Science History Association session honoring her work on the rhetoric of economic history (112).

By thus demonstrating both the constancy of Deirdre's conviction that she is transsexual and her ability to function—and flourish—socially and professionally in the most trying circumstances, McCloskey convincingly overturns the pathology of "inherent distress and impairment" that supposedly characterizes her disorderly transgender identity. It is not a "profound disturbance of identity" that Deirdre suffers; rather, it is a profound disturbance at how the medical establishment that holds the key to "treatment," to the end of dysphoria through the surgical harmonization of gender identity and physiology, degrades those who would receive it in the act of handing it over. For to succeed in obtaining gender reassignment (a success that takes McCloskey two years and more than ninety thousand dollars to achieve) means first to succeed in the psychiatric evaluation and diagnosis of gender identity disorder, a diagnosis that the *Standards of Care* ensures doesn't happen without effort. Yet what type of "success" is this if successful diagnosis is to have oneself labeled "impaired," "distressed," "profoundly disturbed," and, above all, "mentally ill"?

In an argument whose chief persuasive strategy is an agency-defying moment of conversion, McCloskey lays bare the personal and professional misconceptions about gender identity that force the transgendered to strive for these stigmatizing successes. Such clinical antipathies remain the best-case scenario for would-be gender crossers as long as the medical model can persist in asking the deceptively simple question, *why?*, a question that "asks a prudential answer when the matter is identity" (77). Ultimately, it is a question that "doesn't make sense," McCloskey rebuts, for matters of identity—matters of choice and deliberation, but also matters of acceptance and submission—are sometimes beyond prudence.

Identity Constitution as "Gender Education"

At various points in her narrative, McCloskey pauses to relate instances where her transgender evolution provided what "crossdressers call . . . gender education" for those around her (32). A handful of curious bowlers who converse with Deirdre's "mixed league" of fellow cross-dressers, for example, learns not only that these men were *not* gay but also that most of them were in fact married, with wives who supported a behavior that many would think an irreparable breach of any marriage contract. This experience certainly did not reverse every misconception about gender crossing that these patrons brought with them to the alley that night, but perhaps it sent them home with something to think about, something that, at least, caused them to reconsider abstract assumptions in light of the actual experience they now possessed. Real cross-dressers. Real people. Gender education.

McCloskey's memoir of her profound gender transformation seeks to provide just such an educational opportunity for its readership, and many reviews of *Crossing* attest to her success in so doing. Poet Maxine Kumin's comments for the *New York Times Review of Books*, for example, fairly represent the general educational impact of the text on those who have offered their assessment. At first, Kumin puzzled at

> why the editors had not designated it for review by someone gay, or someone involved in the transgendered community. Reading it, I realized that I—a lifelong heterosexual woman—need this book. . . . It had not occurred to me that there was a brisk trade in pornographic magazines targeted at cross-dressers. I did not know that conventions of them assembled regularly in reputable hotels around the country, that chat rooms for cross-dressers provided means for this group to mingle electronically,

> despite geographic distances, and often to arrange to meet offline. . . . I did not know how difficult and how expensive it is to change sex, or that more than 25,000 Americans have done so.

In short, she, like the presumed majority of readers, did not know of the medical and social gauntlet that a Harvard-educated, widely cited, upper-middle-class white male would have to run in order to surgically alter his gender. McCloskey clearly intends this to be central to the text's instruction, so much so that she bravely includes pictures of herself in transformation, from age eleven to present day, including postsurgical snapshots of her face, as she frankly puts it, in a state of "roadkill."

It is perhaps obvious why discussion of these matters predominates in the reception of her text (as in Kumin and in reviews for *Lingua Franca*, *Booklist*, *National Post*, and *Library Journal*, to name a few). A former male's perspective on women's ways of walking, talking, eating, and being, coupled with the vivid details of surgical sex reassignment (how her neo-vagina is constructed out of a fragment of small intestine, for example), are as intriguing as they are unfamiliar. Moreover, these details, combined with the photographs that illustrate them, comprise the most forensic element of the memoir; that is, they stand as the most obvious "evidence" of McCloskey's crossing, "proofs" likely to be scrutinized in a way that other aspects of the text are not.

But these details about "The Operation" and the "conventionally feminine behavior[s]" that McCloskey must subsequently adopt in order to truly "pass" as a woman (what Butler has described as the "stylization of the body" that "constitute[s] the illusion of an abiding gendered self" [*Gender* 142])—are but smaller parts of her broader lesson about gender in *Crossing*. Much more vital than these material factors to the stated rhetorical purposes of her text—the reversal of medical perspectives, the refutation of *why*—is the comparatively intangible lesson of Donald's conversion, a lesson about the nature of identity. The intricate proceedings by which Deirdre rises out of the physical ashes that were Donald comprise a real and quite literal trans*form*ation. But even more poignant to Donald in the text is the transformative realization that first sets these procedures in motion—the conversion of "*I'm a heterosexual crossdresser*" into "*I* am *a transsexual. . . . I am a woman*" (51).

In this conversion, one that asserts the limits of Donald's agency and prudence in matters of gender and identity, McCloskey grounds *Crossing*'s argument that there are limits as well to our agency as a society in our treatment of those who would cross the well-guarded lines of gender. If identity is, as she strategically constitutes it through her narrative, a balance of "made and not made," then the question of *why* we are what we are is fundamentally ambiguous. "Who knows?," McCloskey asks, "Biology or core identity or social role or socially constructed performance of a lifetime?" (133). Given this ambiguity, it becomes harder to make the unswerving judgments about choice and identity that would distinguish legitimate aspects of selfhood from disorder, mental illness, and other imprudences. In the society that would recognize this ambiguity as the precondition of all human identity, it becomes harder for us not to transform our own prejudice and haste into compassion and contemplation.

7

Black Elk Speaks and Is Spoken

The *Dialectic* of Constitutions Revisited

Insofar as situations to which Constitutional clauses were addressed have changed, to that extent they become functions of a different scene and, to that extent, different acts.

Kenneth Burke, "Questions and Answers about the Pentad"

Black Elk is regularly invoked—on the reservation and off—in support of political and religious positions in response to issues that he could not have anticipated. His teachings are continually modified and applied to new situations, as religious practitioners routinely invoke his authority in support of their own.

Clyde Holler, *Black Elk's Religion*

Identity and What Lies Beneath, Above, Outside, Behind

Identities have ambitions. They ask something of those to whom they are addressed. On paper, the identity one constitutes may appear to be little more than a static pronouncement—"this is what I am." But identity's intentions are unmistakably dynamic, and in this sense identity is very much like a constitution. In Burke's analysis, a constitution's attempt to shape human action by declaring "what 'you' may or should and may or should not do" makes it inherently strategic—inherently rhetorical (GM 360). Equally so are the "unique 'constitutions'" of the identities articulated through autobiographical narrative: they decree the substance of a self in a way that might shape and transform the situation this self addresses. As the previous chapters have illustrated, conversion narratives cast this rhetorical dimension of identity in high relief. Like the conversions that "turn" them, these constituted identities demand a turning on our part as well, a turning from convictions or conduct that the narrative of another's transformed selfhood calls into question.

But looking at constitutions as strategic instruments for shaping human relations is but half of Burke's *dialectic* of constitutions. If there is indeed a dialectic in constitutions, then this shaping must work in two directions. Part of what makes a constitution "a dialectical act," Burke reminds, is that a constitution is always "an enactment arising in history." Simply stated, constitutions can shape history, but history can also shape these constitutions in return—a malleability that a constitution naturally papers over, striving by design to be regarded as a "motivational fixity" (GM 357–65). If a constitution is "a strategy for encompassing a situation" in order to transform it, how then might a constitution reciprocally be transformed by the broader situation that encompasses it? How are the principles—the "human wills"—that a constitution would "enact" thus mitigated or altered by the different surrounding "temporal scenes" that this constitution comes to occupy?

As Burke explains, the nature of this dialectical relationship between constitutions and the historical situations in which they arise

> can be easily pictured. Imagine a statue of two fencers, the one lunging forward with his sword aimed at the shoulders. And the other fencer raising his sword to deflect the flow. Imagine next that, in the course of historic change, one of this pair is lost. Only the figure of the parrier remains, with his sword obviously raised to ward off a thrust at the shoulders. Imagine next a change to a new form of duelling. And some sculptor portrays this new opponent, a man let us say with a pistol. And now imagine some academician trying to fit the posture of the swordsman's parry to the posture of the man with the gun. (GM 365)

In Burke's illustration the parrying fencer assumes the role of a constitution, the attacking fencer that of the "situation" or "scene" this constitution addresses. As the attacking situation lunges, advancing some "assertion," the constitution parries with its "answer" to it—its "rejoinder" to this aspect of the situation that it ultimately seeks to defeat (PLF 109). Just as the actions of both of these fencers are required for combat, so a constitution requires the participation of a scene in order to constitute—to enact the particular substance it would decree. In this sense, a constitution can be said to "cooperate" with those elements of the scene it opposes, a give-and-take of thrust and parry through which a constitution strives to "transform . . . behavior" (GM 342). This cooperation between constitution and scene undergirds Burkean constitutional dialectic: any constitution is inevitably a "function of" the scene it would transform, even as this scene is physically external to the constitution ("Questions" 334).[1]

But what Burke particularly emphasizes in illustrating this cooperative dialectic is that the scene external to a constitution is not some passive medium. It is not a tabula rasa upon which a constitution is free to substantiate as it pleases. Quite the contrary, the scene a constitution addresses is an active opponent in this dialectic, an opponent that continually changes its technique of combat, even evolving "new form[s] of duelling." As this scene develops counter-constitutional "assertions" that differ from those that a constitution was originally postured to fend off, this scene might eventually come to overpower the constitution; the parrying fencer at the close of Burke's illustration, no matter how adept a foilsman, can find only defeat at the hand of his now-pistol-wielding opponent. In the same gesture that requires the summoning of "some Academician" to refit the parrying fencer to the altered posture (and altered technology) of his new combatant, constitutions require continual interpretation if they are to remain part of the duel. The "wills" they would "enact" mandate ongoing rearticulations, refashionings—reconstitutions—in order to measure up to the advances of the ever-changing scenes they come to address. This is how scenes can transform constitutions: constitutional enactments by definition work to change the given scene they address, but any such "change of scene," by the turn of the dialectic, "makes it inevitable that [constitutional] enactments become new enactments" (GM 367). This interdependence of constitution and scene, their ability to mutually transform each other, drives Burke's unflagging insistence that a "Constitution . . . must be continually treated as an *act in a scene outside it*"; "We must always consider 'the Constitution *beneath* the Constitution,' or 'the Constitution *above* the Constitution,' or 'the Constitution around the Constitution'" (PLF 111n).

In this chapter I want to more closely consider this dialectic as it applies to the constitution of identities, examining how the scene above, beneath, around, or otherwise external to a constituted identity shapes the "enactment of human wills" that this constituted identity would effect. If Burke is correct in observing that "the quality of [a] Constitutional enactment must change *pari passu* with changes in the quality of the scene in which the Constitution is placed" (GM 362), then it should be possible to observe changes in the constituted identity of an autobiographical text that has similarly been "placed" in, or has come to address, a range of social and historical scenes. More than simply signaling the obvious claim—that the meaning of a text changes with time—this dialectic of constitution and scene would underscore the *motivated* nature of such changes of identity in response to changes of scene. In other words, while the evolution of an autobiographical text through different situations of address ensures that opportunities will arise for an identity to mean different things, these opportunities do not dictate *what* this identity might come to mean or *why* it is altered. Few conversion narratives more clearly demonstrate how a constituted identity is opened to transformation by changes in the scenes it addresses, scenes with new assertions that arise to challenge this constitution, than John G. Neihardt's *Black Elk Speaks.*

First published in 1932, *Black Elk Speaks: Being the Life Story of a Holy Man of the Oglala Sioux* has become one of the most widely read, and most widely contested, narratives of Native American experience. The autobiography's broad readership owes primarily to the miraculous content of the life it narrates, especially the powerful ritual visions of an Oglala Sioux (Lakota) holy man,[2] beginning in his youth and ending with the slaughter of his people at the Battle of Wounded Knee, 29 December 1890. The autobiography's highly contested status, however, owes more particularly to a portion of its subtitle—"as told to John G. Neihardt." In May 1931, Neihardt, a well-known writer of Western-themed lyric and prose—"the Virgil or Milton of the Plains" (Krupat, *For Those* 129)—initiated a series of interviews with then sixty-eight-year-old Black Elk that Neihardt would fashion into the holy man's autobiography. At the heart of Neihardt's rendition is Black Elk's visionary calling, at the age of nine, to be the means of restoring the Lakota to prosperity in their native land, a prosperity that had steadily been undermined by *Wasichu* (white) oppression. In the language of Black Elk's vision, it became his duty to lead the Lakota to "walk . . . in a sacred manner in a good land," to restore the "center of the [Lakota] nation's hoop [and] make it live" so that it might "grow into a shielding tree, and bloom" (BE 31–34).

A critical success but commercial sleeper when it first appeared, *Black Elk Speaks* enjoys immense popularity today for its vivid portrayal of a way of life long outpaced, for its transmission of "the clearest voice from an Indian America that predated the modern era" (Steltenkamp, *Black Elk* 21). Vine Deloria Jr. praises the text for its inspiring documentation of Native American culture and spirituality, proclaiming it "a North American Bible for all tribes . . . perhaps the only religious classic of this century" (xi–xii). More recently, anthropologist Raymond J. DeMallie has heralded the book's singular historical importance, characterizing it as "an American Indian Rosetta stone . . . serv[ing] both Indians and non-Indians of today as an entrance into the traditional native American culture of the nineteenth century, a key to translation from modern American into older American Indian modes of thought" (xx).

But such elevated religious and archaeological analogy has not shielded *Black Elk Speaks* from criticism—criticism that, again, has focused on Neihardt's interlocutory role in the transmission of Black Elk's message. One of the work's most thorough commentators likens the problem of Black Elk's "authenticity" in the narrative to the authenticity of Socrates, a man whom we similarly know only through the textual representations of others, and then only at the double remove of the literary genre (dialogue) into which his utterances have been transmuted (Holler, *Religion* 2). The narrative has been more pointedly criticized as an act of "cultural ventriloquism," as a story "told not by Black Elk through Neihardt, but vice-versa" (Couser, "Forked Tongue" 84). And it has been dismissed entirely as one of the many "fabrications of the white man" that pass for accurate representation of Native Americans (Powers 149). Neihardt remained steadfast throughout his life in declaring that the text represents "what Black Elk would have said if he had been able" (quoted in McCluskey 238). But even Neihardt might have anticipated this controversy over authenticity somewhat: at his request, editions of *Black Elk Speaks* from its 1961 reissue and on bear an emended subtitle, with "as told *to* John G. Neihardt" being changed to "as told *through*" the author (emphasis added in both).[3] This emendation, regardless of Neihardt's reasons for the change, begs the question that contemporary criticism continues to ask: Who, exactly, is speaking in *Black Elk Speaks?*

But my purpose here is not to enter into this sparring over authorship and authenticity in the text, over whether it "is more white than Indian, more fraudulent than factual" (Staub 430). This is already a crowded bout, with contenders weighing in from anthropology, ethnography, history, religion, philosophy, psychology, literary/cultural studies, and Native American studies, to name a few. Rather, I want to draw on this "ongoing interpretive effort to disentangle the voices of Neihardt and Black Elk" (Porterfield 42) as a moment when questions of identity's rhetorical potential are clearly in the foreground. Approaching this debate as a struggle over identity seems as warranted as it does feasible given the range of Black Elks that criticism has depicted: depending on who's counting, pursuits for the "authentic" Black Elk have advanced two, three, and even four distinct contenders for this title (Holler, *Religion* 204; Rice 8; Linden 81–82).

All of these different Black Elks represent differently motivated aims in the contemporary criticism of *Black Elk Speaks*. Accordingly, I want to treat these articulations of who Black Elk "really" is as strategic reinterpretations—strategic *reconstitutions*—of the identity that Neihardt has so influentially depicted. After first clarifying how Neihardt constitutes Black Elk in the service of his broader tragic perspective on Plains Indian history, I will then outline two rival Black Elks that counter aspects of Neihardt's presentation, linking these reconstitutions to changes in the scene of the text's address. Given the differences in these identities that have been fashioned from Black Elk's autobiography and from increased knowledge of his life and interests, the question of who is speaking in *Black Elk Speaks* invites a reformulation, one that turns a *historical* inquiry about authenticity into a *rhetorical* inquiry about identity constitution and purpose: Who is "speaking" these different Black Elks, and why?

Black Elk the Tragic Native American Archetype

When John Neihardt first met Black Elk in August 1930, Neihardt, "a self-styled singer of the grand drama of western expansion" (Kriefall 179), had already acquired a substantial reputation as a writer of plains life. Nebraska's poet laureate since 1921 and the holder of three honorary doctorates in literature (one from the University of Nebraska, granted in a 1917 ceremony that also honored Willa Cather), Neihardt was nearing the completion of what would be regarded as his masterwork, a nearly seven-hundred-page, five-volume epic poem titled *A Cycle of the West*, which he began in 1913. The publication of the third volume in the series, *The Song of the Indian Wars* (1925), earned him a nomination for the 1927 Pulitzer Prize in poetry, and it was during his research for the fourth volume, *The Song of the Messiah* (1935), that Neihardt visited the Pine Ridge Sioux Reservation in South Dakota and made Black Elk's acquaintance. As he relates in his preface to *Black Elk Speaks*, he had come to the reservation to learn more of "what white men have called the 'Messiah craze'—the great Messianic dream that came to the desperate Indians in the middle 80's of the 19th century and ended with the massacre at Wounded Knee." "I had the facts," he clarifies, but "what I needed for my purpose was something to be experienced through intimate contact, rather than received through telling" (BE xv). Black Elk, a respected holy man, second cousin to Crazy Horse, and eyewitness to the infamous Wounded Knee massacre, would eventually provide Neihardt with exactly the sort of intimate knowledge about the end of Plains Indian resistance that he was seeking.

Neihardt wouldn't finish *The Song of the Messiah* for another five years—in part because of his disappointment at not winning the Pulitzer, and in part because he had redirected his efforts toward a book he hadn't planned on writing. "Dear Friend," he wrote to Black Elk three months after their first meeting, "I feel that the whole story of your life ought to be written truthfully by somebody with the right feeling and understanding of your people and of their great history." This story, as Neihardt envisioned it, "would be not only the story of your life, but the story of your people. . . . us[ing] as much of your language as possible" (BE 277–78). Thus began the composition of *Black Elk Speaks*, a translated, transcribed autobiography through which Neihardt sought "to touch his readers with the emotional power of the inexorable struggle between the advancement of white civilization across the American west and the native peoples who had lived there" (DeMallie xx–xxi).

Many have criticized that the previous lyrics of Neihardt's *Cycle*—their praises for "the great race-mood of courage that was developed west of the Missouri River in the 19th century"—render Neihardt "complicit in justifications of violence" against Native Americans (Neihardt, *Indian Wars* 7; Kriefall 183).[4] Others counter that he was nonetheless sensitive to the tragedies that had befallen Native Americans in the name of Manifest Destiny. "Neihardt wished to bring this tragedy into focus by telling the story through the eyes of a single native person," Raymond DeMallie elaborates, a single native person whose life, in representing "the story of [his] people," must be correspondingly tragic (57). By all accounts at the time of the text's original appearance, this poignant embodiment of Native American decline is precisely what the "courageous, racially representative, tragic hero" of *Black Elk Speaks* achieved (Kriefall 183).

What uniquely equips Black Elk for this tragically representative role is a conversion. Neihardt's constitution of Black Elk as the tragic archetype of Plains Indian history centers on an event that transforms his understanding of himself and his nation: the "Great Vision" or "power-vision" of the powers of the earth convening to teach him, endowing him with his mission to redeem the Lakota people. Black Elk had heard peculiar voices calling to him since the age of five (but "what they wanted I did not know," he states). During a period of illness when he is nine, however, he receives his Great Vision and finally senses the purpose for which he is being summoned. "Your nation shall have great troubles," the Spirit of the Earth tells him; his people will walk "a fearful road, a road of troubles and of war," explains the Grandfather of the Earth's South quarter (29–30).

Despite this prophesied tribulation, there is hope yet that his people will become "a good nation walking in a sacred manner in a good land." This hope is Black Elk. "The powers of the four quarters . . . have given you the sacred stick and your nation's hoop . . . and in the center of the hoop you shall set the stick and make it grow," he is commanded; "the living center of a nation I shall give you, and with it many you shall save. . . . By your powers you shall make it blossom" (28–34).[5] But Black Elk's words as the narrative begins reveal that this transforming experience, rather than bringing him the reassurance and wholeness that conversion suggests, will ultimately yield only failure and remorse. "My friend, I am going to tell you the story of my life, as you wish," he begins his autobiography, "the story of a mighty vision given to a man too weak to use it" (1–2). With this lament Black Elk sets in motion the inevitably tragic direction of his life story in *Black Elk Speaks*, "a straight arrow moving towards loss, suffering, and a failed vision" (Staub 436).

Black Elk becomes an adult before he truly begins to grasp the significance of his visionary calling ("and even now I know that more was shown to me than I can tell," he relates). Yet the experience clearly changes him from the youthful moment he receives it: "Nothing I have ever seen with my eyes was so clear and bright as what my vision showed me; and no words that I have ever heard with my ears were like the words I heard," he remarks. "I did not have to remember these things; they have remembered themselves all these years" (49). Foremost among these changes is that Black Elk's unique vision immediately grants him peculiar spiritual power, power with which he works many miraculous benefits for his people, including healing the sick and prophesying of impending dangers that they are then able to escape. But even at age fifteen, Black Elk knows that his duty is much greater than even these miracles. "The Grandfathers had shown me . . . how the nation's hoop would be broken and flowering tree be withered, before I should bring the hoop together with the power that was given me," he tells. "I wondered when my power would grow, so that the rest might be as I had seen it in my vision" (147). The conversion that this vision represents for Black Elk is thus not a conversion in its typical religious sense, as a turning away from a sinful past and toward a consequently more righteous future; Black Elk is not the Jamesian "sick soul . . . who must be twice-born in order to be happy" (163). This experience is a conversion, however, in a more general sense that Lewis R. Rambo outlines: it is an event that "provide[s] a coherent center from which to conduct one's life in a world where that center has been lost" (31). This metaphorical emphasis on conversion as "recenteredness" is in fact the literal message of Black Elk's vision—that the center of the Lakota world itself has been lost, and that it is his divine calling to be that center, to plant the tree around which the sacred hoop might again turn. Despite his eventual failure in this calling, it is a vision that transforms his life into the singular quest for a materially and spiritually blossoming Lakota nation. This visionary transformation is a transformation of Black Elk's identity in a Burkean sense as well—"a change in substance or principle, a qualitative shift in the nature of motivation." For with his gradually increased understanding of his duty comes an increased sense that *who* he is centers on *what* he has been chosen to perform for the Lakota; the restoration of the nation's broken hoop becomes the "ultimate motivation" around which he now understands and defines himself (GM 355–57).

But as Black Elk's own words have repeatedly foretold, it is an ultimate motivation he does not materialize. Toward the end of the narrative, he speaks in the present tense about his regret at not having done more to bring his vision to life: "Now when I look about me upon my people in despair, I feel like crying and I wish and wish my vision could have been given to a man more worthy. I wonder why it came to me, a pitiful old man who can do nothing. Men and women and children I have cured of sickness with the power the vision gave me; but my nation I could not help. If a man or woman or child dies, it does not matter long, for the nation lives on. It was the nation that was dying, and the vision was for the nation; but I have done nothing with it" (180). Black

Elk's lament at his personal inability to match the greatness of his vision—his mournful self-appraisal as "a pitiful old man"—is repeated elsewhere in the narrative, most significantly, in his autobiography's final paragraph. In the closing chapter, "The End of the Dream," he contemplates the horrors he has witnessed in the previous chapter, "The Butchering at Wounded Knee." After reflecting on the gory finality of the scene, he utters his life story's bitter (and oft-quoted) conclusion: "A people's dream died there. It was a beautiful dream. And I, to whom so great a vision was given in my youth—you see me now a pitiful old man who has done nothing, for the nation's hoop is broken and scattered. There is no center any longer, and the sacred tree is dead" (270). In Black Elk's almost causal connection here of his failure to achieve his vision and the ignominy of Wounded Knee—"the most devastating of Sioux historical memories," the "Lakota Auschwitz" (Staub 436; Wise, "Speaking" 19)—the tragic course that he foreshadows at the narrative's opening reaches its fruition. It is a course that seals his identity as the pitiable victim of a failed conversion, a holy man who, however devoted to preserving his culture, simply could not save it from Wasichu encroachment. More than just tragic, his identity as constituted in *Black Elk Speaks* represents "tragedy in the greatest sense" (Castro 86).

Neihardt's rendering of this tragedy in *Black Elk Speaks* typifies what Alfred Kazin has described as "the preponderance of descriptive nonfiction" in early-1930s literature that sought to give representation to "the dispossessed and the marginal" in American society and history (quoted in Staub 425–26). The almost total dissolution of the Lakota at the hands of failed or disingenuous U.S.–Indian relations (a dissolution given its most memorable form in the Wounded Knee massacre) certainly qualifies as a story of dispossession and marginalization worth telling. In Black Elk, Neihardt found an ideal vehicle for telling it, for representing a people whose history, like Black Elk's, was one of loss and unrealized potential. That Neihardt intended Black Elk's autobiography to serve such a representative function for the Lakota as a whole is evident both in his correspondence with Black Elk and in the autobiography itself. As he had remarked to Black Elk a year prior to the interviews that produced *Black Elk Speaks*, "this book would be not only the story of your life, but *the story of the life of your people*"; consequently, it is less than surprising that Black Elk begins to tell "the story of my life" in the text by qualifying that "if it were only the story of my life I think I would not tell it" (*Black Elk* 278, emphasis added; 1). More than simply the tragedy of a single life and a singular vision unrealized, *Black Elk Speaks* is itself the tragedy of the Lakota at the end of the nineteenth century, an autobiography that, in constituting the failed ambitions of its holy man subject, constitutes as well the failed dream of a people at the voiceless margins of American history.

With this "story of a mighty vision given to a man too weak to use it"—and, through his failed conversion, the parallel story of his nation's decline—Neihardt struck just the tragic chord with readers that he aimed to intone. A 1932 review in the *New York Times Book Review*, for example (aptly titled "A Sioux Indian Tells a Tragic Story"), noted how "what will immediately strike the reader is the obvious, but nonetheless terribly poignant, anti-climax of Black Elk's life" (Chamberlain 4). *New Republic*, in a review titled simply "Morituri" ("we who are about to die") similarly praised how "the power and beauty of Black Elk's 'Great Vision' are so compelling as to overshadow even the heroic proportions of the narrative, with its inevitably tragic conclusion" (Childs 161). And the complex pathos of Black Elk's visionary entitlement and visionary failure was most succinctly encapsulated in the *Saturday Review of Literature* review, its title pronouncing Black Elk "A Maladjusted Soul" (Vestal 551).

As these reviews at the time of the text's publication further attest, Neihardt succeeded not only in evoking pity for the self-proclaimed "pitiful old man who [could] do nothing" to save the Lakota from tragedy; he also succeeded in transmitting his autobiography with what appeared to be exacting verisimilitude. "No unprejudiced reader will doubt that John Neihardt has set down honestly what Black Elk told him," claimed a reviewer for *Books* (Skinner 3). "Neihardt has set his sensitive poet's mind to the task of recording faithfully and without intrusion Black Elk's words. . . . a keen and scrupulous editor," concurred *New Republic*. And in the most straightforward assertion of his unbiased transcription, *Saturday Review* lauded how Neihardt, the transparent "as told to" of Black Elk's vision, "almost completely submerges himself, his rhetoric . . . and allows the Indian to speak for himself" (Vestal 551). In the world beyond the academic infighting over identity and authenticity, the impotent holy man of John G. Neihardt's *Black Elk Speaks is* Black Elk. He is the tragic synecdoche of the end of Plains Indian resistance, invoked in this representative capacity in texts as diverse as Dee Brown's immensely popular *Bury My Heart at Wounded Knee* (1970), where Black Elk's concluding lament of his failed vision appears verbatim as the conclusion of this "Indian History of the American West" (446); and in Paula Gunn Allen's more recent *The Sacred Hoop* (1986), where Black Elk's failure becomes a rallying cry for the revitalization of Native American spirituality. The transformed vessel of a holy duty to unite his people, Black Elk is likewise the vessel of the consequences of his failure in this holy duty: he *is* the broken and centerless hoop, the withered tree of a scattered nation, the "dream" that "died . . . in the bloody mud" (BE 270). Perhaps the obviousness of Black Elk's constitution as the embodiment of this tragic Lakota history, as "the very symbol of his people" (DeMallie 57), is what ultimately dissuaded Neihardt from the heavy-handed metaphorics of his working title for Black Elk's autobiography—"The Tree That Never Bloomed."

Black Elk the Catholic Regenerate

As I have already noted, Burke's insistence that constitutions be viewed dialectically, as "enactment[s] arising in history," is a way of emphasizing what might be called the "checks" on the substantiating powers of constitutions. Inasmuch as a constitution arises as an address to the demands of a specific temporal situation, the simple passage of time guarantees that a constitution will inevitably find itself addressing scenes it could not have anticipated, with results it could not have foreseen. (As Burke's anecdote of the fencers illustrates, the very "opponent" that a constitution seeks to thwart or hedge off might even disappear.) Such changes in the "supporting, extra-constitutional scene into which the constitution has survived as an enactment" entail changes of constitutionality, the transformation of the individual "oughts" a constitution would substantiate as its wishes are weighed against the realities of specific circumstances (GM 380). It is in this sense that scenes come to shape constitutions, with a constitution's "enactment of human wills" necessarily becoming a "new act" in the evolving extra-constitutional scenes of human history.

By the time that the question of Black Elk's identity—the question of who he *really* is—becomes a subject of debate, the scene this constituted identity now addresses differs significantly from the scene in which the autobiography first arose. If preserving the memory of Lakota history (and preserving it as a decidedly *tragic* history) was central to Neihardt's purposes in *Black Elk Speaks*, then the "opponent" that this enactment once addressed, the historical elision of the Lakota's tragic story, has indeed retreated. By the early 1980s, when questions about authenticity in *Black Elk Speaks* first began to emerge, there seemed little danger that injustices against Native Americans would fade from public memory—an accomplishment of popular texts such as Brown's *Bury My Heart at Wounded Knee* and, notably, *Black Elk Speaks* itself, which experienced an explosive resurgence of popularity in the early 1960s.[6] This attention to Native American history increases over time, with the late 1980s–early 1990s exhibiting what Couser cites as a "dramatic upsurge in the visibility of native Americans in mainstream American culture" (a visibility attributable in part to highly successful films such as *Dances with Wolves*, which was about the Lakota, and *The Last of the Mohicans*—both films that vilify the oppression of Native Americans) ("Speaks Again" 273). Inasmuch as history no longer seems to threaten to forget the tragedy of the Lakota (at least, for the moment), Black Elk's identity as Neihardt constitutes it no longer addresses or "cooperates" with this "opponent" in determining its significance. The absence of this opponent creates a "new scene" of address for this constitution; consequently, "the enactments that derived their significance from the old scene must change accordingly" (GM 364). In other words, Black Elk's constitution as a "racially representative, tragic hero" of the Lakota (Kriefall 183)—his strategic constitution for ensuring a Lakota presence in public memory—opens to the possibility of becoming some kind of "new act." The "scene" of popular awareness of America's native peoples shifts in the last quarter of the twentieth century, and so do the interests to which a figure such as Black Elk might speak.

Foremost among these new interests is the study of how the emergent genre of the "Indian autobiography" manifests the "complex, cross-cultural collaboration" behind the production of Native American texts (Krupat, *For Those* xi).[7] As Arnold Krupat explains, "Native American literature presents itself exclusively in the form of oral performances, not textual objects; no matter how scrupulous a transcription may be, it is inevitably a declension from the narrative act." Thus the focus in reading the autobiographies of Native American "authors" such as Black Elk widens to examine not merely "what they said" but "how they said it" as well, an effort to more fully apprehend both the performative character of orality and the inevitable mutations this orality undergoes as it is transcribed into written narrative (2–3). A text such as *Black Elk Speaks*, then, one that was "long accepted as the authentic utterance of an unreconstructed Lakota holy man" (Couser, "Speaks Again" 276), suddenly finds itself the object of scrutiny regarding the reconstruction that Black Elk necessarily experiences at the hands of his literary mouthpiece, John Neihardt. Under such scrutiny, previous assertions of Neihardt's transparency in telling Black Elk's story—assertions of his total self-effacement in letting him "speak for himself" (Vestal 551)—become naive impossibilities, as do claims that Neihardt's influence in the text's production simply doesn't affect the significance of Black Elk's story. This significant change in the scene surrounding *Black Elk Speaks* mounts a powerful argument about how the text should be read—or rather, how it should *not* be read: as Holler summarizes, "the days are now past when an uncritical conflation of Neihardt and Black Elk will pass for serious scholarship" (*Religion* 2).

With the 1985 publication of the original transcripts of the Black Elk–Neihardt interviews of 1931, *Black Elk Speaks* becomes a crucible for questions of textual representation and Native American autobiography, a status it maintains today. In particular, the mounting "debate over the identity and beliefs of Black Elk" (Couser, "Speaks Again" 276) gains tremendous steam as these transcripts help to clarify how both *what* Black Elk said and *how* he said it were, in Neihardt's own words, "*transform[ed]* . . . so that [they] could be understood by the white world" (quoted in McCluskey 238, emphasis in original). Easily the most significant aspect of what is "transformed" in Neihardt's narrative is his omission of the fact that Black Elk, the "pitiful old man" who tragically could not save traditional Lakota spirituality from white acculturation, was a baptized Christian. Not only was he a Christian—and had been for nearly thirty years prior to meeting Neihardt—he was an officially endowed Roman Catholic catechist to the Lakota at the Pine Ridge Reservation. This new awareness of Black Elk's Christianity, a pivotal change of scene since the appearance of *Black Elk Speaks*, seems to fatally compromise Neihardt's original constitution of Black Elk as the embodiment of Lakota tradition. How can Black Elk function as the "decentered or marginalized other" who represents Plains Indian culture when he is discovered to have spent the last half of his life as an active proselytizer for the most prominent and powerful religion of the European-American world? Inquiry into his Christian involvement, an involvement not known to the original readership of *Black Elk Speaks*, remains highly problematic, for it "leave[s] us with two essentially incommensurable Black Elks—a traditionalist and a Catholic—where there should be one whole person" (Holler, *Religion* 204).

Taken together, the growing general awareness of Native American history, the increased attention to the collaborative authorship of Indian autobiographies, and the publicizing of Black Elk's Catholic allegiance all but reverse the long-standing and unproblematic reception of *Black Elk Speaks* as an unprofaned glimpse of a vanished culture. With these formidable changes in the scene that the narrative now addresses, changes that open the text to a host of new critiques, the identity of Black Elk himself invites a corresponding latitude of novel interpretations. At the fore of those who challenge the unmitigated traditionalism of Neihardt's Black Elk are Jesuits who, having worked with Black Elk or with the Lakota generally, seek to fill in the blanks of Black Elk's life as a proselytizing Catholic. Paul Steinmetz, for example, a Jesuit missionary-cum-anthropologist who worked with the Lakota at Pine Ridge during the 1960s and 1970s, draws on Black Elk's life story to refute the common claim that Native Americans on reservations accept Christianity for purely social reasons, as a way of "pleas[ing] their conquerors" (Rudolf Kaiser, quoted in Steinmetz, *Pipe* 179). There is "genuine conversion" among Native Americans such as the Lakota at Pine Ridge, he argues, and the figure who is the "starting point" in proving this fact is none other than Black Elk (179). In *Black Elk Speaks* Neihardt's chief strategy for constituting Black Elk as an archetype of Lakota tragedy was his depiction of Black Elk's "Great Vision"—his conversion into the holy man that would restore his nation's sacred hoop—as a conversion that he fails to live up to. Similarly, those who challenge Black Elk's traditionalist identity, seeking to reconstitute him as a devoted Catholic, also draw upon this moment of transformation as a defining moment of his life. The difference, of course, is in just *how* this moment of conversion is used to define him.

From this Catholic perspective Black Elk's conversion defines him as a proto-Christian, a devoted Lakota spiritualist who would later find the true object of this spirituality in finding Catholicism. Through a detailed reading of the published Neihardt–Black Elk transcripts (recovering therein the Catholic elements of Black Elk's life that Neihardt deliberately "left out"), Steinmetz explains how the "Great Vision" of *Black Elk Speaks* is actually "a Messiah manifestation," a "vision . . . [of] the Christ of [the] Catholic faith" (*Black Elk* 180–81). While this Catholic reading of the Great Vision differs vastly from the vision's original presentation in *Black Elk Speaks,* it does not alter the god-term or "ultimate motivation" of Black Elk's transformed identity through this vision: he was then, and remained after embracing Catholicism, a spiritually "chosen" individual with a sacred "duty" to lead his people. What changes in Steinmetz's rearticulation, however, is Black Elk's *means* for accomplishing this duty to his people, for leading them "to walk in a sacred manner in a good land" (36). This means is not traditional Lakota spirituality, as Neihardt would have it; rather, it is "a total commitment to Christ," a commitment that Black Elk clearly made as a Catholic, "as was evident from his life as a catechist" (Steinmetz, *Pipe* 188).

Black Elk's converting vision was by Neihardt's hand a failure, a tragic hesitation to act that leaves him "poised, seemingly helplessly, on the brink of civilization . . . sorrowing over the destruction of his people" (DeMallie 56–57). But to Steinmetz, this tragic "failure" is nothing more than Black Elk's failure to have yet encountered the Christian teaching that would reveal to him what his Great Vision really meant; "Only after Black Elk had explicitly known Christ," after his catechism on the reservation in the early 1900s, "could he realize that he had actually seen Him without knowing it" in his Great Vision (*Pipe* 182). From this point of view, the supposed "pitiful old man who could do nothing" of Neihardt's creation had, in fact, by the 1930s, done quite a bit more than "nothing" to lead his people "to walk in a sacred manner." That sacred manner was Catholicism, and Black Elk was nothing if not a powerful leader for the cause: in his capacity as catechist, he had personally taught and facilitated the baptism of an estimated four hundred Lakota at the Pine Ridge Reservation alone, to say nothing of his frequent travels well beyond the reservation to teach.

For those who have thus worked to recover the Christian elements of Black Elk's discussions with Neihardt, the "authentic" Black Elk is a devoted Catholic, a Black Elk that Neihardt likely recognized, yet carefully excised from *Black Elk Speaks* (Kaye 159).[8] Proving Black Elk's Catholicism is more than simply a matter of fidelity to history (with *prove* being the right word, given that this Catholicism is, according to Steltenkamp, "empirically verifiable" [*Black Elk: Holy Man* 173]). In this reconstituted identity of sincere Lakota Catholic, Black Elk becomes a powerful argument for causes that are foreign—if not wholly antithetical—to the purposes of his original constitution in *Black Elk Speaks.* No longer just a synecdoche of traditions passed, something of a Lakota last (holy) man standing, Black Elk instead becomes an argument for the *subordination* of Native tradition: as the representative "genuine convert" of Native American Christianity, he becomes the "touchstone" and "prime example" of how Christianity *subsumes* traditional spirituality in fulfilling it—of how Lakota religion is "an Old Testament reaching its fulfillment in Christ" (Steinmetz, "Missiology" 280–81). Black Elk is even a prescient forerunner of the spirit of Vatican II, which proclaims its respect for the "validity . . . [of] non-Christian religions" while the purpose of "the Church" yet remains to "absorb non-Christian religions into itself" (264). For many of the Jesuits who knew him, Black Elk's turn from misguided tradition to Christianity makes him nothing short of a Lakota Paul (Enochs 80), complete with a change of name, from the simple "Black Elk" of his traditional identity to the Black Elk of his Catholic baptism, *Nicholas* Black Elk.

Through a reconstitution of identity that centers on an alternate interpretation of his converting vision, Black Elk is ultimately transformed from a representation of the death of Lakota dreams of unity into an argument for a renewed Lakota hope—the hope of Catholic practice. Unlike the unworthy and defeated messenger of *Black Elk Speaks*, this regenerate Black Elk yet works to make good on his conversion, to realize his vision of restored Lakota holiness; and that "tree blooming in the center of the sacred hoop" he was divinely called to plant, that he has planted, and that his story continues to nurture is "a Lakota Christian religion" (Steinmetz, "Missiology" 281).

Black Elk the Strategic Syncretist

The case for a staunchly Catholic Black Elk to rival the tragic traditionalist of Neihardt's creation is compelling. But Jesuits are not alone in responding to the reconstitutive opportunity that changes in the situation surrounding *Black Elk Speaks* have created—an opportunity to constitute "authentic" Black Elks that support different attempts to "shape . . . human relations" (GM 341). The identity politics that has been leveraged toward creating a more culturally inclusive literary canon has also called attention to yet another Black Elk, one whose ability to authentically represent Lakota culture is of paramount importance. As multiculturalism attempts to diversify the canon through increased attention to historically "marginalized . . . identity based discourses," Carl Silvio relates, "the identity of the author becomes a matter of crucial significance insofar as it serves as the guarantor of a text's efficacy as authentically representing the concerns of a given identity category." Whatever the debatable merits of any particular minority-based discourse, it is this "capacity to represent a given group" that ultimately "serves as the motivation for decisions to include or exclude [a text] from the canon." Within this conception of literary multiculturalism, the question of the canonicity of *Black Elk Speaks* becomes the question of whether Black Elk's identity in the text can yet be "the canonical representative . . . of the cultures to which [he] belong[s]" (143). It becomes the question of what "authentic" Black Elk can account for both his identity as constituted in *Black Elk Speaks*—that of tragic Lakota representative—and the dramatic changes of scene outside the text (such as the discovery of his Catholicism) that vitiate his identity as a representative Lakota.

This final authentic Black Elk is the most rhetorically interesting of all. Rather than simply a passed and passive figure whose identity is strategized in the service of different contemporary arguments, this Black Elk strategized about his own identity. He saw in his unique combination of allegiances an opportunity to accomplish purposes of his own choosing, purposes that guided his collaborations with Neihardt in producing *Black Elk Speaks*. This Black Elk is "an ingenious, syncretic Lakota–Christian," a combiner of cultures for whom Lakota tradition and Catholicism were not mutually exclusive (Rice 8). While he seems to have found in Catholicism (a Catholicism that "all Indian people were aggressively urged to embrace," Rice notes) a spirituality he both practiced and reverenced, he also saw in it a way of working more effectively for the preservation of Lakota tradition amid the strictures of reservation life (1). Understanding how Black Elk "found channels in Church practice through which to continue Lakota tradition" thus frees the question of his identity, of who he *really* is, from the either/or binary of traditionalism vs. Catholicism: he was a Catholic catechist, yes, and one who "spent his last years working actively to preserve the Lakota religion using every available vehicle," including Catholicism (3–4). Chief among the vehicles available to him was the powerful story of his own converting vision, and it is by clarifying his purposes in sharing this vision with Neihardt that an authentic, syncretic, self-strategizing, and culturally representative Black Elk is constituted.

To understand how Black Elk sought to use his vision on behalf of the Lakota later in his life, however, we must also ask *why* Black Elk said what he did—why he revealed his vision to Neihardt in their 1931 interviews. *Black Elk Speaks* itself makes clear why Neihardt thought Black Elk took him into his confidence in this way—no small gesture, Black Elk points out in the autobiography, considering that he had never before revealed the entirety of his vision to anyone.

> I had never told anyone all of it, and even until now [during their interview] nobody ever heard it all. Even my old friend, Standing Bear, and my son here have heard it now for the first time when I have told it to you. . . . It has made me very sad to do this at last, I have lain awake at night worrying and wondering if I was doing right; for I know I have given away my power when I have given away my vision, and maybe I cannot

> live very long now. But I think I have done right to save the vision in this way, even thought I may die sooner because I did it; for I know the meaning of the vision is wise and beautiful and good; and you can see that I am only a pitiful old man after all. (206)

As Black Elk states, he is deeply troubled at the thought of revealing his vision to Neihardt, wondering if full disclosure respects the sacredness of it, and wondering as well if he hasn't hastened his own demise in speaking its fullness. But giving his vision to Neihardt ultimately merits this sacrifice in that it allows Black Elk to "save" his vision in some sense—that is, to keep it from perishing in the grave with him, as he believes he might shortly do. "Soon I shall be under the grass and it will be lost," Neihardt quotes him in the preface. "You were sent to save it" (xviii).

But Black Elk is troubled by more than simply the thought of the vision's disappearance. As he also relates, sharing the vision amounts to a relinquishing of his powers as a holy man, powers that, as he has stated from the very outset of his autobiography, are already all but gone. As the simultaneous relinquishing of his powers, sharing his vision becomes his personal atonement for his failure in the service of this vision, an abdication of divine calling that cements his status as a fallen and tragic figure. A reader's sympathy and pity for Black Elk seem even more aroused at this moment of sacrifice than at the narrative's concluding vignette of the "bloody mud" of Wounded Knee. Through this final act of self-sacrifice, the tragedy of Black Elk becomes a tragedy not just of the past but of the present as well, the holy man once and for all admitting his defeat as a savior for Lakota culture, then sealing it by vesting Neihardt with the stewardship of a vision he is no longer worthy to hold. In Neihardt's account Black Elk's power-vision assumes the status of an artifact devoid of power; it is a "beautiful and good" relic that Neihardt gently picks up from the dust of Lakota tradition and shrouds in the pathos of a literary lament. *Black Elk Speaks*, then, essentially serves as something of a museum case in which this Great Vision artifact is preserved, a container that would hermetically seal its tragic significance in narrative. Indeed, encasement is an accurate description of how Neihardt's text binds the vision in tragedy: Black Elk's repeated laments at his "pitiful" and failed status, laments that frame the autobiography as both its opening and concluding chapters, were not Black Elk's words; they were Neihardt's own additions.

But for those who argue Black Elk's syncretic identity as a holy man who, even as a "converted" Catholic, strove for the preservation of Lakota tradition, treating Black Elk's sharing of his vision as a tragic admission of failure willfully misrepresents his intentions. Quite the opposite, Black Elk's meetings with Neihardt to discuss Lakota history and culture, meetings that he carefully arranged and prepared for,[9] might be considered in the same terms as his unlikely union with Catholicism. That is, just as Black Elk pursued Catholicism on the reservation in part to open "channels . . . through which to continue Lakota tradition"—as "a strategy . . . for protecting his people"—so Neihardt's interest in writing about the Lakota might have provided Black Elk with a similar channel for further tradition-building, a strategic opportunity for advancing the promise of his vision (Rice 8; Holler, *Religion* 204). Such a purpose would likely have gone unrecognized by Neihardt, especially considering the overriding project of the *Cycle of the West* (with its depiction of Plains Indian decline as a "fortunate fall") he was composing at the time he interviewed Black Elk.[10] In "treat[ing] the story of Black Elk's life as a description of a noble way of life that had vanished forever," Amanda Porterfield explains, Neihardt "did not appreciate the tenacity of Black Elk's faith in Lakota religion, or take seriously his commitment to its future contribution to the world. He took Black Elk's story of having a vision . . . and assigned the relevance of that vision to a culture of the past. He never considered . . . [that] retelling the vision was a significant part of its development and realization. He never considered the stories Black Elk told him about the vision and its impact on the life of his people as a statement about the ongoing vitality of Lakota culture" (40). Whether because of his own focus on using Black Elk as a tragic symbol or due to his inability to fully understand Black Elk, Neihardt did not grasp that Black Elk might have found in the sharing of his vision an opportunity to disseminate it, to tap its powers yet toward restoring the center of the Lakota nation. In Holler's words, Neihardt simply could not see Black Elk, or perhaps chose not to see him, as "an active creator of his people's present rather than as a passive victim of acculturation and an informant on the past" (*Religion* 204).[11]

Materials external to *Black Elk Speaks* demonstrate that Black Elk likely saw the sharing of his vision in this way, as an effort on behalf of his visionary calling. But the most telling evidence of this claim is present on the cover of *Black Elk Speaks* itself—Neihardt's parenthetical reference to himself in the text's author line as "Flaming Rainbow." Through a ritual renaming that Black Elk himself performed, declaring Neihardt "Flaming Rainbow" served as a necessary preparation before he could receive Black Elk's vision. While this renaming has the immediate effect of rendering Neihardt a much more credible author of an Indian autobiography—one ritually legitimated to his readership by the very man whose life he records—the name's significance attests to Black Elk's perception of Neihardt as a participant in the fulfillment of his duty to the Lakota. As DeMallie explains, "The flaming rainbow was the power that marked the entryway to the home of the six grandfathers [as seen in Black Elk's vision]; . . . Neihardt was to enact the role of this power on earth by making the vision 'go out'—like the flames from the rainbow—so that people would understand its meaning" (37). For Black Elk his vision was not a static museum piece at all but rather a vessel of power, one that could yet bring the Lakota their promised transformation into a people of prosperity. Interestingly, Black Elk's ritual renaming of Neihardt might itself be considered a constitutive act, one that would define Neihardt not simply as a historian, poet, or (auto)biographer, but as an active partner in the fruition of Black Elk's vision. This ritual renaming would place as the circumference of Neihardt's identity the same ultimate motivation that defines Black Elk: the restoration of the sacred hoop, a duty that Neihardt now shares with the holy man whose powers he has received.

Seeing Neihardt as a ritually endowed participant in Black Elk's vision dramatically reverses the tragic finality that characterizes the vision's depiction in *Black Elk Speaks*. As Couser asserts, "it was Neihardt, not Black Elk, who pronounced Lakota culture dead" ("Speaks Again" 287). Consequently, Black Elk's identity as the embodiment of this tragic failure is reversed as well. Whatever his regrets in falling short of his duty, Black Elk yet held hope for the vitality of Lakota tradition. Sharing his vision with Neihardt, rather than an atonement for his failed conversion, instead becomes the strategic incorporation of a new "vehicle" or "channel" for Lakota advancement—literature. The product of a collaboration now understood to have occurred largely at cross-purposes,[12] *Black Elk Speaks* thus emerges as a text with virtually antithetical readings: the autobiography originally embraced as a holy man's eulogy for a culture of the past-tense becomes instead, through attention to Black Elk's regenerative aims, "an effort, through Neihardt as 'Flaming Rainbow,' to bring into history the ritualistic forces that will stop history itself as the white man has shaped it and restore . . . the Sioux people" (Olson 22). No longer the tragic admission of defeat it was so long held to be, sharing his vision with Neihardt and bringing about its dissemination might have been Black Elk's most profound ritual performance as a Lakota holy man, a means not of eulogizing a vanished past but rather of speaking it back into being.

Constituted in this way, Black Elk's identity is defined by an "ultimate motivation" for the endurance of traditional Lakota culture and spirituality, a god-term of preservation without assimilation. The Catholicism that certain Jesuits would argue is much more central to Black Elk's sense of self thus becomes one of several voluntaristic principles of his identity—the "willed" aspects of his actions on behalf of renewed Lakota prosperity; Catholic practice, whatever Black Elk's sincerity, simply does not define the overall substance of his identity in the way that his enduring Lakota heritage does. Moreover, this Black Elk is, from the multiculturalist perspective I noted earlier, a culturally representative (and hence canonical) Black Elk. Given that Black Elk apparently never ceased in his duty to materialize a restored Lakota nation—a duty that motivated his embrace of Neihardt's interest in documenting Lakota culture—he certainly qualifies as one whose identity manifests "the sense of authenticity that multicultural revisionists demand" (Silvio 149). In this interpretation the Catholicism of his later life, rather than undermining his Lakota authenticity, instead makes him all the more unique and interesting as a Lakota spokesman. The fact that he would accept a catechist's duties in a belief system so seemingly contrary to his tradition can only magnify a reader's sense of how important his visionary duty was, important enough to be advanced through "every available vehicle" (Rice 4).

As Black Elk thus "show[s] how Christianity could be embraced without sacrificing Lakota identity," his identity becomes something other than either Catholic regenerate or monocultural traditionalist. He becomes instead a "creative religious thinker," a man who is the "principal visionary behind the modern revitalization of Lakota religion" (Holler, *Religion* 38; Porterfield 39). Constituted in response to a contemporary critical situation's emphasis on questions of authenticity and representation, his identity is that of cultural strategizer, and an "ingenious" one to boot, seeing in his own conversion an opportunity to voice an argument for the power that yet obtained in Lakota tradition. And the story of this holy man whose divine responsibility to his people defines his very sense of self, *Black Elk Speaks* has become transformed as well. Having achieved a prominence that belies its initially tepid public reception, this subject of both high school and college instruction alike is nothing short of a literary classic, "an acknowledged masterpiece of religious literature" (Holler, "Introduction" xxiii).

Conclusion: "Black Elk Speaks Again"

In the winter of 1933 Black Elk, then age seventy, was thrown from a wagon he was driving and run over by his team, suffering two broken ribs. After receiving the last rites in the hospital and apparently wanting to make a final profession of his beliefs, he dictated a statement in Lakota to two Jesuit fathers of Holy Rosary Mission, who then translated and typed it. The resulting document, after it was signed by Black Elk, was released as "Black Elk Speaks Again—The Final Speech." Roughly two pages long, the text presents a Black Elk who strongly asserts that, as concerns Catholicism, "I am a believer. . . . Thirty years ago I knew little about the one we call God. . . . but now I think I am better. St. Paul also became better after his conversion. I know that the Catholic religion is good, better than the Sun dance or the Ghost dance. . . . The Indian religion of long ago did not benefit mankind. . . . I want to go straight in the righteous way that the Catholics teach us so my soul will reach heaven. This is the way I wish it to be" (quoted in DeMallie 59–61). A declaration by Black Elk himself, it would indubitably appear to be the "final" word, just as it is titled, on questions of his Catholic sincerity. The holy man of *Black Elk Speaks* who once prayed to the Six Grandfathers of his vision in *Black Elk Speaks* still prays, yet much differently: "I have converted . . . and say in my own Sioux Indian language, 'Our Father, who art in heaven . . .'" (60).

But recent archival work confirms that more appears to have motivated Black Elk's speaking again in this final profession than his "true" identity of converted Catholic. Whatever his reasons for collaborating with Neihardt in 1931, the Jesuits at Pine Ridge were less than pleased with the holy man's depiction in *Black Elk Speaks*, released the following year; "shocked and horrified at the suggestion that one of their most valued catechists still harbored beliefs in the old Indian religion," they realized that "to accept *Black Elk Speaks* at face value necessarily called into question the genuineness of their success in converting the Lakota" (DeMallie 58). Jesuits immediately criticized Neihardt for telling a slanted story, protesting that Black Elk's final profession of faith "should stand in every new edition of *Black Elk Speaks*" as a corrective. Black Elk was removed from his position as a catechist of more than twenty years, and the Jesuits officially terminated their efforts to employ native catechists. In addition, this controversy over who Black Elk really was—"pagan" traditionalist or Catholic—set the stage for what would become his above-cited "Final Speech" the next winter, following his accident. His half of a quid pro quo, Black Elk agreed to prove his Catholic fidelity by authoring and signing an official renouncement of Lakota religion. In exchange, the Jesuits agreed to give him the last rites (Vecsey 277–78).

"The more we learn about Black Elk, the more controversial he becomes," Holler observes, "a development that would hardly have seemed possible twenty years ago" ("Introduction" xiii). In this reaction to the unanticipated ways that Black Elk has been taken up by contemporary readers, Holler implies precisely the relationship between constitution and scene—between constitution and the "Constitution-beneath-the-Constitution"—that defines Burke's "*Dialectic* of Constitutions." That is, the constitution that would transform a given scene can find itself transformed by this scene as well, changed by its own changed surroundings; the "unique 'constitution'" of an identity that once represented a certain kind of "enactment" finds that, with its "perpetuat[ion] through subsequent variously altered scenes" (RM 21; GM 362), what it seeks to enact becomes "variously altered" as well. Simply put, it is transformed in ways that "would hardly have seemed possible" in the scene of its original constitution.

Certainly this has proven true for *Black Elk Speaks*. The narrative of a Great Vision, a conversion, once held as "an open door to the traditional Lakota world" (DeMallie 94), this same conversion narrative has become instead an "open door" to many different Black Elks. As the scene that surrounds *Black*

Elk Speaks continues to change, and as the life and identity of the man it narrates are "continually modified and applied to new situations" (Holler, *Religion* 3), who knows how Black Elk will yet speak, or how he will be spoken? In this ongoing, mutually transforming dialectic between selves and the scenes into which identity exists—above, beneath, outside, and behind it—could even the "authentic" Black Elk himself have the "final" word?

8

Conclusion

Identity and the Rhetorical Self

. . . we notice only its banality and fail to appreciate its argumentative value.

Chaim Perelman and Lucie Olbrechts-Tyteca, *The New Rhetoric*

Identity is nothing if not banal. Daily, unremarkable, even trite, and unapologetically so: it is these things not by chance, but by definition. Even the most cursory survey of popular discourse suffices to underscore the ubiquity of "the myriad ways in which we can tell others 'who I am'" (Deaux 224). Bookstore shelves sag with autobiographies and memoirs, from gilt-edged classics such as Augustine's *Confessions* and Thoreau's *Walden* to modern permutations of these genres such as Lucy Grealy's *Autobiography of a Face* and Jeannette Angell's *Callgirl: Confessions of an Ivy League Lady of Pleasure*. Movies and song lyrics across the spectrum tell the triumph and tragedy of learning who one really is. The *New Yorker* and the *National Enquirer* alike brandish tales of self-discovery and self-transformation that we seem ever ready to consume. And through these and other means of their conveyance some identities achieve such notoriety that they become their own marketing campaigns—the "branding" of self whereby celebrities become fragrances, athletes become apparel, and the world becomes Oprah. Banal? It is perhaps too erudite an adjective. Identity is common.

Yet being banal or common does not mean being inconsequential. As I have argued, the banality of a facet of experience such as identity may itself be the very key to its consequentiality. To be so basic, so assumed as to be taken for granted is a rhetorical status with a powerful rhetorical warrant. For no rhetorical enterprise materializes ex nihilo: rhetors construct persuasive discourse out of what they find available, and what they labor to build with these available means must stand upon something. As a doxastic rhetorical tradition since Aristotle has asserted, best that the persuasive edifice stand upon a foundation that is not even conspicuously part of one's argument, something that neither invites disputation nor requires explanation. In other words, it is best that persuasion rest upon "the 'given'" (*Rhetoric* 1355b). Such givenness in discourse, its potential as a grounding for persuasive acts, is one vital sense in which the banal possesses the "argumentative value" that Perelman and Olbrechts-Tyteca adjure us not to neglect. But gauging this rhetorical function can be a difficult errand, given that masking cultural, intellectual, and argumentative value is exactly what banality does. Add to this the efficacy with which contemporary theoretical perspectives outfit us to explore that which is common specifically *not* in its own common terms, and it is easy to see why mention of "identity" becomes derisive and naive—an anachronism devoid of nostalgic appeal. Do we feel less open to accusations of banality ourselves if our inquiries into how people negotiate personal definition and significance in the world are accomplished through the comparably urbane vocabularies of power and subjection, of shifting and colligated subject positionalities, of rhizomatic interbeing? In the face of such compelling scholarship—and its equally compelling terminologies—there may be times when it feels that identity is beneath us. But as the doxastically attuned rhetorician reminds, so are foundations.

For what I hope by now are obvious reasons, I have tried to make this case for identity, a case through banality to rhetorical importance, by way of autobiographical narratives. In autobiography, and especially in those narratives of conversion experiences such as I have considered in the previous chapters, the first-person constitution of identity is central, conspicuous; indeed, identity constitution is equally the means and the ends of these texts. Accordingly, these narratives lend themselves to examining the means and ends of identity constitution, which I have approached as a poetics of identity's textual making and a rhetoric of the ends these constituted identities seek in the audiences they address. In fairness to the complexity of the texts I have analyzed, however, it seems appropriate in conclusion to acknowledge the possible, less patently rhetorical ends of these conversion narratives—in other words, those potential purposes that are less about audiences than they are about the authors themselves. A recent study of autobiography, *Turns in the Road: Narrative Studies of Lives in Transition*, summarizes some of these more personal reasons why we tell stories about the dramatic changes "in the trajectory . . . of our lives" that we experience, changes that include conversions. As the study asserts, "the stories we make and tell about the major transitions in our own lives contribute to our identities, help us cope with challenges and stress, shape how we see the future, and help to determine the nature of our interpersonal relationships and our unique positionings in the social and cultural world" (xv). I believe this is true for each of the narratives I have considered. For Dorothy Day, *The Long Loneliness* was clearly an act of "cop[ing] with challenges": this third accounting of her life helped her face the struggles of the weakening Catholic Worker Movement, and to face as well the recent death of its cofounder and her closest friend, Peter Maurin. David Brock's still-contested memoir publicly repudiates the neoconservatism that once dictated his sense of self, but it is every bit as much an effort to further solidify the dramatic recasting of identity and character he narrates—to definitively "reset [his] moral compass," as he indicates ("Unliving" 75). *Crossing* is nothing if not a "contribution" to Deirdre McCloskey's identity, articulating for the benefit of both author and audience alike a clearer sense of the agential constraints that animate "being" a gender. And the Black Elk of John G. Neihardt's *Black Elk Speaks* similarly tells his own life story in a way that would help him make greater sense of his own identity as an endowed vessel of his people's preservation. Whatever his disputed motives for making Neihardt the literary mouthpiece of his holy vision, Black Elk's need to understand his own changing role in the changing future of the reservation-bound Lakota nation can unquestionably be numbered among them.

I do not dispute—and do not know how to dispute—such autotelic aims of these first-person narratives. I grant them their probable presence and function, in Burke's words, as part of their authors' individual "rebirth rituals" (ATH 265). But I do hope to have demonstrated that something more is afoot in these identity narratives as well. More than just therapeutic in their self-representations, these texts disclose "realities" of self-understanding in more broadly purposeful, "stylized" ways; the sense of "who one is" they articulate is also an "answer or rejoinder to assertions current in the situation in which [they] arose" (PLF 109). That is, these constitutions of identity are strategic constitutions. The work of Kenneth Burke has been my foundation for developing this view of identity's strategy, particularly Burke's "The Dialectic of Constitutions" and his corpus-scattered descriptions of identity as a function of language—as "a set of inter-related terms," an "individual substance . . . or constituted act," a "unique 'constitution'" (RM 21–23).

One merit of following Burke's cue in likening the substance of an identity to the substance or enactment of a constitution is that this conjunction informs the joint poetics and rhetoric of identity in language that I have elaborated. The poetic dimension of this perspective centers on conceptual tools that "The Dialectic of Constitutions" can yield to help explain how an identity is structured or assembled textually—how it is constituted. The concepts of circumference and god-term, the agon of voluntaristic and necessitarian principles, the addressed nature of constitutions, and the mutually transformative dialectic between constitution and "Constitution-beneath-the-Constitution" (GM 373) all enable a fuller discussion of how identity is exhibited in rhetorical discourse. Given how quickly (and correctly) first-person expressions of self-understanding are labeled identity statements or identity discourse, but then are left as though such a label somehow renders this discourse rhetorically accounted for, concepts that can show more at work in the making of identity are an essential step toward more robust analysis—toward more fully appreciating identity's argumentative value.

In the rhetoric of identity that these concepts also inform, the "substance" of identity becomes exactly that of a constitution: a body of wills, or "mutually-adjusted terms" (RM 23), that together act as "motives for the shaping or transforming of behavior" (GM 342). Constitutions are agonistic, admonitory "instruments" whose very nature is to effect the transformation of those to whom they are addressed. The substance of a constitution thus cannot be passive, nor can the substance of a constituted identity. It cannot be an "essence" that one "has," untouched by the forces of history, language, and culture—just the ontological mystification that contemporary theory has sought to overturn in dismantling identity. On the contrary, it is only within these forces of history, language, and culture that identity can come to be. As an "answer" or "rejoinder" to assertions in the situations that surround it, as a way of "encompassing" and "addressing" these situations so as to transform them, identity requires these seemingly "external" mediums for its substance to take shape. As a rhetorical strategy, a way of working transformations through language, identity only exists in tension with that which can be transformed. Viewed from this rhetorical perspective, the substance of a constituted identity manifests the same nature that Burke identifies in substance generally: it is, just as it was in the "old philosophies," an "*act*" (RM 21). Identity always has a reason behind its constitution—a purpose that, like any constitution, it exists to enact. Identity thus can never simply "be" for rhetorical inquiry. It must *do*.

The intention I declared at the outset was to argue for identity as an important concept within rhetoric's critical vocabulary of the person. Put another way, I am arguing for a transformation of rhetoric's thinking at the level of what I have described as Burke's grammatical "problem of identity": my concern is a concern with the "terms" and "resources" available to rhetoric in "siz[ing] up" the discursive situations of human conduct (GM xvi). I hope to have demonstrated identity's analytical merits clearly enough to create a sense of the need for what the concept can offer in the study of persuasive self-presentation. Moreover, I have tried to situate identity in relation to another vital concept in this vocabulary—ethos—and especially to suggest why neither term alone will suffice in the task that Alcorn spiritedly advances, the task of "grasp[ing] the self as a rhetorical entity" (13). My focus on inferential relationships between discursively created impressions of who we are and how we act has illustrated one way in which identity and character interact toward achieving rhetorical effects. In light of how ethos and its common referent of "character" both continue to evolve in significance, much remains to be explored toward better understanding the "intrinsicness" that identity and ethos manifest (Swearingen 115). Such explorations will surely enhance our understanding of these terms of persuasive self-presentation, as well as their possible interconnections, toward better assessing how the person of the rhetor is a factor in persuasion.

Another vital term and resource of this vocabulary is, again, that for which Burke is well known: *identification.* Burke's "key term" for exploring questions of identity and persuasion, a name for both the process and product of substance-sharing between rhetor and audience, *identification* has in many ways become the rhetorical–conceptual stand-in for identity. Burke himself is at least partially responsible for this emphasis, having said much more about identification than "identity" per se—or, at least, having treated identification with a greater focus that has translated into greater accessibility. "The poetic house is built of *identifications*" (RM 84–85), Burke states in asserting discourse's identificatory framework, where these poetic houses can be any "linguistic structure" (GM 218), from "the individual poem" to "the individual person" ("Addendum" 222). From speeches to speakers, from autobiographies to autobiographers, what language builds, it builds out of identifications.

But what are identifications built of? Substance. And, as Burke makes clear, substance has but one origin: "A thing's substance is that whereof it is constituted. Hence a concern with substance is a concern with the problems of constitutionality" (GM 337–38). While deeply concerned with both identification and substance, to what extent is rhetorical theory concerned with these problems of constitutionality, a constitutionality that is the very precondition of substance, consubstantiality, and identification? If the general absence of "The Dialectic of Constitutions" from discussion of these issues is any barometer (despite it being Burke's representative text on substantiation), then a clear opportunity exists to consider how Burke's constitutional theory might enrich inquiry that opts for the now well-worn analysis of identification in rhetorical discourse. Moreover, this theory also stands to complement current work in constitutive rhetoric, allowing for the same careful scrutiny of a rhetor's acts of self-constitution that the constitution of audience identity currently enjoys. However these opportunities are pursued, continued discussion of identity, substance, and constitution promises to counter how little Burke's thinking on identity has been developed, cited in ways often too vague to be productive.[1]

As helpful as I believe this use of Burke to rhetorically question identity may be, it is not without its hazards. In particular, failing to bear in mind the dialectical nuances of constitutions in Burke's analysis can reintroduce stumbling blocks that rendered identity theoretically suspect in the first place. Chief among these potential problems is the myth of the sovereign self that identity often connotes. Self-interpretation, self-definition, self-constitution—such phraseology might easily be taken as support for that fiction of unchecked power in self-fashioning, reifications of the myopia that we are what we make ourselves to be. And, to be sure, between the covers of an autobiographical narrative lies great freedom—and perhaps great temptation—to make oneself as one wants, to constitute a desired identity with little more effort than the wave of a scepter. A too-quick reading of Burke might misread this sovereign myth in constitutions, especially in Burke's attention to the conscious deliberation that forms "voluntaristic principles" into the "enactment of human wills" a constitution represents. Worse yet, Burke's description of a constitution as a "motivational fixity" (GM 357) might impute identity to be something even more dangerous: established, unchanging, essential, as though the "circumference" of shared substance that holds its terms together were an impermeable biosphere, or the god-term that represents a shorthand of its designs a lexical deity that indeed somehow sat on high.

But identity is not that simple, nor are the constitutions to which I have likened them. The remedy against both misreadings of sovereignty and fixity is agonistic vigilance. The agon that a constitution contains in the molten fluidity of its circumfered principles; the broader, encompassing agon that is a constitution's dialectical relationship with the historically evolving scenes it addresses: both ultimately hold court over the "wishes" and "wills" a constitution would enact. More accurately, these dialectical forces co-rule with the human wills a constitution seeks to substantiate. If there is any sovereignty in identity from a Burkean rhetorical perspective, the scepter of its exercise is borne in the unbreachable collaborative grasp of human purpose, linguistic ambiguity, and temporal change. And if there is any fixity in this identity, its indomitability is only as enduring as a discursive situation's desire to see it as such, a desire more transient than the words that commit it to the page. As a final caution against the knee jerk that would see these claims about identity and textuality as expressions of ontology, it bears repeating that Burke's interest, as mine has been, is "with the analysis of *language* rather than with the analysis of '*reality*'" (GM 317). That there are differences between what *is* and what *is said* about "identity" is obvious.[2] That both are thus differently crucial to appreciating our lives as language-learned animals is as much so.

"In all places of the world," Holland et al. observe in *Identity and Agency in Cultural Worlds*, "there are ways of talking about what we might call a person's self (or selves)" (19). This is true of that place in the world we call the academy: we have *The Saturated Self* (Gergen), *The Scripted Self* (Christie et al), *The Evolving Self* (Keegan)—all of which might be seen as different ways of *Situating the Self* (Benhabib), which we better understand as we hearken to the *Voices of the Self* (Gilyard). Is there room in this swelling taxonomy for yet another self, a *rhetorical* self? Its possibility—and its indispensability—both begin to emerge when, as Calvin Schrag does in *The Self after Postmodernity* (yet another self there), we ask *who* questions of the human self rather than *what* questions. The ontologically motivated "what" questions, he explains, aim to discern "abstract universal nature." "Who" questions, however, instead seek to render "a praxis-oriented self," "the who of our quotidian and lived-through communicative practices of speaking, listening, narrating, acting, working, and playing" (4–9). This self of communicative praxis is "a rhetorical animal . . . an engaged rhetorical self" (29). Unique among its kindred selves, this is a self that allows us to focus on how the self makes itself known in language, how it expresses the realities of its experience, and how it does so with specific designs upon those with whom it speaks, listens, narrates, acts, works, plays. To such a rhetorical self, identity matters, for articulating "who I am" is one prominent linguistic means by which it can address, and perhaps even transform, the scenes it inhabits and the other selves therein. In this sense, as Charles Taylor has suggested, identity for the rhetorical self can be understood not just as an answer to the question of "who I am" but rather as "an answer to the question of who I am through a definition of where I am speaking from and to whom" (36); the self's identity is thus the "horizon" in which it is "capable of taking a stand" (Taylor, *Sources* 27).[3] And the rhetorical self is as much a practiced audience for expressions of identity as it is an astute producer of them: "The way we practice identity narrative makes a difference," Paul John Eakin asserts, because "identity narratives generate identity judgments" (141).

Taken together, these invocations of speaker, audience, and an address that elicits judgment tell us what even an obliquely rhetorical perspective, let alone a Burkean one, would conclude: identity is a rhetorical situation. All told, then, the rhetorical self may in part be characterized (identified?) by discursive commitments that prevent its coalescence into other selves that theory has helped us to name—selves for whom language may matter, but very differently so. For the theorist combating the essentialization that mortifies the self at play, "writing is . . . the black-and-white where all identity is lost" (Barthes 49).

For the theorist who would appreciate symbolic action, writing might be precisely where identity *comes to be*. For rhetorical selves, writing is clearly one place where identity comes to matter as well. Banal, common, and yet a potentially powerful persuasive strategy: as long as identity remains such a given of human experience, rhetoric must be, in some sense, given to identity.

NOTES

Chapter 1: Introduction

1. "To see anything honest in such a man as Paul . . . when he converts an hallucination into a *proof* of the resurrection of the Saviour, or even to believe his tale that he suffered from this hallucination himself—this would be a genuine *niaiserie* in a psychologist. Paul willed the end; *therefore* he also willed the means. What he himself didn't believe was swallowed readily enough by the idiots among whom he spread *his* teaching. What *he* wanted was power" (*Antichrist* 120–21).

2. The rhetorical sophistication I impute to Paul is one clear reason why Augustine admires him. In his own conversion narrative, the *Confessions*, Augustine praises Paul for demonstrating how "the defeat of the enemy is all the more conspicuous when one wins over from him a man of whom he has a particular hold *and through whom he can particularly influence others*" (167, emphasis added).

3. Several New Testament scholars have written at length about the issue of contradiction in Paul's writings generally and in the accounts of his conversion specifically (see especially Betz and Segal). For a brief review of scholarship on the likelihood and level of Paul's rhetorical education, see Kern's introduction in *Rhetoric and Galatians*.

4. Marlon B. Ross summarizes this sentiment well in a recent forum on identity politics in *New Literary History*. Ruminating in response to the question "Is there life after identity politics?," Ross notes how "behind the anxiety over the afterwards of 'identity politics' is a deeper anxiety fueling a desire to be finished with all identity for good" (834). Calhoun, Wagner, and Hall each offer helpful summaries of the issues contributing to identity's problematic theoretical status.

5. This shift I am suggesting toward examining *identity* as an experiential term or as a term of self-interpretation is akin to Terry Eagleton's call that "we begin to grasp the decentering of the subject as a transitive social action rather than some curious ontological condition" (269).

6. While Aristotle did not invent the idea that rhetoric requires "an ability to aim at commonly held opinions" (*Rhetoric* 1355a), his treatment of persuasion's reliance upon doxa (in works such as the *Rhetoric, On Sophistical Refutations*, and the *Topics*) is the earliest and most systematic. Consequently, Aristotle has most influenced contemporary rhetorical considerations of doxa (as in the work of pragmatic theorists such as Chaim Perelman and Lucie Olbrechts–Tyteca, Oswald Ducrot, Ruth Amossy, and Anne Cauquelin).

7. Distinguishing *arkhai* from *doxa*, Aristotle explains that "things are true and primary which command belief through themselves and not through anything else; for regarding the first principles of science it is unnecessary to ask any further question as to 'why'" (*Topics* 100b). Complementing Aristotle's use of *endoxa* as "commonly held opinions" or as "the 'given'" in discourse, the Liddell & Scott's *Greek-English Lexicon* notes the additional senses of *doxa* as "a notion, true or false" and "expectation."

8. As Amossy stresses, "there can be no social life, no verbal communication, no mutual persuasion without a solid background of shared opinions and beliefs" ("How" 465). Both Aristotle and those theorists who have further advanced the doxastic grounding of rhetoric acknowledge that such backgrounds of shared belief (and their attendant obviousness) are culturally specific, observing that bodies of shared beliefs can be further particularized to groups or audiences much more diminutive than an entire culture. In discussing the meaning of *endoxa* as "acceptable" in his edition of Aristotle's *Topics*, Robin Smith elaborates that "to be acceptable is to be acceptable *to someone*, or to some *type* of person." Accordingly, "the *endoxa* . . . do not form a single list; instead, there are various lists of typical beliefs associated with types of person" (xxiii).

9. Psychological and philosophical literatures most commonly treat the sense of identity I am elaborating here as "self-identity," "personal identity," or "ego identity." The terms *identity* and *self* are often used interchangeably, within this literature as much as in both rhetorical studies and contemporary culture. Because the "conceptual morass" that such loose synonymy has fostered is one key obstacle to clearer theoretical uses of identity (Leary and Tangney 7), I follow Charles Taylor's more precise formulation of their relationship. Taylor defines identity as "the identity of the self, and the self is understood as an object to be known"; identity is thus "the self's understanding of itself" (*Sources* 49; see especially Taylor's chapter "Self-Interpreting Animals" in *Human Agency and Language*). Such approaches to identity as a term of interpretation are not unique to the humanities. As Peter Wagner notes in his survey of social-scientific treatments of the concept, "the safeguarding of identity entails steady work at the maintenance of continuity and coherence or, in other words, at the interpretation of one's own life" (47). Many contend, following Taylor, that such interpretive understanding of self and identity is the only kind of self-knowledge to which we can aspire. Given that the self "is not like an object in the usually understood sense" in that "we don't have selves in the way we have hearts or livers," as matters of physiological fact, "to ask what a person is, in abstraction from his or her

self-interpretations, is to ask a fundamentally misguided question, one to which in principle there couldn't be an answer" (*Sources* 34).

10. For further illustration of the nature and function of what I am calling "personal truths" and "personal realities" in self-interpretation, see Carol Winkelmann's engaging rhetorical analysis of the "personal theologies" of battered women. Also helpful in understanding how identity is shaped and expressed in light of these personal realities is Karen Tracy's *Everyday Talk,* in which Tracy enacts a stated "rhetorical perspective" on identity, or one that "assumes that people talk in particular ways in order to accomplish desired identities" (26). As to the specifically narrative nature of people's expression of defining personal truths or experiences, see especially Dan McAdams's *The Stories We Live By* and Paul John Eakin's excellent *How Our Lives Become Stories.*

11. Psychologist and autobiography scholar Jerome Bruner refers to this broader cultural discourse in which I am situating identity as the "folk psychology" or "ethnopsychology" of a given culture—"a culture's account of what makes human beings tick" (*Acts* 13). Demonstrating the complementarity of his approach and my own rhetorical treatment of this cultural discourse in terms of doxa, Bruner notes that folk psychology is something that most who share it would simply call "common sense" (*Acts* 35).

12. For reasons of focus I only mention here rhetorical treatments of identity that are most explicitly relevant to a constitutive approach. For a brief review of "constitutive" perspectives on rhetoric, see Jasinski. Further worth consulting, while not labeling itself "constitutive" in the approaches it demonstrates, is the Fall 1997 special issue of *Argumentation and Advocacy* on "Argument and Identity." Wayne Booth helpfully articulates what are now basic premises about viewing identity dialectically and rhetorically in *Modern Dogma and the Rhetoric of Assent.* Especially pertinent to constitutive rhetoric is Booth's discussion of "The Self as a Field of Selves" (126–37) and his discussion there of the self as "literally constituted of other selves who are in turn unthinkable except in matrices of human converse" (132). See also Frederick J. Antczak's extension of Booth in *Thought and Character: The Rhetoric of Democratic Education.*

13. "Constitutive rhetorics . . . capture alienated subjects by rearticulating existing subject positions so as to contain or resolve experienced dialectical contradictions between the world and its discourses. The process by which an audience member enters into a new subject position is therefore not one of persuasion. It is akin more to one of conversion that ultimately results in an act of recognition of the 'rightness' of a discourse and of one's identity with its reconfigured subject position" (Charland 142). Black's description of this process in "Idioms of Social Identity" reads as a patent definition of *conversion,* especially in its emphasis on "crisis" in identity formation and transformation: "The choice of social identity rarely occurs in tranquility . . . [and is] commonly manifested as an urgent crisis. . . . The crisis may culminate finally in political disassociation, and the displacement of previous associations by a different configuration of social attachments, sometimes a new invention, sometimes a rehabilitated memory" (23).

Chapter 2: Kenneth Burke's "Problem[s] of Identity"

1. This is not to say that identity in Burke has gained no attention whatsoever. Frank Lentricchia's *Criticism and Social Change*, for example, an early effort to utilize what Burke has said about identity, offers a thoughtful consideration of Burke's notions of identity in relation to contemporary theoretical interrogations of the "'free' subject" (71). In a similar vein, Christine Oravec's "Kenneth Burke's Concept of Association and the Complexity of Identity," which limits its consideration to Marxian aspects of identity in Burke, illuminates "association" in *A Rhetoric of Motives* as one important mechanism by which identities are constructed. For the best recent discussions of identity in Burke, see Crusius's treatment of identity as one of three key Burkean "postPhilosophical themes" (34–64); and Beth Eddy's *The Rites of Identity*.

2. The effort to bring Burke's "Symbolic of Motives" to print is nothing short of epic. Commenting on its problematic status, William Rueckert, who worked actively with Burke in assembling prospective versions of the volume, notes that "it was really mostly finished by the mid-fifties, though parts of it were not published until later." Granting that "we will never know what else Burke might have written as part of the 'Symbolic,'" he nevertheless asserts that "Burke's dramatistic poetics is certainly 'complete' in the sense that all the essential elements of it are present in the existing published essays. . . . In other words, anyone who wishes to study the 'Symbolic'—certainly Burke's major statement on the nature of literature, its function and significance as an act of language, and his most comprehensive presentation and demonstration of the methodology developed for the dramatistic analysis and interpretation of literature—can readily do so" (*Encounters* 77–79; see also "Kenneth Burke's" in *Unending Conversations*). Rueckert makes available an additional version of the symbolic in *Essays toward a Symbolic of Motives*. However, given his observation that we still "lack . . . a definitive version of it as selected and arranged by Burke" ("he would not agree to any arrangement of it while he was alive"), I yet prefer to regard "A Symbolic of Motives" as unfinished. Regardless of this question of the text's completion, Rueckert notes that all three known versions of "A Symbolic of Motives" (including an incomplete manuscript version found at Burke's home in Andover) "fulfill . . . his own definition that the original *A Symbolic of Motives* should be devoted to the study of individual, self-contained symbolic actions and structures," as I have emphasized here in discussing the text's contribution to a Burkean inquiry into identity (*Essays* xiv–xxi).

3. The emphasis on interpretation in *A Grammar of Motives* is more clearly signaled in *Permanence and Change*, where Burke inaugurates his defining concern with "motive" by introducing the concept in the book's first section, "On Interpretation" (PC 18). As Barbara A. Biesecker concurs, the *Grammar* can be summarized as an inquiry into "the practical art of interpreting symbolic acts" (24). The function of Burke's grammatical perspective as the grounding of his rhetorical and symbolic perspectives finds expression in 1953's "Curriculum Criticum," in which he indicates that "the *Grammar* is the grounding of the *Motivorum* project" (218).

4. "Looking at the matter from the dramatist point of view, we should expect instruments of precision not to avoid the paradox of substance, but to confront it more precisely" (GM 260).

5. As Burke further explains, "the classical notion of clear persuasive intent isn't an accurate fit . . . for describing the ways in which the members of a group promote social cohesion by acting rhetorically upon themselves and others" (RM xiv).

6. While "substance" is not a key concept of Burke's discussion of motive in *Permanence and Change,* Burke does discuss in this text the essentially persuasive nature of any statement about motives that the *Rhetoric* later develops—the fact that "the assigning of motives is a matter of *appeal.*" In addition Burke describes this process of appeal, of how a writer "translate[s his thesis] into a system of motivations which will be cogent with his readers," in terms that presage his use of identification to question the relationship between consciousness and persuasion: this process of translation in appeal, Burke notes, "happens so spontaneously that the writer may even learn to think 'naturally' in the terms of such motivations" (PC 24–25).

7. Efforts to make such distinctions between different possible senses of identification have been common since the *Rhetoric* first appeared. L. Virginia Holland's *Counterpoint: Kenneth Burke and Aristotle's Theories of Rhetoric* similarly describes the function of identification as both the means and ends of rhetoric (21–38, especially 28–30). Lentricchia discusses identification differently, distinguishing between "identification with" and "identification of" in discourse (148–49). And Burke himself notes that "the term 'identification' can be applied in at least three ways" (*Dramatism* 28). This flexibility in application seems to be precisely the merit of the term for Burke.

8. Burke continues: "Here are ambiguities of substance. In being identified with B, A is 'substantially one' with a person other than himself. Yet at the same time he remains unique, an individual locus of motives. Thus he is both joined and separate, at once a distinct substance and consubstantial with another" (RM 21). While the *Rhetoric* develops senses of identification in relation to ambiguity and substance that are not drawn out in *Attitudes toward History,* these senses certainly seem implicit in Burke's general treatment of identification there. More specifically, Burke's later rhetorical specifications of identification (as both an analytical tool to "mark off the areas of rhetoric" and a productive strategy of rhetorical discourse) might be seen as fruitions that lend the principle even more to his interest in the "characteristic responses of people in their forming and reforming of congregations" (RM xiii; ATH 1).

9. Burke hints at the differences between "the character of the individual poem and the character of the individual person" in referring to them as the "poetic . . . dimension" and the "ethical dimension" of language, respectively. In *Language as Symbolic Action*'s "Poetics in Particular, Language in General" (the second of this volume's "Five Summarizing Essays" and a text that was to be included in "A Symbolic of Motives"), Burke further defines this "ethical dimension of language" as "the ways in which, through language, we express our characters, whether or not we intend to do so" (28). As he explains in his 1967 "Addendum" to *Counter-Statement*'s

"Curriculum Criticum," the Symbolic almost became two separate volumes on the poetic and the ethical dimensions of language; "but now that so many of my speculations about Poetics have been treated in the theoretical and analytical pieces of which *Language as Symbolic Action* is comprised, I dare believe I can revert to my original plan and finish the project in one more book" (222). My merger here of text and individual beneath the head of poetics appeals to me inasmuch as it represents the same type of merger between key concepts that Burke tries to establish in the motives texts I have previously discussed: between motive and substance in the *Grammar* (where substance is motivating and motive is substantiating); and between persuasion and identification in the *Rhetoric* (where identifications are persuasive and persuasion is the result of "stylized identifications") (RM 46).

10. An appendix to *Permanence and Change*, "On Human Behavior Considered 'Dramatistically,'" for example, claims that "man being a generically biological organism, the ideal terminology [for "the discussion of . . . social behavior"] must present his symbolic behavior as grounded in biological conditions" (274–75). *Permanence and Change* offers a thorough discussion of these metabiological groundings: see especially "Outlines of a 'Metabiology'" (232–36) and "Recalcitrance" (255–61). In the latter, Burke asserts that the choice of poetics as his "*starting point*" in human relations—"*the situation common to all, the creative, assertive, synthetic act*"—is a choice based upon "the most undeniable point of reference we have; the biological . . . a point of view biologically rooted seems to be as near to 'rock bottom' as human thought could take us" (261).

11. As Burke summarizes the purpose of his three planned motives texts: "the whole project aims to round out an analysis of language in keeping with the author's favorite notion that, man being the specifically language-using animal, an approach to human motivations should be made through the analysis of language" ("Curriculum Criticum" 218). Psychological aspects of the individual thus represent one area of concern within this broader interest in language. "The individual in his uniqueness falls under the head of Symbolic," Burke explains, "but one should not thereby assume that what is known as 'individual psychology' wholly meets the same test" (RM 37).

12. So quips Burke's dialectically attired Impresario in introducing the "Prologue in Heaven," reminding us of the "vexing fact" that any "'solution' raises further problems. (Confidentially, that's 'the dialectic')" (*Rhetoric of Religion* 275).

13. Greig Henderson states that "in Burke's way of thinking, the various levels of discourse—grammatical, rhetorical, symbolical, and ethical—intersect ambiguously" (153). But rather than merely intersecting *ambiguously*, they intersect precisely *in their concern with ambiguity itself*—in their focus on the workings of verbal dialectic in each of these levels of discourse (see, for example, "Position Epitomized" [GM 335–38], particularly the concluding paragraph of the section). This inexorable dialectic between merger and division at the heart of language demonstrates one sense of Burke's claim that rhetoric "is rooted in an essential function of language itself, a function that is wholly realistic and is continually born anew" (RM 43).

Chapter 3: Toward a Poetics and Rhetoric of Identity

1. The importance of "The Dialectic of Constitutions" in demonstrating Burke's approach to substance and motive is often missed, and the section is commonly misread as merely another "application" of the pentad—as in Vitanza, for example ("Thought" 166). Burke specifically counters this misreading by asserting the constitutional grounding of the pentad in his "Questions and Answers about the Pentad."

2. Burke remarks in his 1971 Heinz Werner lecture, "Biology, Psychology, Words": "Recently, in going over reviews that appeared when the *Grammar* was first published, I was struck by the fact that no reviewer, to my knowledge, discussed the section on 'The Dialectic of Constitutions.' Yet several reviewers raised objections that would have been irrelevant had this portion of the book been systematically considered" (*Dramatism* 23–24).

3. Unfortunately, a text of Burke's presentation is not known to exist.

4. As Burke states at the outset of "The Representative Anecdote," the section that opens part 2 of *A Grammar of Motives,* "Scope and Reduction," "Men seek for vocabularies that will be faithful *reflections* of reality" (GM 59).

5. An additional illustration of how Burke sees the constitutive as the basis for the admonitory—how *what is* leads to *what should be*—can be found in "Dialectician's Hymn," in which Burke discusses the relationship between "declarative" and "optative" statements: "a very clear way to illustrate the meaning of an act is to say, 'The actor, by this act, is saying, in effect . . .'—then give the equivalent in a declarative sentence. Thus the practice of shaking hands after a game says in effect: 'There are no hard feelings. The rivalry does not extend beyond the confines of the game.' A declarative sentence, in turn, may often be best illustrated by the optative, as in resolutions and petitions. Thus, the function of the statement, '*There are* no hard feelings . . . etc.' can be most clearly conveyed by translation into a different grammatical idiom, '*Let there be* no hard feelings . . . etc.'" (PLF 447).

6. A constitution, as Burke notes, "is 'binding' upon the future in the sense that it has centered attention upon one calculus of motivation rather than some other" (GM 368).

7. This claim counters, or at least complicates, the fact that the pentad is typically seen as the most important theoretical contribution of Burke's *Grammar.* The pentad might indeed be the most accessible or applicable element of the text, but, in a sense, the pentad itself is an extension of the more foundational theory of substance and constitutionality in "The Dialectic of Constitutions" that subtends it: "In the pentad, all roads lead to the act," Wess notes, "that is, *to the constitution*" (*Rhetoric* 181, emphasis added).

8. "A Constitution is but a partial act; the only truly total act would be the act of a Supreme Founding Father who founded the Universal Substance, the Constitution-beneath-the-Constitution, the scene in which the Constitution of 1789 was an enactment" (GM 374)

9. As Burke notes elsewhere, "The 'same' act can be defined 'differently,' depending upon the 'circumference' of the scene or overall situation *in terms of which* we choose to locate it" (*Language* 360); "Any change of the circumference in terms of which an act is viewed implies a corresponding change in one's view of the quality of the act's motivation" ("Dramatism" 446).

10. In addition to his extensive remarks in *A Grammar of Motives*, Burke explicitly argues the importance of circumference in "Questions and Answers about the Pentad," "Biology, Psychology, Words" (from *Dramatism and Development*), and "What Are the Signs of What?: A Dramatistic Theory of 'Entitlement'" (*Language as Symbolic Action* 359–79), to name a few prominent sources.

11. "But ideals are never practicable; indeed, they are *by definition* something that you don't attain; they are merely *directions* in which you aim. (You can't hit 'North,' for instance, though you may hit a target placed to the north of you)" (GM 344).

12. As Burke further notes, constitutional *ideals* and *principles*, "as terms bearing upon motivation, . . . contain the ambiguities of the 'substantial' and the 'potential'" (GM 360). Stephen Bygrave develops this sense of ambiguity helpfully, and particularly its relevance to Burkean constitutions, in his discussion of the "alchemic center" of Burke's work (89–93). Virginia Anderson also discusses how the inherent ambiguity within and between constitutional principles is mitigated by what Burke terms "proportionalizing" and "essentializing" strategies (see also GM 380–84). For an exceptionally clear summary of the legal ramifications of Burkean constitutional ambiguity, see Witteveen and van Klink.

13. Burke originally planned to begin his "material on rhetorical strategies and symbolic acts" with a section entitled "The Constitutional Wish." Regressions into the "preparatory groundwork" that this section seemed to require led Burke to the pentad as an explanation of "why I thought I should begin a study of *human* relations with a study of *constitutional* relations." Thus Burke's remarks on the idea of a constitution as a "representative anecdote" for the study of human relations, "The Dialectic of Constitutions," now sit as the penultimate section of the *Grammar* (GM 323–24). Wess provides a more detailed account of this development of "The Dialectic of Constitutions"—what Burke describes as "the saga of what all was involved in my getting that first draft [of the *Grammar*] turned around" ("Questions" 333). See Wess, *Rhetoric* 138–39.

Chapter 4: Religious Radicalism Becomes Her

1. Day recalls of Spellman's staunch anti-Communism, "He was a member of the church militant. I think he'd have gladly gone off to lead a march on the Kremlin, if he only could have found others to join him" (quoted in Coles, *Dorothy Day* 82).

2. While nearly all of Day's writings are autobiographical in some sense, I refer specifically here to *The Eleventh Virgin* (1924), *From Union Square to Rome* (1939), *On Pilgrimage* (1948), *The Long Loneliness* (1952), and *Loaves and Fishes* (1963). *The Long Loneliness* has been in near-continuous print since its original appearance, while texts such as *From Union Square to Rome* have long been unavailable. The most recent edition of *The Long Loneliness* (1997, Harper San Francisco) further attests

to the importance of this text through an amended subtitle on the cover that declares it "the autobiography of the legendary Catholic social activist." For more on how Day's autobiographical writings throughout her life bespeak different attempts "to construct a 'life' that enacted her beliefs and that appealed to various readerships," see Jablonski (196).

3. As many of Day's biographers note, the *Catholic Worker* staff were generally disconcerted by the presence of Dwight MacDonald at their headquarters, given that the article represented both the movement's and Day's "first introduction to a general segment of the educated public." MacDonald's reaction to what he saw at the *Catholic Worker* was more than approving, however. In fact, he was so impressed with Dorothy Day personally that he broke with journalistic practice and allowed her to read and even to alter the text of his two articles before they went to press (Miller, *Dorothy Day* 429–30).

4. Nancy Roberts's *Dorothy Day and the Catholic Worker* provides the most comprehensive index of circulation rates for the *Catholic Worker* from its appearance in May 1933 (see especially "Appendix: The Circulation of the *Catholic Worker*, 1933–1983," 179–82). These rates are compiled from various sources, including Day's personal notes, and competing records often exist for circulation in any given month.

5. The week prior to the publication of *The Long Loneliness*, Day was participating in an Insurance and Allied Workers protest against a court order that the fraternal insurance organization be liquidated for fear that its Marxist-affiliated leadership would surrender its assets to Moscow in the event of a war. In the weeks immediately following the appearance of her autobiography, she was engaging in a nine-date speaking tour in cities that included Washington, D.C., Pittsburgh, Louisville, Phoenix, St. Louis, and Memphis (traveling by bus, as was her custom) ("On Pilgrimage," February 1952, 4). Given such constant promotion of her movement and its ideals, Day was most decidedly disturbed at what were becoming frequent references in the past tense to the Catholic Worker Movement's social viability. Even MacDonald's praising essay distinguishes the movement's present state from its more notable past, "back in the days when the Catholic Workers were playing a conspicuous part in the labor movement, the fight for racial justice, and in the political struggle with the Communists" (October 11, 1952, 52).

6. Day elsewhere resists labeling *The Long Loneliness* an autobiography and further hints at the purpose-driven character of her autobiographical writings I discuss here: "It is always called my autobiography but it is really a selection of periods of my life searching for God and not at all a story giving the whole truth. . . . It is not the truth about me . . . [but] only part of the truth" (quoted in Forest 213).

7. Day's time in the Village, as Miller notes, was a "high point" of her life (*Dorothy Day* 82). In one of her most interesting assignments for the *Call*, Day interviewed Leon Trotsky in New York prior to his return to Russia. Less than a month later, on 21 March 1917, she joined the throng at Madison Square Garden in celebrating the fall of Czar Nicholas and the beginning of the Russian Revolution. Leaving her position at the *Call* after seven months, Day next began work at a much more renowned New York paper, the *Masses*, where she soon became fast friends with this

left-wing Greenwich Village weekly's editors—Max Eastman and Floyd Dell, two of the early twentieth century's most important figures in liberal advocacy journalism. She further enjoyed the close companionship of Village habitués such as fellow journalist Hypolite Havel, Terry Carlin (an Irish anarchist and former acquaintance of the Haymarket martyrs), poet Max Bodenheim, Caroline Gordon, Kenneth Burke, Malcolm Cowley, Peggy Baird (soon to become Peggy Baird Cowley), John Dos Passos, and Eugene O'Neill. As Malcolm Cowley reminisces, Day was a valued companion both for her enthusiastic conversation and her equally enthusiastic tippling: at a basement nook where they often convened (known by its familiars as the Hell Hole), she is reputed to have drunk the local gang of "petty thieves and small-time gamblers," the Hudson Dusters, under the table (69).

8. Day humorously recalls her role in this trial: "I was a bad witness for the state and a good one for the defense" (LL 87).

9. As Day also notes in her description of life in the Village, "Certainly I felt again and again the need to go to church to kneel, to bow my head in prayer. It was a blind instinct, one might say, and I was not conscious of praying. But I went. I put myself there in the atmosphere of prayer—it was an act of the will" (LL 85).

10. For example, Day does not mention her pregnancy through an affair she began in 1918. She had an abortion in 1919, leading her to a "rebound marriage" and European passage with Berkeley Tobey in 1920. The marriage dissolved after only a year, and Day and Tobey parted company without ever officially divorcing. Much of this material is referenced in Day's thinly veiled autobiographical novel, *The Eleventh Virgin*.

11. Forster Batterham was also, coincidentally, Kenneth Burke's brother-in-law.

12. Mark S. Massa observes in *Catholics and American Culture* that Day "never considered herself as other than a dutiful daughter of the church: it would never have occurred to her that she was crafting a 'radical' or 'left-wing' brand of Catholicism. She was simply implementing the commands of the gospel and of every pope since 1891" (127). Similarly, Piehl comments extensively on the singularity of the Catholic Worker Movement in that it "enthusiastically embraced the orthodox tradition as the fount and strength of its radical social attitudes and actions" (*Bread* 138).

13. As Day details, there are both Spiritual and Corporal Works of Mercy, each comprising seven specific practices. "The Spiritual Works of Mercy are: to admonish the sinner, to instruct the ignorant, to counsel the doubtful, to comfort the sorrowful, to bear wrongs patiently, to forgive all injuries, and to pray for the living and the dead. The Corporal Works are to feed the hungry, to give drink to the thirsty, to clothe the naked, to ransom the captive, to harbor the harborless, to visit the sick, and to bury the dead" (quoted in Ellsberg 89). In a remark that nicely illustrates the religious and radical synthesis of the Catholic Worker Movement, Day notes that "we have always classed picket lines and distribution of literature among these works" as well (LL 220).

14. Burke's most sustained discussion of conversion ("Secular Conversions," in *Permanence and Change*) describes such transformations in a way that maps perfectly onto his later constitutional concepts, as I am applying them to define conversion.

Burke notes how Paul, the figure in whom "we find the phenomena of conversion at their intensest," illustrates conversion as a "symbolic reconstruction" whereby "old linkages were ripped apart, [and] new linkages were welded" because of "the forceful collapse of his earlier orientation." Further validating my description of conversion as the overall transformation of an identity's substance, Burke observes that "when a man so vigorous as Saul had of a sudden ceased to be Saul, in that dramatic interim between the loss of his old self and his rebirth as Paul, we may expect to find his structure shaken to its very roots" (156). See also Burke's description of conversion in psychoanalysis as the creation of "a fresh terminology of motives to replace the patient's painful terminology of motives . . . of cause, purpose, and prophecy," earlier in this chapter of *Permanence* (125). These same observations pervade Burke's later excursus on conversion's other defining father (and his longest treatment of a single author), "Verbal Action in St. Augustine's *Confessions*" (*Rhetoric of Religion* 43–171).

Chapter 5: Ethos, Identity, Lies

1. Ethos as a specifically rhetorical concept predates Aristotle's *Rhetoric*, as Eckart Schütrumpf illustrates, although its usage is limited (it appears a total of six times in the writing of Isocrates, for example, as Rosa Eberly has discussed). Ethos serves important critical functions in disciplines other than rhetoric, but character remains a dominant aspect of its meaning there as well. Clifford Geertz, for instance, summarizes *ethos* in anthropological usage in noting that "a people's ethos is the tone, character, and quality of their life, its moral and aesthetic style and mood" (126).

2. As Brock clarifies in defining *neoconservatism* (what he also refers to as the "Third Generation of conservatives"): "Barry Goldwater made the GOP a conservative party; Ronald Reagan made it a winning electoral majority; now it was our turn." Neoconservatism's agenda, he explains, "was pretty much Reagan's: militant anti-Communism, tax cuts to benefit corporations and the rich, dismantlement of affirmative action and social welfare programs, deregulation, and union-busting" (BR 32, 24).

3. This is not to say, however, that physically observable features do not lead to judgments about identity, which they often do. In a more robust sense, however, *identity* involves not just observable attributes but also aspects of self-understanding or self-interpretation that cannot be accessed until they are made available by the person whose identity is in question. For a clear articulation of *character* in its doxastic sense as moral agency that I treat here, see Lester Hunt.

4. See especially Baumlin's entry on "Ethos" in the *Encyclopedia of Rhetoric* for a review of conceptions of the term from classical rhetoric to the present, considered in light of the models of selfhood predominant in each historical period.

5. As Johnson explains, "the overall emphasis of rhetoric treatises designed for the academy and for the general public since the Middle Ages has maintained the Aristotelian–Ciceronian approach to ethos, which stress[es] the importance of adjusting presentation of character to audience and subject." In opposition to the positions

of Plato, Quintilian, and Augustine, who regard virtue as necessarily "intrinsic" to the speaker "even before the rhetorical process begins" if it is to be present in discourse, "the modern pedagogical tradition in rhetoric has been governed by the pragmatic and relativistic interpretation of ethos formulated by Aristotle" ("Ethos" 244–45; see as well Johnson's "Ethos and the Aims of Rhetoric").

6. For an especially helpful discussion of Aristotle on the problems of inferences between real and artistic ethos, see Garver 195–201.

7. While *persona* (literally, a "mask") originates as a term of inquiry in literary studies, the concept has been part of rhetorical theory as well at least since Edwin Black's influential consideration of "the second persona." For what is still the clearest discussion of the differences between ethos and persona, see Cherry.

8. While I do not intend to find theoretical motes in the eyes of others, some illustration of this subsumption or collapse seems warranted. See, for example, the vague confluence of ethos and identity in Blair and Michel; and Frobish. Halloran encapsulates this indistinct interchangeability well in his observation that "the ritual acts that manifest our group identity or ethos are the very same acts that form it" (60). There are obvious reasons for the hypertrophy of *ethos*, a venerable term of rhetorical theory, to supplant *identity*, a comparatively modern term driven more by culture than theory. (*Identity* recently titled both a major motion picture and an NBC television game show; when was the last time *ethos* graced a marquee or a prime-time lineup?) Another contributing factor is surely *identity*'s enduring stigma as a theoretical naïveté, whereas *ethos* has much more successfully made the transition from Aristotle to a postmodern aesthetic, as in the work of Foucault (see, for example, Foucault's use of *ethos* in "What Is Enlightenment?" and Vitanza's "Concerning a Postclassical *Ethos*").

9. Emphasizing his longing for some secure sense of identity, a longing heightened by this question of his biological origin, Brock recalls that "I made up stories to myself, and occasionally to others, about where I might have come from" (BR 12).

10. In fairness to the text, Brock does at various points depict if not a rational basis for some of his actions then at least his conscious awareness of some of the "moral wrongs" he perpetrates. However, these acknowledgments seem more like concessions to readers who expect him to own something of his actions than they do challenges to the overriding message of the narrative: that he does what he does because, as he summarizes, "the conservatives had bought my brain" (BR 162).

11. For example, relating his fight not to be ousted from the *Daily Cal*, Brock claims that "all I understood was that I was being targeted in a campaign by the left to recall me from my post as editor for speaking my mind. . . . I was determined to stand my ground and fight, all the more so because, as I saw it, the fight was not about Grenada, but about the First Amendment" (BR 6).

12. In saying that identity claims meet with increased acceptance and decreased scrutiny in comparison to character, I am again not saying that identity cannot be fictionalized where character can: speakers or writers can make pretenses about *who they are* just as easily as they can about *how they act*. I can manipulate discourse to create the impression that I am Norwegian, or Mennonite, or a mother, or a Holocaust

survivor—even if I am none of these things—in much the same way I can manipulate discourse to persuade you that I am trustworthy, or prudent, or lecherous, or greedy—even if I similarly possess no such virtues or vices. But whatever the circumstances that prompt us to question the realness or authenticity of the identity that a writer or speaker advances, they are much less common than those that provoke our questioning of the authenticity of character, the "inherence" that may or may not inform its "artistic accomplishment" in discourse (Hyde xvi).

13. Brock tells, "I received the following email, under the heading 'XXX.' Drudge wrote: 'Laura [Ingraham] spreading stuff about you and me being fuck buddies. I should only be so lucky'" (BR 283).

14. My discussion of persona emphasizes its literary origin and function as a "mask," or that which is understood in discourse to hold some distance from the actual person of the author or speaker. For obvious reasons, such a concept falls flat in the analysis of autobiographical conversion narratives, which can only create a convincing sense of personal transformation to the degree that distance between the real author and the author in the text is collapsed. Ethos, however, is much more fluid in its ability both to stand apart from and to align itself with the actual person of the rhetor. Beyond the use of "second persona" in the rhetorical criticism of Black, Hammerback, and Jensen that I have already mentioned, see Michael Leff and Ebony Utley's use of both *ethos* and *persona* in analyzing "the constitution of self and the instrumental uses of character" in Martin Luther King Jr.'s "Letter from Birmingham Jail" (37).

Chapter 6: Identity beyond Agency

1. Butler notes the indebtedness of this claim about gender and identity to Nietzsche's familiar tenet that "there is no 'being' behind doing, effecting, becoming; 'the doer' is merely a fiction added to the deed—the deed is everything" (quoted in *Gender Trouble* 25).

2. In keeping with McCloskey, I use the terms *transgender* and *transsexuality* interchangeably throughout (although, as she rightly observes, *transsexuality* has more pronounced medical connotations than *transgenderedness*).

3. *Crossing* is written almost entirely in the third person, with "Donald," "Dee," and "Deirdre" referring to McCloskey before her converting realization of her female gender identity, during her legal and surgical transition period, and after her completed gender transformation, respectively (the memoir is divided into three corresponding parts). I use "McCloskey" throughout to refer to present-day Deirdre McCloskey as the author of the memoir, as distinct from the "Deirdre" constituted in the text itself. While I am unable to reproduce the text's original typography here, McClosky represents all her internal monologues in bold italics. This strategy ultimately complements the rhetorical aims of her text, for it amplifies the reality and importance of the interiority—the "felt" character—that she argues is an essential component of gender identity.

4. The moment of conversion in *Crossing* seems particularly constructed around this idea of the absence of agency, as I have identified it. Indeed, as Donald submits

to his realization that "*I* am *a woman*," the entirety of Donald's ability to act seems to disappear, even to the extent that, as McCloskey notes, "the car *drove itself*" (51, emphasis added).

5. In their discussion of "conversion as a non-religious phenomenon," Christopher Lamb and M. Darrol Bryant note how "coming out as a gay man or lesbian woman frequently leads to a complete transformation of life" such as that traditionally associated with religious conversion experiences (15). While their remarks are specific to homosexuality, McCloskey's epiphany illustrates that this observation seems equally true in relation to transsexual comings-out as well.

6. McCloskey's article ultimately obtained a much wider readership than the field of economics. Her remarks there were later reprinted in *Lingua Franca* in the early spring of 1996, and then again in shortened form in *Harper's* in July 1996.

7. McCloskey frequently criticizes this assumption that the more or less permanent nature of surgical reassignment justifies the extensive psychiatric gatekeeping of the *Standards of Care*. As she asserts in an extended argument by analogy, "Having a baby is well and truly irreversible more so than gender reassignment. A new human being is brought into the world. Well, shouldn't everyone have many years of psychological-psychiatric counseling before having a child? And getting married, though reversible at some cost, like cheek implants, is pretty serious too. So likewise is choosing a career, or buying a house, or taking up golf" (146).

8. McCloskey expresses her disenchantment both with the *Standards of Care* and with the Harry Benjamin International Gender Dysphoria Association generally, given how "the self-appointed committee that had issued [the *Standards*] tried in 1997 to make them worse, with no scientific evidence and no representation from gender crossers" (72).

9. Both the American Psychiatric Association and American Psychological Association have endorsed such definitions of homosexuality, and McCloskey draws on them heavily to argue that the continued diagnosis of gender identity disorders contradicts these definitions. As Katherine K. Wilson explains, "if homosexuality and transgender identity were classified as disorders for essentially the same reasons [prior to 1973 in the DSM], then it remains unclear how those reasons uphold the continued inclusion of diagnostic categories for Gender Identity Disorder . . . in the DSM-IV today" (Online). McCloskey, however, in keeping with her goal of gender education, suggests that this continued inclusion is primarily a problem of awareness; it persists because, unlike the prevalence of homosexuality, "there are so few crossers that no one bothers to care" (CM 147).

10. As Leslie Feinberg explains in *Trans Liberation*, the ineffective handling of transsexual patients is not simply a problem of prejudice: "Even well-intentioned health care providers can be hampered in their approach to trans patients based on what they've been taught is natural" (83).

11. After hearing about Donald's arrest at the Chicago SSHA conference, the Speech Communication Association, demonstrating the "usually timid" character of academic organizations, cancelled his participation. (The SSHA, however, much to McCloskey's clear appreciation in the text, helped Donald find a lawyer in Chicago,

showed up at his trial in protest, and passed a resolution condemning his unreasonable seizure [117].)

Chapter 7: Black Elk Speaks and Is Spoken

1. Burke elaborates this sense of *constitution* as a "dialectical term" in *The Philosophy of Literary Form* by distinguishing "dialectical terms" from "positive terms." Positive terms, such as "apple . . . do not require an opposite to define them"; "we do not require, to understand it, the concept of a 'counter-apple" (109n). But a constitution, as an "answer" or "rejoinder" to assertions in a surrounding situation, is clearly a different matter. In the case of the U.S. Constitution, for example, the framers articulated rejoinders or "principles" that were "dialectically defined" in response to a very specific opposition: "the Crown." "The position of the Crown," as Burke notes, "was a necessary term in giving meaning to the people's counter-assertions," an opposition that can thus be said to "cooperate" with the Constitution in making it meaningful (110n).

2. The terms *Sioux* and *Lakota* are often used interchangeably, but *Lakota* is held by the Native Americans to whom it refers as the more authentic designation of their culture. (*Sioux,* as Steltenkamp notes, is "the shortened form of an Ottawa word" for the Lakota, and it "eventually became the colloquial English word used when Lakota referred to themselves" [*Black Elk* 4].) *Oglala* refers to one of seven different tribal distinctions within the Lakota.

3. A more accurate reading of the reasons for Neihardt's emendation seems to be not that he wanted to problematize the text's authorship but rather that he sought to call attention to his own "creative and editorial" function in this "work of art with two collaborators"; "I was the tool—no, the medium—he needed for what he wanted to get said" (qtd. in McCluskey 238).

4. As Kaye summarizes, "The poetic logic of the whole [*Cycle of the West*] is that the defeat of the Lakotas becomes a kind of fortunate fall giving rise to the new nation of the Jedediah Smiths and Hugh Glasses who, in conquering the land and the people, themselves assume the virtues of their valiant but defeated foes" (162).

5. The complexity of Black Elk's vision merits a more detailed summary than what I am able to present here. There are several existing discussions that do this complexity justice—see, for example, R. Todd Wise, "The Great Vision of Black Elk as Literary Ritual," as well as "The Great Vision" in DeMallie's *Sixth Grandfather* (111–42), where DeMallie comments at length on the differences between the transcripts of Black Elk's retelling of his vision and its representation in Neihardt's *Black Elk Speaks.*

6. Such questions of authenticity likely arose in response to Deloria's observation in his 1979 introduction to *Black Elk Speaks* that "it is, admittedly, difficult to discover if we are talking with Black Elk or John Neihardt" (xiv). The classically held starting point for the debate that ensued is David H. Brumble and Karl Kroeber's "Reasoning Together" (1981). Kaye notes that "although the book did not sell particularly well in its first edition, its reissue . . . at the beginning of the 1960s made it not only a campus classic among hippies but also an instrument of rebirth for the Red

Power movement" (158). McCluskey comments in 1972 that *Black Elk Speaks* "is an underground classic fast coming above ground" (231). Her speculation as to the reason for this "recent popularity" further indicates how the "situation" of the text's address had shifted significantly from that of its original appearance: whereas its (critical) success in the early 1930s had been primarily in its representation of "the plight of the disempowered . . . designed to shock a middle-class readership into a greater awareness of widespread suffering" (Staub 425–26), McCluskey locates its newfound appeal in how it "seems to speak deeply to the twentieth-century yearning for simpler times and a more coherent universe" and in "the beauty with which that time and that view are presented" (231).

7. The term is Robert Sayre's from his early attempt to distinguish different genres of Native American literature, a literature that, as Krupat notes in 1985, was not yet part of the American literary canon. Krupat distinguishes "Indian autobiographies" such as *Black Elk Speaks*—texts produced through "three-part collaboration between a white editor-amanuensis," "a Native 'subject," and "a mixedblood interpreter/translator"—from "autobiographies by Indians," or "texts . . . [that] are indeed written by those whose lives they chronicle" (Krupat, "Introduction" 3–5).

8. Michael Steltenkamp, for example (who, like Steinmetz, is also a Catholic priest), has been instrumental in providing additional biographical backing for claims of Black Elk's sincerity as a converted Catholic. In his "final reckoning" on the question of who Black Elk really was, Steltenkamp quotes Black Elk's last surviving child, Lucy Looks Twice, who claimed that Neihardt had not presented an accurate picture of her father. "My father related to John Neihardt an addition to his book, but they never put it out. Afterward, he realized this and wanted the last part of his life also told—his life as a Christian man praying" (*Black Elk* 20). As Steinmetz concurs with her assessment, "certainly, she knew more about her father and his true feelings than anyone reading about Black Elk today" ("Missiology" 269).

9. Heflin persuasively suggests that Black Elk knew quite a bit about how anthropologists had preserved other Native Americans' stories, and that this knowledge led him to carefully select Neihardt, a poet, as a collaborator who might more effectively disseminate his vision. "Is it too outrageous to speculate," she queries, "that Black Elk understood the potential, and lasting, impact of a story with literary value as opposed to one collected by an anthropologist? Was Black Elk consciously looking for a larger audience and a more influential transmitting medium, recognizing the power of the written word because of his knowledge of the Bible's power given Christianity's scope around the world?" (4). Neihardt himself stated that "I think he knew the kind of person I was when I came to see him—I am referring to the mystical strain in me and all my work" (quoted in McCluskey 238).

10. As Rice clarifies this idea of "fortunate fall" in Neihardt's work, the overall purpose of the *Cycle of the West* is to depict the decline of the Lakota as a "transition to Christian enlightenment. The progression through defeat, and the loss of the Lakota traditional culture, are tragic only in the sense that the crucifixion is tragic. . . . The Lakota suffer at Wounded Knee as Christ suffered on the cross, so that a lesser understanding can be transformed to unifying love" (18–19, 49).

11. Krupat, for example, suggests that Neihardt intentionally kept any sense of Black Elk's ongoing efforts on behalf of Lakota culture out of his autobiography. "Even in 1931, Black Elk was engaged in traditional ritual means to influence the fate of the Lakota. This is not at all how Neihardt presented the matter; indeed, he edited and deleted those portions of Black Elk's narration that would emphasize his persisting desire for a return to the old ways" (*For Those* 128–29).

12. "From Neihardt's perspective, he had come to write what Black Elk wished to teach him about the Lakota people before the Wounded Knee massacre; from Black Elk's perspective, he had invited Neihardt in order to instruct him in the old Lakota religion. There has been a misunderstanding of purpose: Neihardt conceived of the project as writing Black Elk's life story, whereas Black Elk conceived of it as making a record of the Lakota religion" (DeMallie 62).

Chapter 8: Conclusion

1. Even Christine Oravec's insightful look at identity and association in Burke produces primarily broad statements about identity in his work—for example, the observation that "language . . . actively create[s] meaning and hence identity" (183).

2. Burke forcefully states the importance of this distinction between language and "reality," especially as it concerns the reality of lived experience, in arguing that we should "not for the world make literature and life synonymous since, by comparison in such terms, the merest life is so overwhelmingly superior to the noblest poem that illiteracy becomes almost a moral obligation" (*Counter-Statement* x).

3. Jerome Bruner phrases this case in similar terms: "Given that autobiography is also a form of 'taking a stand,' it is perforce rhetorical" ("Self-Making" 35).

BIBLIOGRAPHY

Alcorn, Marshall W., Jr. "Self-Structure as a Rhetorical Device: Modern *Ethos* and the Divisiveness of the Self." In *Ethos: New Essays in Rhetorical and Critical Theory*, edited by James S. Baumlin and Tita French Baumlin, 3–36. Dallas: Southern Methodist University Press, 1994.

Alter, Jonathan. "From Cold War to Steamy Sex." *Newsweek*, July 9, 2001, 36.

American Federation of Labor and Congress of Industrial Organizations. "Constitution of the American Federation of Labor and Congress of Industrial Organizations." *First Constitutional Convention Proceedings*. New York, 1955.

American Psychiatric Association. "COPP Position Statement on Therapies Focused on Attempts to Change Sexual Orientation (Reparative or Conversion Therapies)" (September 1, 2006). http://www.psych.org/pract_of_psych/copptherapyaddendum83100.cfm.

———. *Diagnostic and Statistical Manual of Mental Disorders*. 4th ed., revised. Washington, D.C.: American Psychiatric Association, 2000.

American Psychological Association. "Answers to Your Questions About Sexual Orientation and Homosexuality" (March 26, 2006). http://www.apa.org/pubinfo/answers.html.

———. "Resolution on Appropriate Therapeutic Responses to Sexual Orientation" (October 20, 2006). http://www.apa.org/pi/sexual.html.

Amossy, Ruth. "*Ethos* at the Crossroads of Disciplines: Rhetoric, Pragmatics, Sociology." *Poetics Today* 22 (2001): 1–23.

———. "How to Do Things with Doxa: Toward an Analysis of Argumentation in Discourse." *Poetics Today* 23 (2002): 465–87.

———. "Introduction to the Study of Doxa." *Poetics Today* 23 (2002): 369–94.

Anderson, Virginia. "Antithetical Ethics: Kenneth Burke and the Constitution." *Journal of Advanced Composition* 15 (1995): 261–79.

Antczak, Frederick J. *Thought and Character: The Rhetoric of Democratic Education*. Ames: Iowa State University Press, 1985.

Arac, Jonathan. "Toward a Critical Genealogy of the U.S. Discourse of Identity: *Invisible Man* after Fifty Years." *Boundary* 2, no. 30 (2003): 195–216.

Aristotle. *Nicomachean Ethics*, translated by Hippocrates G. Apostle. Grinnell, Iowa: Peripatetic, 1984.

———. *On Rhetoric: A Theory of Civic Discourse*, translated by George A. Kennedy. New York: Oxford University Press, 1991.

———. *Topics*. Vol. 2 of *Aristotle in Twenty-Three Volumes*, translated by E. M. Forster. Cambridge, Mass.: Harvard University Press, 1960.

———. *Topics: Books I and VII with Excerpts from Related Texts*, translated by Robin Smith. Oxford: Clarendon, 1997.

Augustine, St. *The Confessions*, translated by Rex Warner. New York: Signet, 1963.

Barthes, Roland. *The Rustle of Language*, translated by Richard Howard. New York: Farrar, Straus & Giroux, 1986.

Battaglia, Deborah. "Problematizing the Self: A Thematic Introduction." In *Rhetorics of Self-Making*, edited by Battaglia, 1–15. Berkeley: University of California Press, 1995.

Baumlin, James S. "Ethos." In *Encyclopedia of Rhetoric*, edited by Thomas O. Sloane, 263–77. Oxford: Oxford University Press, 2001.

———. "Introduction: Positioning *Ethos* in Historical and Contemporary Theory." In *Ethos: New Essays in Rhetorical and Critical Theory*, edited by James S. Baumlin and Tita French Baumlin, xi–xxxi. Dallas: Southern Methodist University Press, 1994.

Baumlin, Tita French. "A Good (Wo)Man Skilled in Speaking: *Ethos*, Self-Fashioning, and Gender in Renaissance England." In *Ethos: New Essays in Rhetorical and Critical Theory*, edited by James S. Baumlin and Tita French Baumlin, 229–64. Dallas: Southern Methodist University Press, 1994.

Bellow, Adam. "'Blinded by the Right': An Exchange." *New York Review of Books*, October 10, 2002, 23.

Benson, Thomas W. Series editor's preface to *The Ethos of Rhetoric*, edited by Michael J. Hyde, ix–x. Columbia: University of South Carolina Press, 2004.

Betz, Hans Dieter. *Galatians: A Commentary on Paul's Letter to the Churches in Galatia*. Philadelphia: Fortress, 1979.

Biesecker, Barbara A. *Addressing Postmodernity: Kenneth Burke, Rhetoric, and a Theory of Social Change*. Tuscaloosa: University of Alabama Press, 1997.

Black, Edwin. "Idioms of Social Identity." In *Rhetorical Questions: Studies of Public Discourse*, edited by Black, 21–51. Chicago: University of Chicago Press, 1992.

———. "The Second Persona." *Quarterly Journal of Speech* 56 (1970): 109–19.

Blair, Carole, and Neil Michel. "The Rushmore Effect: *Ethos* and National Collective Identity." In *The Ethos of Rhetoric*, edited by Michael J. Hyde, 159–96. Columbia: University of South Carolina Press, 2004.

Blanshard, Paul. *American Freedom and Catholic Power*. 2nd rev. ed. Boston: Beacon, 1959.

Bolin, Anne. *In Search of Eve: Transsexual Rites of Passage*. South Hadley, Mass.: Bergin & Garvey, 1988.

Booth, Wayne. *Modern Dogma and the Rhetoric of Assent.* Chicago: University of Chicago Press, 1974.

Bozell, L. Brent, III. "David Brock's Bitter Little Book." *Human Events* 58 (April 2002): 10.

Brock, David. *Blinded by the Right: The Conscience of an Ex-Conservative.* New York: Crown, 2002.

———. "Unliving a Lie." *Fast Company* 86 (September 2004): 75.

Brown, Dee. *Bury My Heart at Wounded Knee: An Indian History of the American West.* New York: Holt, Rinehart & Winston, 1970.

Browne, Stephen Howard. *Angelina Grimké: Rhetoric, Identity, and the Radical Imagination.* East Lansing: Michigan State University Press, 1999.

Brumble, David H., and Karl Kroeber. "Reasoning Together." *Canadian Review of American Studies* 12 (1981): 253–70.

Bruner, Jerome S. *Acts of Meaning.* Cambridge, Mass.: Harvard University Press, 1990.

———. "Self-Making and World-Making." In *Narrative and Identity: Studies in Autobiography, Self, and Culture,* edited by Jens Brockmeier and Donal Carabaugh, 25–37. Amsterdam & Philadelphia: John Benjamins, 2001.

Bruni, Frank. "Sorry about That." Review of *Blinded by the Right,* by David Brock. *New York Times,* March 24, 2002, 14.

Burke, Kenneth. "Addendum." In *Counter-Statement.* 1931. 2nd ed., 220–25. Berkeley: University of California Press, 1968.

———. "Appendix: On Human Behavior Considered Dramatistically." In *Permanence and Change: An Anatomy of Purpose.* 1935. 3rd ed., 274–94. Berkeley: University of California Press, 1984.

———. *Attitudes toward History.* 1935. 3rd rev. ed. Berkeley: University of California Press, 1984.

———. *Counter-Statement.* 1931. 2nd ed. Berkeley: University of California Press, 1968.

———. "Curriculum Criticum." In *Counter-Statement.* 1931. 2nd ed., 213–25. Berkeley: University of California Press, 1968.

———. "Dramatism." In *International Encyclopedia of the Social Sciences,* edited by David L. Sills, 445–51. New York: Macmillan & Free Press, 1968.

———. *Dramatism and Development.* Barre, Mass.: Clark University Press, 1972.

———. *Essays toward a Symbolic of Motives,* edited by William H. Rueckert. West Lafayette, Ind. Parlor Press, 2007.

———. *A Grammar of Motives.* 1945. Berkeley: University of California Press, 1969.

———. *Language as Symbolic Action: Essays on Life, Literature, and Method.* Berkeley: University of California Press, 1966.

———. Letter to William Chesebro. N.d. Kenneth Burke Papers, Pattee Library, Pennsylvania State University.

———. *Permanence and Change: An Anatomy of Purpose.* 1935. 3rd ed. Berkeley: University of California Press, 1984.

———. *The Philosophy of Literary Form: Studies in Symbolic Action.* 1941. 3rd ed. Berkeley: University of California Press, 1973.

———. "Questions and Answers about the Pentad." *College Composition and Communication* 19 (1978): 330–35.

———. *A Rhetoric of Motives.* 1950. Berkeley: University of California Press, 1969.

———. *The Rhetoric of Religion: Studies in Logology.* Berkeley: University of California Press, 1961.

Butler, Judith. *Bodies That Matter: On the Discursive Limits of "Sex."* New York: Routledge, 1993.

———. *Gender Trouble: Feminism and the Subversion of Identity.* New York: Routledge, 1990.

Bygrave, Stephen. *Kenneth Burke: Rhetoric and Ideology.* London & New York: Routledge, 1993.

Calhoun, Craig. "Social Theory and the Politics of Identity." In *Social Theory and the Politics of Identity*, edited by Calhoun, 9–36. Cambridge, Mass.: Blackwell, 1994.

"Cardinal Brings to End N.Y. Cemetery Strike." *Catholic Worker,* April 1949, 1–2.

"Cardinal Says He'll Dig Graves with Clergy in Cemetery Strike." *New York Herald Tribune,* March 3, 1949, 1, 18.

Castro, Michael. *Interpreting the Indian: Twentieth–Century Poets and the Native American.* Albuquerque: University of New Mexico Press, 1983.

Chamberlain, John. "A Sioux Indian Tells a Tragic Story." Review of *Black Elk Speaks,* by John G. Neihardt. *New York Times Book Review,* March 6, 1932, 4, 14.

Charland, Maurice. "Constitutive Rhetoric: The Case of the *Peuple Québécois.*" *Quarterly Journal of Speech* 73 (1987): 133–50.

Cheever, Susan. *Note Found in a Bottle: My Life as a Drinker.* New York: Simon & Schuster, 1999.

Cherry, Roger D. "Ethos versus Persona: Self-Representation in Written Discourse." *Written Communication* 15 (1998): 384–410.

Childs, Marquis W. "Morituri." Review of *Black Elk Speaks,* by John G. Neihardt. *New Republic,* June 22, 1931, 161.

Clark, Gregory. *Rhetorical Landscapes in America: Variations on a Theme from Kenneth Burke.* Columbia: University of South Carolina Press, 2004.

Clinton, Bill. *My Life.* New York: Knopf, 2004.

Coleman, Simon. "Continuous Conversion? The Rhetoric, Practice, and Rhetorical Practice of Charismatic Protestant Conversion." In *The Anthropology of Religious Conversion,* edited by Andrew Buckser and Stephen D. Glazier, 15–28. Lanham, Md.: Rowman & Littlefield, 2003.

Coles, Robert. *Dorothy Day: A Radical Devotion.* Reading, Mass.: Merloyd–Lawrence, 1987.

Coles, Robert, and Jon Erikson. *A Spectacle unto the World.* New York: Macmillan, 1973.

Cooper, Ilene. Review of *Blinded by the Right,* by David Brock. *Booklist* 15 (March 2002): 1186.

Couser, G. Thomas. "Black Elk Speaks Again: Self-Representation in Contemporary Native American Autobiography." *Auto/Biography Studies* 7 (1991): 273–91.

———. "Black Elk Speaks with Forked Tongue." In *Studies in Autobiography*, edited by James Olney, 73–88. New York: Oxford University Press, 1988.

Cowley, Malcolm. *The Exile's Return: A Literary Odyssey of the 1920s*. New York: Viking, 1951.

Crusius, Timothy. *Kenneth Burke and the Conversation after Philosophy*. Carbondale: Southern Illinois University Press, 1999.

Cunneen, Sally. "Dorothy Day: The Storyteller as Human Model." *Cross Currents* 34 (1984): 283–93.

Day, Dorothy. *The Eleventh Virgin*. New York: A. & C. Boni, 1924.

———. *From Union Square to Rome*. Silver Spring, Md.: Preservation of the Faith, 1938.

———. *House of Hospitality*. New York: Sheed & Ward, 1939.

———. Letter to Francis Cardinal Spellman. March 4, 1949. Dorothy Day–Catholic Worker Collection, Marquette University Library Archives.

———. *Loaves and Fishes*. New York: Harper & Row, 1963.

———. *The Long Loneliness: The Autobiography of Dorothy Day*. New York: Harper, 1952.

———. *On Pilgrimage*. New York: Catholic Worker Books, 1948.

———. "On Pilgrimage." *Catholic Worker*, April 1949, 1–2.

———. "On Pilgrimage." *Catholic Worker*, February 1952, 4.

———. "To Our Readers." *Catholic Worker*, May 1933, 4

Deaux, Kay. "Identity." In *A Dictionary of Psychology*, edited by Andrew M. Colman, 222–25. New York: Oxford University Press, 2001.

Deloria, Vine, Jr. Introduction to *Black Elk Speaks: Being the Life Story of a Holy Man of the Oglala Sioux*, by John G. Neihardt. 1932. Lincoln: University of Nebraska Press, 1979.

DeMallie, Raymond J., ed. *The Sixth Grandfather: Black Elk's Teachings Given to John G. Neihardt*. Lincoln: University of Nebraska Press, 1984.

De Waele, J.-P., and Rom Harré. "Autobiography as a Psychological Method." In *Emerging Strategies in Social Psychological Research*, edited by G. P. Ginsburg, 177–224. New York: Wiley, 1979.

Dorsey, Peter. *Sacred Estrangement: The Rhetoric of Conversion in Modern American Autobiography*. University Park: Pennsylvania State University Press, 1993.

Eagleton, Terry. "Self-Undoing Subjects." In *Rewriting the Self: Histories from the Renaissance to the Present*, edited by Roy Porter, 269–87. New York: Routledge, 1997.

Eakin, Paul John. *How Our Lives Become Stories: Making Selves*. Ithaca & London: Cornell University Press, 1999.

Eberly, Rosa. "Ethos and Tropos: Isocrates and the Possibility of Rhetorical Agency." Paper presented at the conference of the Rhetoric Society of America, San Antonio, Texas, May 2004.

Eddy, Beth. *The Rites of Identity*. Princeton & Oxford: Princeton University Press, 2003.

Ehardt, George C. "Memorandum." January 14, 1949. Dorothy Day–Catholic Worker Collection, Marquette University Library Archives.

Ellsberg, Robert. Introduction to *By Little and by Little: The Selected Writings of Dorothy Day*. New York: Knopf, 1983.

Enochs, Ross. *The Jesuit Mission to the Lakota Sioux: Pastoral Theology and Ministry, 1886–1945*. Kansas City: Sheed & Ward, 1996.

Feehan, Michael. "Kenneth Burke's Dualistic Theory of Constitutions." *Pre/Text* 12 (1991): 39–59.

Feinberg, Leslie. *Trans Liberation: Beyond Pink or Blue*. Boston: Beacon, 1998.

Forest, Jim. *Love Is the Measure*. New York: Paulist, 1986.

Foucault, Michel. "What Is Enlightenment?" In *The Foucault Reader*, edited by Paul Rabinow, 32–50. New York: Pantheon, 1984.

Frobish, Todd. "Sexual Profiteering and Rhetorical Assuagement: Examining *Ethos* and Identity at Playboy.com." *Journal of Computer-Mediated Communication* 9, no. 3 (April 2004). http://jcmc.indiana.edu/vol9/issue3/frobish.html.

Gaffney, Edward R. Letter to Francis Cardinal Spellman. 15 February 1949. Dorothy Day–Catholic Worker Collection, Marquette University Library Archives.

Gager, John G. *Reinventing Paul*. New York: Oxford University Press, 2000.

Garver, Eugene. *Aristotle's Rhetoric: An Art of Character*. Chicago & London: University of Chicago Press, 1994.

Geertz, Clifford. *The Interpretation of Cultures*. New York: Basic, 1973.

Goldstein, Richard. "The Primal Lie." *Village Voice*, March 27, 2002, 45.

Graves, Florence George. "The Real David Brock?" Review of *Blinded by the Right*, by David Brock. *Women's Review of Books* 19 (May 2002): 1–2.

Gunn Allen, Paula. *The Sacred Hoop: Recovering the Feminine in American Indian Traditions*. Boston: Beacon, 1986.

Hall, Stuart. "Introduction: Who Needs 'Identity'?" In *Questions of Cultural Identity*, edited by Hall and Paul Du Gay, 1–17. London: Sage, 1996.

Halloran, Michael S. "Aristotle's Concept of Ethos, or if not His Somebody Else's." *Rhetoric Review* 1, no. 1 (1982): 58–63.

Hammerback, John. "Creating the 'New Person': The Rhetoric of Reconstitutive Discourse." *Rhetoric Review* 20 (Spring 2001): 18–21.

Hammerback, John, and Richard Jensen. *The Rhetorical Career of César Chavez*. College Station: Texas A&M University Press, 1998.

Hanafin, Patrick J., and Melissa S. Williams. Introduction to *Identity, Rights, and Constitutional Transformation*, edited by Hanafin and Williams. Brookfield, Vt.: Ashgate, 1998.

Harry Benjamin International Gender Dysphoria Association. *Standards of Care for Gender Identity Disorders, Sixth Version* (September 12, 2006). http://www.hbigda.org/socv6.html.

Harte, Thomas J. *Papal Social Principles: A Guide and Digest*. Gloucester, Mass.: Peter Smith, 1960.

Haughton, Rosemary. "Formation and Transformation." In *Conversion: Perspectives on Personal and Social Transformation*, edited by Walter E. Conn, 23–26. New York: Alba House, 1978.

Hawkins, Anne Hunsaker. *Archetypes of Conversion: The Autobiographies of Augustine, Bunyan, and Merton*. Lewisburg, Pa.: Bucknell University Press, 1985.

Hazen, Michael David, and David Cratis Williams. "Introduction: Argument and Identity." *Argumentation and Advocacy* 34 (Fall 1997): v–viii.

Heflin, Ruth J. "Black Elk Passes on the Power of the Earth: Black Elk's Purpose and Use of Lakota Literary Tradition in Creating *Black Elk Speaks*." In *The Black Elk Reader*, edited by Clyde Holler, 3–18. Syracuse: Syracuse University Press, 2000.

Henderson, Greig E. *Kenneth Burke: Literature and Language as Symbolic Action*. Athens: University of Georgia Press, 1988.

Hertzberg, Hendrik. "Can You Forgive Him?" Review of *Blinded by the Right*, by David Brock. *New Yorker*, March 11, 2002, 85.

Hesford, Wendy. *Framing Identities: Autobiography and the Politics of Pedagogy*. Minneapolis: University of Minnesota Press, 1999.

Holland, Dorothy, et al. *Identity and Agency in Cultural Worlds*. Cambridge, Mass.: Harvard University Press, 1998.

Holland, L. Virginia. *Counterpoint: Kenneth Burke and Aristotle's Theories of Rhetoric*. New York: Philosophical Library, 1959.

Holler, Clyde. *Black Elk's Religion: The Sun Dance and Lakota Catholicism*. Syracuse: Syracuse University Press, 1995.

———. Introduction to *The Black Elk Reader*, edited by Holler, xiii–xxvi. Syracuse: Syracuse University Press, 2000.

Holte, James Craig. *The Conversion Experience in America: A Sourcebook on Religious Conversion Autobiography*. New York: Greenwood, 1992.

Hoover, Bob. "The View from Left Field: Confessions of a Disillusioned Right-Wing Hero." Review of *Blinded by the Right*, by David Brock. *Pittsburgh Post-Gazette*, March 10, 2002, E8.

Hunt, Lester. *Character and Culture*. Lanham, Md.: Rowman & Littlefield, 1997.

Hyde, Michael J. "Introduction: Rhetorically, We Dwell." In *The Ethos of Rhetoric*, edited by Hyde, xiii–xxviii. Columbia: University of South Carolina Press, 2004.

Jablonski, Carol J. "Declining Honors: Dorothy Day's Rhetorical Resistance to the Culture of Heroic Assent." In *Doing Rhetorical History: Concepts and Cases*, edited by Kathleen J. Turner, 191–206. Tuscaloosa: University of Alabama Press, 1998.

Jacobs, David M. *Secret Life: Firsthand, Documented Accounts of UFO Abductions*. New York: Fireside, 1993.

James, William. *The Varieties of Religious Experience: A Study in Human Nature*. New York: Modern Library, 1902.

Jameson, Fredric R. "The Symbolic Inference; or, Kenneth Burke and Ideological Analysis." In *Representing Kenneth Burke*, edited by Hayden White and Margaret Brose, 68–91. Baltimore & London: Johns Hopkins University Press, 1982.

Jasinski, James. "Constructing American Identity/Identities." *Rhetoric and Public Affairs* 3, no. 1 (2000): 71–129.

Jelinek, Estelle C. "Introduction: Women's Autobiography and the Male Tradition." In *Women's Autobiography: Essays in Criticism*, edited by Jelinek, 1–20. Bloomington: Indiana University Press, 1980.

Jenkins, Peter. *A Walk across America*. New York: Morrow, 1979.

Johnson, Nan. "Ethos." In *Encyclopedia of Rhetoric and Composition: Communication from Ancient Times to the Information Age*, edited by Theresa Enos, 243–45. New York: Garland, 1996.

———. "Ethos and the Aims of Rhetoric." In *Essays on Classical Rhetoric and Modern Discourse*, edited by Robert J. Connors, Lisa Ede, and Andrea Lunsford, 98–114. Carbondale: Southern Illinois University Press, 1984.

Kaye, Francis W. "Just What Is Cultural Appropriation, Anyway?: The Ethics of Reading *Black Elk Speaks*." In *The Black Elk Reader*, edited by Clyde Holler, 147–68. Syracuse: Syracuse University Press, 2000.

Keller, Christopher J. "The Ecology of Writerly Voice: Authorship, Ethos, and Persona." In *Ecocomposition: Theoretical and Pedagogical Approaches*, edited by Christian R. Weisser and Sidney I. Dobrin, 193–208. Albany: State University of New York Press, 2001.

Kern, Philip H. *Rhetoric and Galatians: Assessing an Approach to Paul's Epistle*. Cambridge: Cambridge University Press, 1998.

Kinneavy, James L., and Susan C. Warshauer. "From Aristotle to Madison Avenue: *Ethos* and the Ethics of Argument." In *Ethos: New Essays in Rhetorical and Critical Theory*, edited by James S. Baumlin and Tita French Baumlin, 171–90. Dallas: Southern Methodist University Press, 1994.

Kriefall, Andreas. "Ethics of Polyphony: The Example of *Black Elk Speaks*." *Western American Literature* 33 (1998): 179–203.

Krupat, Arnold. *For Those Who Come After: A Study of Native American Autobiography*. Berkeley: University of California Press, 1985.

———. Introduction to *Native American Autobiography: An Anthology*, edited by Krupat. Madison: University of Wisconsin Press, 1994.

Kumin, Maxine. "The Metamorphosis." *New York Times*, November 14, 1999. http://www/pfc.org.uk/cgi/printit.pl?/reviews/mcc-nyt.htm.

Lamb, Christopher, and M. Darrol Bryant. Introduction to *Religious Conversion: Contemporary Practices and Controversies*, edited by Lamb and Bryant. London & New York: Cassell, 1999.

Lauerman, Kerry. "The Apostate." Review of *Blinded by the Right*, by David Brock. *Salon* (October 31, 2006). http://www.salon.com/books/feature/2002/03/08/brock/index_np.html.

Leary, Mark R., and June Price Tangney. "The Self as an Organizing Construct in the Behavioral and Social Sciences." In *Handbook of Self and Identity*, edited by Leary and Tangney, 3–15. New York: Guilford, 2003.

Leff, Michael, and Ebony A. Utley. "Instrumental and Constitutive Rhetoric in Martin Luther King, Jr.'s 'Letter from Birmingham Jail.'" *Rhetoric & Public Affairs* 7 (2004): 37–52.

Leigh, David J. *Circuitous Journeys: Modern Spiritual Autobiography*. New York: Fordham University Press, 2000.

Lentricchia, Frank. *Criticism and Social Change*. Chicago: University of Chicago Press, 1983.

Lercaro, Giacomo Cardinal. "Christian Concept of Work." In *The Church and Social Progress*, edited by Benjamin L. Masse, 69–73. Milwaukee: Bruce, 1966.

Lie, John. *Modern Peoplehood.* Cambridge, Mass.: Harvard University Press, 2004.

Linden, George W. "John Neihardt and *Black Elk Speaks:* A Personal Reminiscence." In *The Black Elk Reader,* edited by Clyde Holler, 79–86. Syracuse: Syracuse University Press, 2000.

MacDonald, Dwight. "Profiles: The Foolish Things of the World." *New Yorker,* October 4, 1952, 37–56; October 11, 1952, 37–52.

Mason, Mary G. "Dorothy Day and Women's Spiritual Autobiography." In *American Women's Autobiography: Fea(s)ts of Memory,* edited by Margo Culley, 185–217. Madison: University of Wisconsin Press, 1992.

Massa, Mark S. *Catholics and American Culture: Fulton Sheen, Dorothy Day, and the Notre Dame Football Team.* New York: Crossroad, 1999.

Maurin, Peter. "Easy Essays." *Catholic Worker,* May 1, 1933, 1, 8.

McAdams, Dan P. *The Stories We Live By: Personal Myths and the Making of the Self.* New York & London: Guilford, 1997.

McAdams, Dan P., Ruthellen Josselson, and Amia Lieblich, eds.*Turns in the Road: Narrative Studies of Lives in Transition.* Washington, D.C.: American Psychological Association, 2001.

McCloskey, Deirdre. *Crossing: A Memoir.* Chicago: University of Chicago Press, 1999.

———. "Some News That at Least Will Not Bore You." *Eastern Economic Journal* 21, no. 4 (1995): 551–53.

McCluskey, Sally. "Black Elk Speaks: and So Does John Neihardt." *Western American Literature* 6 (1972): 231–42.

Miller, William D. *Dorothy Day: A Biography.* San Francisco: Harper & Row, 1982.

———. *A Harsh and Dreadful Love: Dorothy Day and the Catholic Worker Movement.* New York: Liveright, 1973.

Moya, Paula M. L. "Introduction: Reclaiming Identity." In *Reclaiming Identity: Realist Theory and the Predicament of Postmodernism,* edited by Moya and Michael R. Hames-Garcia, 1–26. Berkeley: University of California Press, 2000.

Mulvey, Michael, and Carl Stech. "Do-It-Yourself Investing: Exploring the Ethos of Online Trading." *Advances in Consumer Research* 28 (2001): 87.

Namaste, Viviane K. *Invisible Lives: The Erasure of Transsexual and Transgendered People.* Chicago: University of Chicago Press, 2000.

Neihardt, John G. *Black Elk Speaks: Being the Life Story of a Holy Man of the Oglala Sioux, as Told through John G. Neihardt (Flaming Rainbow).* 1932. Lincoln: University of Nebraska Press, 1979.

———. *The Song of the Indian Wars.* New York: Macmillan, 1925.

Nietzsche, F. W. *The Antichrist,* translated by H. L. Mencken. New York: Knopf, 1920.

Nock, A. D. *Conversion: The Old and the New in Religion from Alexander the Great to Augustine of Hippo.* London: Oxford University Press, 1933.

Olson, Paul A. "*Black Elk Speaks* as Epic Ritual Attempt to Reverse History." In *Vision and Refuge: Essays on the Literature of the Great Plains,* edited by V. Faulkner and F. C. Luebke, 3–37. Lincoln: University of Nebraska Press, 1982.

Oravec, Christine A. "Kenneth Burke's Concept of Association and the Complexity of Identity." In *The Legacy of Kenneth Burke,* edited by Herbert W. Simons and Trevor Melia, 174–95. Madison: University of Wisconsin Press, 1989.

Olmstead, Wendy. "Invention, Emotion, and Conversion in Augustine's *Confessions.*" In *Rhetorical Invention and Religious Inquiry: New Perspectives,* edited by Walter Jost and Olmstead, 65–86. New Haven & London: Yale University Press, 2000.

Pauley, John L., II. "Reshaping Public Persona and the Prophetic Ethos: Louis Farrakhan at the Million Man March." *Western Journal of Communication* 62 (1998): 512–36.

Perelman, Chaim, and Lucie Olbrechts-Tyteca. *The New Rhotoric: A Treatise on Argumentation,* translated by John Wilkinson and Purcell Weaver. Notre Dame & London: University of Notre Dame Press, 1969.

Perry, John. *Identity, Personal Identity, and the Self.* Indianapolis: Hackett, 2002.

Piehl, Mel. *Breaking Bread: The Catholic Worker and the Origin of Catholic Radicalism in America.* Philadelphia: Temple University Press, 1982.

———. "The Catholic Worker and American Religious Tradition." *Cross Currents* 34 (1984): 259–69.

Pile, Steve, and Nigel Thrift. Introduction to *Mapping the Subject: Geographies of Cultural Transformation,* edited by Pile and Thrift, 1–51. London & New York: Routledge, 1995.

Pleszczynski, Wlady. "You've Got a Friend." *American Spectator,* July/August 2002, 82.

Porterfield, Amanda. "Black Elk's Significance in American Culture." In *The Black Elk Reader,* edited by Clyde Holler, 39–58. Syracuse: Syracuse University Press, 2000.

Powers, William K. "When Black Elk Speaks, Everybody Listens." In *Religion in Native North America,* edited by Christopher Vecsey, 136–51. Moscow: University of Idaho Press, 1990.

Rambo, Lewis R. *Understanding Religious Conversion.* New Haven & London: Yale University Press, 1993.

Rice, Julian. *Black Elk's Story: Distinguishing Its Lakota Purpose.* Albuquerque: University of New Mexico Press, 1991.

Rich, Frank. "Ding, Dong, the Cultural Witch Hunt Is Dead." *New York Times,* February 24, 2002, 36.

Robbins, Blaine. "'That's Cheap': The Rational Invocation of Norms, Practices, and an Ethos in Ultimate Frisbee." *Journal of Sport and Social Issues* 28 (2004): 314–37.

Roberts, Nancy. *Dorothy Day and the Catholic Worker.* Albany: State University of New York Press, 1984.

Ross, Marlon B. "Commentary: Pleasuring Identity, or the Delicious Politics of Belonging." *New Literary History* 31 (2000): 827–50.

Rueckert, William. *Encounters with Kenneth Burke.* Urbana: University of Illinois Press, 1994.

———. *Kenneth Burke and the Drama of Human Relations.* Berkeley: University of California Press, 1963.

———. "Kenneth Burke's 'Symbolic of Motives' and 'Poetics, Dramatistically Considered.'" In *Unending Conversations: New Writings by and about Kenneth Burke,* edited by Greig Henderson and David Cratis Williams, 99–124. Carbondale & Edwardsville: Southern Illinois University Press, 2001.

Rueckert, William, ed. *Letters from Kenneth Burke to William H. Rueckert, 1959–1987*. West Lafayette, Ind.: Parlor, 2003.

Sarfati, Georges-Elia. "Cultural Study, Doxa, and Dictionaries: The Case of Jewish Identity." *Poetics Today* 23 (2002): 489–512.

Said, Edward. "Between Worlds." *London Review of Books* 20 (May 7, 1998): 3–7.

Sayre, Robert. "Vision and Experience in *Black Elk Speaks*." *College English* 32 (1971): 509–35.

Schauffler, Marina F. *Turning to Earth: Stories of Ecological Conversion*. Charlottesville: University of Virginia Press, 2003.

Schrag, Calvin O. *The Self after Postmodernity*. New Haven & London: Yale University Press, 1997.

Schütrumpf, Eckart. "The Model for the Concept of *Ethos* in Aristotle's *Rhetoric*." *Philologus* 137 (1993): 12–17.

Schwartz, Howard S. "Grandiose Unhappiness." Review of *Blinded by the Right*, by David Brock. *Sexuality & Culture*, Spring 2003, 79–83.

Segal, Alan F. *Paul the Convert: The Apostolate and Apostasy of Saul the Pharisee*. New Haven: Yale University Press, 1990.

Shelley, Thomas J. "Proud Legacy." *Catholic New York* (April 27, 2006). http://www.cny.org/archive/ft/ft122399.htm.

Silvio, Carl. "*Black Elk Speaks* and Literary Disciplinarity: A Case Study in Canonization." *College Literature* 26, no. 2 (1999): 137–50.

Skinner, C. L. Review of *Black Elk Speaks*, by John G. Neihardt. *Books*, February 21, 1932, 3.

Smith, Craig R. "*Ethos* Dwells Persuasively: A Hermeneutic Reading of Aristotle on Credibility." In *The Ethos of Rhetoric*, edited by Michael J. Hyde, 1–19. Columbia: University of South Carolina Press, 2004.

Smith, John E. "The Concept of Conversion." In *Conversion: Perspectives on Personal and Social Transformation*, edited by Walter E. Conn, 55–72. New York: Alba House, 1978.

Spacks, Patricia Meyer. "Selves in Hiding." In *Women's Autobiography: Essays in Criticism*, edited by Estelle C. Jelinek, 112–32. Bloomington: Indiana University Press, 1980.

Spigelman, Candace. "Argument and Evidence in the Case of the Personal." *College English* 64 (2001): 63–87.

Spivak, Gayatri Chakravorti. Translator's preface to *Of Grammatology*, by Jacques Derrida, iv–xxi. Baltimore: Johns Hopkins University Press, 1987.

Staub, Michael E. "(Re)Collecting the Past: Writing Native American Speech." *American Quarterly* 43 (1991): 425–56.

Steinmetz, Paul B., S.J. "New Missiology and Black Elk's Individuation." In *The Black Elk Reader*, edited by Clyde Holler, 262–81. Syracuse: Syracuse University Press, 2000.

———. *Pipe, Bible and Peyote among the Oglala Lakota: A Study in Religious Identity*. Syracuse: Syracuse University Press, 1990.

Steltenkamp, Michael F. *Black Elk: Holy Man of the Oglala.* Norman: University of Oklahoma Press, 1993.

———. "A Retrospective on *Black Elk: Holy Man of the Oglala.*" In *The Black Elk Reader,* edited by Clyde Holler, 104–26. Syracuse: Syracuse University Press, 2000.

Stromberg, Peter. *Language and Self-Transformation: A Study of the Christian Conversion Narrative.* Cambridge: Cambridge University Press, 1993.

Stuart, Charlotte L. "The Constitution as 'Summational Anecdote" *Central States Speech Journal* 25 (1974): 111–18.

Swearingen, Jan C. "*Ethos:* Imitation, Impersonation, and Voice." In *Ethos: New Essays in Rhetorical and Critical Theory,* edited by James S. Baumlin and Tita French Baumlin, 115–48. Dallas: Southern Methodist University Press, 1994.

Taft, Philip. "The Contributions of Leo XIII and Pius XI." In *The Church and Social Progress,* edited by Benjamin L. Masse, 33–38. Milwaukee: Bruce, 1966.

Taylor, Charles. *Human Agency and Language.* Cambridge: Cambridge University Press, 1985.

———. *Sources of the Self: The Making of the Modern Identity.* Cambridge, Mass.: Harvard University Press, 1989.

Too, Yun Lee. *The Rhetoric of Identity in Isocrates: Text, Power, Pedagogy.* Cambridge: Cambridge University Press, 1995.

Tracy, Karen. *Everyday Talk: Building and Reflecting Identities.* New York & London: Guilford, 2002.

"An Unmistakable Verdict." *Commonweal,* January 18, 1952, 363.

Valenta, Markha Gabriela. "The Radical Folly of Love in (Post)Modern America: The Autobiographical Narratives of Dorothy Day." 2 vols. Ph.D. diss., University of Iowa, 1999.

Vecsey, Chris. "A Century of Lakota Sioux Catholicism at Pine Ridge." In *Religious Diversity and American Religious History: Studies in Traditions and Cultures,* edited by Walter H. Conser Jr. and Sumner B. Twiss, 262–95. Athens: University of Georgia Press, 1997.

Vestal, Stanley. "A Maladjusted Soul." Review of *Black Elk Speaks,* by John G. Neihardt. *Saturday Review of Literature,* February 27, 1932, 551.

Vitanza, Victor J. "Concerning a Postclassical *Ethos* as Para/Rhetorical Ethics, the 'Selphs,' and the Excluded Third." In *Ethos: New Essays in Rhetorical and Critical Theory,* edited by James S. Baumlin and Tita French Baumlin, 389–432. Dallas: Southern Methodist University Press, 1994.

———. "A Mal-Lingering Thought (Tragic-Comedic) about KB's Visit." *Pre/Text* 6 (1965): 163–67.

Wagner, Peter. "Identity and Selfhood as a Probélmatique." In *Identities: Time, Difference, and Boundaries,* edited by Heidrun Friese, 32–55. New York: Berghahn, 2002.

Wess, Robert. *Kenneth Burke: Rhetoric, Subjectivity, Postmodernism.* New York: Cambridge University Press, 1996.

———. "Kenneth Burke's 'Dialectic of Constitutions.'" *Pre/Text* 12 (1991): 9–30.

Williams, Robin. *Making Identity Matter: Identity, Society, and Social Interaction.* Durham, N.C.: Sociologypress, 2000.

Wilson, Katherine K. "The Disparate Classification of Gender and Sexual Orientation in American Psychiatry" (May 5, 2006). http://www.priory.com/psych/disparat.htm.

Wilson, Robin. "Leading Economist Stuns Field by Deciding to Become a Woman." *Chronicle of Higher Education* (February 16, 1996). http://www.pfc.org.uk/news/1996/mcloskey.htm.

Winkelmann, Carol L. *The Language of Battered Women: A Rhetorical Analysis of Personal Theologies.* Buffalo: State University of New York Press, 2003.

Wise, R. Todd. "The Great Vision of Black Elk as Literary Ritual." In *The Black Elk Reader,* edited by Clyde Holler, 241–61. Syracuse: Syracuse University Press, 2000.

———. "Speaking through Others: *Black Elk Speaks* as Testimonial Literature." In *The Black Elk Reader,* edited by Clyde Holler, 19–38. Syracuse: Syracuse University Press, 2000.

Wisse, Jakob. *Ethos and Pathos: From Aristotle to Cicero.* Amsterdam: Hakkert, 1989.

Witteveen, Willem, and Bart van Klink. "Why Is Soft Law Really Law? A Communicative Approach to Legislation." *RegelMaat* no. 3 (1999): 126–40.

INDEX

ABOUT THE AUTHOR

Dana Anderson is an assistant professor of English at Indiana University and an editor of the *KB Journal.* His work has appeared in *Philosophy and Rhetoric*, *College Composition and Communication*, *Rhetoric Society Quarterly*, *Queen*, and *Journal of Popular Culture.*